GOING TO CHURCH

It's Not What You Think!

Susan Mann Flanders

To Aabra,
With fond memories,
Susan

S‖P

ST. JOHANN PRESS
Haworth, NJ

ST. JOHANN PRESS

Published in the United States of America
by St. Johann Press
P.O. Box 241
Haworth, NJ 07641
www.stjohannpress.com

The paper used in this publication meets the minimum requirements
of the American National Standard for Information Sciences—
Permanence of Paper for Printed Library Materials,
ANSI/NISO Z39/48-1992

Composition and interior design by Susan Ramundo
(susan@srdesktopservices.com)
Cover design by G&H Soho Inc., Elmwood Park, NJ
(ghsoho.com)
Author's photo by Taisie Berkeley

ISBN 978-1-937943-22-6

Manufactured in the United States of America

for Bill

my partner in the quest

Table of Contents

Acknowledgments

A number of people have helped me with the actual writing and editing of this book, and I am grateful for their time, their insights, their honest criticisms and positive encouragement and support. First among these is Sara Taber whose memoir workshops over several years nurtured my work and gave me faith that it would become a book. Other members of the group, Kaja Weeks, Jeanne Lemkau, Irene Landsman, Peggy Treadwell, Anne Varnum, and Oliver Tessier read and critiqued my work at various stages. Friend and fellow theologian, Richard Rubenstein offered comments and suggestions along the way as did friends and neighbors Norman and Ellen Sinel, over coffee or stronger drink, often in front of their fireplace. My step-daughter, Lili Flanders, a published author and memoirist in her own right, provided ongoing support and was especially helpful in recasting the chapter "Tearing Apart." Liz and Noble Richards, Truro friends with backgrounds in high school English and literature, volunteered to read the whole manuscript and provided affirmation that my story could be of interest to people outside of the church. Friends Rebecca Milliken and Tucker Clark read sections of the work and also bolstered my confidence. My sister, Marty Mann, was invaluable in helping me sort out how to handle those places where family members are part of the story and how to balance honesty with respect for their feelings and their own versions of events.

David Biesel at St. Johann Press has been a trusted advisor, editor and publisher. His experience and professionalism have been invaluable to me in this first venture into publication.

Various clergy mentors and colleagues, all mentioned in the book, helped to shape my priesthood and the way my theology and life in the church has evolved. Bill Opel, Jim Steen, Jim Adams especially, Bill Baxter, Benjamin Pratt, Alan Jones, Harrison West, and Paul Abernathy have all been invaluable companions along this pathway of faith. In addition, Fred Plumer, Director of ProgressiveChristianity.org, has sharpened my understanding and articulation of incarnational theology and given me hope for the future of the church.

More than anyone, the people in the congregations where I have served have made my quest possible. No one can be a priest without other people, and the communities of faith where I have loved and been loved have prompted these reflections and been the very embodiment of church and Christianity for me. I thank the people of St. John's Broad Creek, St. Patrick's in Washington, St. Mark's on Capitol Hill, Grace Cathedral in San Francisco, and St. John's Norwood Parish in Chevy Chase, Maryland.

Four generations of family have supported me in my work and writing, even though most of them, except for my mother, Betty Mann, don't go to church. Siblings and children and grandchildren seem to respect what I do, and my children actually like having a Mom who is a priest. Bill's family have entered the story in the last ten years and have been curious, loyal and loving as this work has unfolded.

My husband Bill has read every word, known every doubt, listened to every boast and discussed and argued theology with me for countless hours over meals, walks and long drives. He is a true partner in going to church and all that that means to both of us. I am full of love and thanks for his presence in my life and in this story.

Introduction

He is small and blue and barely alive—born way too soon. And, after twenty minutes, he dies. His parents are bereft, grieving, and the comfort they afford each other isn't enough. The mother is empty, has no plan for the future except to wait for another child. She has recently become interested, mostly intellectually, in Christianity, and so, to pass the time and occupy her restless soul, she signs up for some classes at a nearby seminary.

She goes for an interview and then begins to page through the course catalog. On that bright autumn day, standing on some stone steps under flaming leaves like her own personal burning bush, her heart and mind come alive. She knows this is where she wants to be, what she wants to learn—this language of faith she has avoided for so long. And slowly, gradually, over several years, a vocation to ministry is born—a new way for her life and generativity to flourish. And that little premature boy is raised, resurrected in the only way she can understand that—born into new life in his mother and used, not only to heal her, but to be a blessing to many.

This is, at the deepest level, how my long and winding path as an Episcopal priest began. It has been a thicketed passage, never simple, not a conventional story. My experience of God has been bound up in the events of my life, nurtured through darkness and light, complexity and doubt, and welcome times of gladness and joy. I claim neither orthodoxy nor heresy, only my own honesty about the faith I have tried to live.

That living has included two divorces, three marriages, three sons and a large step-family. It has included a successful run as a parish priest over twenty-five years, despite a protested ordination and various skirmishes with church policies and authority. My account is contrary to what many assume about clergy and life in the church, especially those who have pretty much written them off. I believe Christianity to be different from what so many reject, and I mourn the sorry descent of the church as more and more people simply don't believe what they think it offers.

And so, my story. It is for all who have ever wondered about faith and how it can make any difference in your life. It is for all who are curious about ministers. It is for all who would embrace one woman's odyssey for what it might tell them about their own.

1

A Young Girl and God

I was thirteen, and my grandmother had died. The funeral was in a distant city, and my parents deemed me too young to go. And so my imagination took over. I envisioned, or dreamed, a huge vaulted space, very high, full of colored streaming light—like vertical rainbows, and somehow my grandmother was enveloped in all that light and color. I never made logical sense of this, didn't even try, but for me it was an intimation of some kind of holiness, some extraordinary dimension of reality, a religious experience.

A few years later, desperate to complete an assignment for tenth grade English class during a spring break, I tried to write about the most spectacular sunset I had ever seen. I sat cross-legged on a broad white beach on the western coast of Florida where our family was vacationing. As I watched, the sky filled with gold and pink, and blue and green and purple, all shooting through clouds and lighting the whole sky. Never had I felt such a profound sense of the grandeur of this world, of a creator capable of such glory. My description of that experience won a space in my high school literary journal that year. It had no title, and when I asked my teacher what to call it, she suggested "Theophany."

"What does that mean?"

"Look it up."

"Theophany: An appearance of a god to a man; divine manifestation" (from *American Heritage Dictionary*)

1

These seemingly religious intuitions were quite different from the conventional exposure to Christianity that my Presbyterian childhood afforded. Just
as nearly everyone in our suburban Philadelphia neighborhood in the late 40s
and 50s did, we went to Sunday School while our parents went to church. We
heard stories; we colored pictures; we learned songs about Jesus, and we were
constantly encouraged to be good and to love our neighbors and love God by
giving money to Him in his House, where we should be quiet and respectful.
Much of it I liked, at least through grade-school, and I did have one truly
inspiring role model in the lovely church soloist, Beth Ann Oughton. She
was tall and beautiful with long red hair, and she wore a pure white robe and
looked so serene, sitting up front, waiting to sing her anthem.

I was a shy and serious little girl. One report card came back saying "Susan
should smile more." I loved school and excelled in my classes, and I was super
conscientious most of the time, seeking approval through grades and doing
the right thing. I pretty much kept my religious questions and definitely my
religious experiences to myself, a private realm of the spirit that was then in-
choate, fledgling and unspoken.

As I grew into my teens, the whole church experience began to grate on
me. My questions about how to possibly understand all the literally unbelievable stuff in the Bible were inevitably met with something like "Well you
just have to make a leap of faith." That answer was so inadequate for all my
misgivings about a virgin birth, a bodily resurrection, walking on water, seas
parting, cripples walking and lepers cured! I simply couldn't make myself
make that leap. Further, neither my parents nor my Sunday School teachers
nor any other adults I knew ever admitted to not believing in the literal truth
of these stories, so I figured they either had somehow been able to make the
leap or else were pretending. Either way, I was left out of that game.

The moral lessons put forth in church grew more onerous, warning against
all the seductive pitfalls of adolescence. I saw the teachers and church ladies as
"do-gooders" always bustling about smiling and helping one another. There
was cheery, bright-eyed Mary Louise Johnson, wife of the organist, in her
matronly housedresses and fussy hats, way too appreciative of everyone and
everything. There was earnest young Gil Lincoln, tasked with teaching junior
high Sunday School, but so gentle and seemingly naïve that we pretty much
discounted his efforts to make disciples of us. These and others were reverse

role models—people I never wanted to grow up to be like. Meanwhile I would hear my parents talking about the Pastor as a severe alcoholic. He often showed up on Sunday mornings looking red and bloated, but then again people loved his erudite sermons and wouldn't have considered confronting him or offering him any kind of help with his problem. In some strange way I actually admired him; I loved the fact that he had wanted to be an actor before he went to seminary.

I did feel that my father was a serious Christian. He was an engineer, highly rational, emotionally restrained, but he had thought deeply about Christianity and accepted it. He tried to talk to us children about the importance of church-going and reading the Bible and trying to follow Jesus. He actually did these things himself and visited prisoners as part of his church's ministry. He believed in disarmament and the possibility of world peace and worked for these with the World Federalists, an advocacy group for global governance. He was active in the civic life of our community and gave generously to the church and other charities. On many Sundays, he would preface dinner by asking one of us to read a short Bible passage which we would then talk about. It seemed a little corny and boring, but it was certainly better than the arguments that usually went on with my two younger brothers about eating peas or squash, and I did respect what my dad was trying to do.

On the other hand, I felt my mother's church involvement to be more conventional. She didn't seem to have much serious interest in or understanding of what Christianity was about except that she always wanted to do the right thing in terms of how she and her four children were perceived by others. We had to dress right for church. My sister and I had pretty dresses from our grandmother, Easter hats and coats, black patent leather "Mary Jane" shoes with ankle straps. My brothers had little clip-on bow ties and white shirts with round collars. We went to Sunday School every week, often enough to get the little round pins with yearly bars beneath for good attendance. My mother insisted that when we were teenagers we were to help serve at Lenten dinners, passing out some kind of plain food at long tables of middle-aged people who felt these simple meals were somehow important to God or perhaps the "starving Armenians" who were actually still talked about in those days. To my mind they were boring wastes of an evening, forced acts of charity. Despite Mom's concern about our going to church, I never got a sense of where God was for her in any of this.

Prayer at home was automatic, said briefly by rote before dinner, usually by my mother, "Thank thee Lord, that Thou dost give, our daily food that we may live. Amen." As we went to bed each night, we dutifully recited, "Now I lay me down to sleep, I pray the Lord my soul to keep. God bless Mommy and Daddy and Susan and Marty and Bobby and Tommy. Amen." These weren't much different from church prayers, repetitive utterances that suggested that God would listen and reward us according to our prayers, and that if things didn't go well and we prayed hard enough, we could expect relief. If that didn't come, well, it was probably because we hadn't prayed enough or in the right way, or because we just deserved our misfortunes because of our sins. It was an ungenerous, ungracious theological stance, but it was never laid out as theology, just as the way good Christians did things, or at least the good Christians of the tame and tidy churches outside of Philadelphia and Pittsburgh where I was raised.

This tidy tameness, of necessity, excluded sex. Although we were taught the basics of human reproduction, it was swathed in fear and taboo. All the horrible things, from venereal disease to a bad reputation to unwanted pregnancy, were used as constant warnings to keep us from falling into disgrace. Unlike today's more nuanced recognition of the healthy role of sexuality and of how people mature into sexual beings, we were simply told that married sex was good and any other kind of sex was wrong, completely.

Even so, my own religious instincts and experiences had persisted. I still distinctly remember one very long night when I was 14. I was alone in my bedroom, after being awake for hours. I had been wrestling with a terrible guilt—guilt because I had been, heaven forbid, necking, with my very first boyfriend. We had kissed, a few times, on our living room couch., and one sunny afternoon, in an old barn in the woods in back of our house, I had let him touch one breast, one time. "It's pretty" he had said, blushing red through his freckles. Nothing more, but still, more than what my parents would have approved and what my Sunday School God would have allowed. Finally, that night as I lay in bed and then paced my room, cowering really, in shame and fear, a wave of relief flowed around and through me. I didn't actually hear anything, but it was as if a voice said "You are not terrible; you are loved, and good." I associated this with God, as an actual someone then, a presence now, reaching to my unfolding sexuality and blessing it.

Despite that powerful experience, I continued to struggle to figure out what to do about necking and petting and trying to have a boyfriend and set appropriate limits. Church was of no help. In fact, it added to my confusion. My boyfriend in senior year of high school, Jim, was Roman Catholic and had to attend mass and confession regularly. We had never talked about religion during all the weeks when our limited experiments in drive-in movies were keeping us safe from the perils our parents feared but definitely not as "pure" as the Roman church would demand. After a New Year's Eve, when we'd been to a party after attending midnight mass, I never heard another word from that boyfriend. Since in those days, girls weren't supposed to call boys because it was too "forward," I spent several months of hopeless wondering, not even knowing what I had done to cause this rejection which was as desperate and painful as any first love lost. I later discovered through a third party that Jim had been counseled by his priest never to see me again after he'd confessed that we'd been "making out." He felt he had to obey. Such a God, such a church.

As I moved through my teen years, there was also a growing boredom with the whole church enterprise. Services, except for the occasionally interesting and meaningful sermon, were routine, dry, pious. I felt a growing disconnect between my intuitions of God and goodness and the constraining cloak of dogma and tradition and what seemed to me a smug moralism, wafting from the folds of this dated garment.

2

Liberation

My adolescent years were an ongoing struggle for acceptance in my own eyes and by my parents and peers. We moved to Sewickley, a suburb of Pittsburgh, when I was thirteen, and I had a hard time fitting in there with the mostly wealthy, private school crowd I tried to enter. I continued to excel in my academic work and was proud of that, even though I felt I was considered a bit of a "grind" and a "square" by the more athletic and socially popular girls in my classes. I remember them all as tall and blond and slender, while I was on the short side, brown haired and curvy. They were full of talk of upcoming debutante parties and who was going to which boarding school. Starting in tenth grade, I commuted to Ellis, a girls' private day school in Pittsburgh, a forty-five minute drive each way. Ellis was the fourth new school I'd attended in as many years and the first one where I didn't end up in tears during the first day. It was a struggle to feel a part of my class. I was new and didn't live locally and was horrible at field hockey. I did make a few close friends in those years, but mostly I studied and read and practiced the piano, having taken lessons since I was seven. One girl friend and I thought the finest Saturday night ever was to have a roast beef and chocolate sundae dinner at the University Club (her father's treat), followed by a Pittsburgh symphony concert (my father's treat).

When it came time to apply for college, I sent in an application for early admission to Wellesley College. I loved its beautiful campus, and I wanted the prestige of going to a top school. Two of my best friends in the class had also applied, so I was sure we wouldn't all get in. One December morning, during English class, the headmistress showed up and asked the three of us to come forward. As we did so, she announced, "You're all in Wellesley!." We literally jumped for joy at the incredible news, and I felt my life opening out before me into a realm of excellence, acceptance and things I was really interested in. I would no longer feel bogged down as a social loser, no longer even care about all those "preppies" back in Sewickley. I was going to Wellesley!

I arrived on campus in the fall of 1961, and from the beginning, I felt at home. I loved my classes and the intellectual excitement they generated in me. I remember running headlong up the walkway to my dorm for lunch one day just euphoric after a particularly interesting lecture on St. Augustine's *Confessions*. It was the philosophical rather than the religious content that stirred me then. I loved thinking about what I considered the big questions of life: Is there a God? Why are we here? What is the Good? How do we find meaning and value in life? I also loved Art History, which I declared as a major early on. I was particularly interested in architecture and the social history that gets expressed in art. In those classes, I gained a sense of how Christianity had shaped Western civilization in wonderful as well as horrific ways. That people without any modern building technology could design and build the soaring cathedrals of the high Gothic period spoke to me of the intense yearning of the human spirit to seek the good and perfect, to express beauty in stone and glass, and to dedicate this art to God. I was fascinated by the ways that the visual arts showed us the values and aspirations and belief systems of people over the centuries, and here again, the questions about meaning and beauty and ultimate purpose engaged me.

Religion did not. I was free of it—of my parents and their Presbyterianism and the whole dutiful exercise of going to church. I think I went once to a service on campus and once to an organ concert in the chapel. That was it. Sundays were free, for social life, or for recovering from Saturday's social life, or preparing for Monday's classes. I didn't miss church in the least, and didn't feel guilty for not going. None of my friends went except Roman Catholics, and, of course, they had to.

During my first Christmas vacation, I went to the midnight service back in Sewickley at the Episcopal Church with my boyfriend Wif and his family.

Everyone in those days called him Wif, based on his initials, instead of Walter, so for me it remained the name I've always used for him. We had fallen impetuously in love during the previous summer, and we spent most weekends of that fall traversing the state of Massachusetts between Wellesley and Williams College where he was a senior. Now back at home, we did what was expected. We sat in church all dressed up, with our elders, many of whom had had too much to drink at the boozy party that preceded this display of sentimental religiosity. And then Wif and I just left, preferring to be alone together on this supposedly holy night, feeling our young love a better celebration of God's presence with us than ornate pageantry and social ostentation.

The young love continued, but with much uncertainty once Wif graduated from Williams and began to figure out what was next for him. He finally joined an Air Force program that would lead to a career in intelligence and headed off to basic training in San Antonio. I received a picture of my beloved with all of his beautiful blond hair shaved off and a military crew cut in its place, signed "Yul" for the then-famous bald actor (Yul Brynner). I didn't really see an immediate future for us, so I applied, with some ambivalence, to spend my junior year in Paris as part of a Smith College plan. After much negotiating with a reluctant dean over whether I could go since I was an art rather than a French major, permission was granted, and I began to plan for this great adventure, that is until an even greater adventure presented itself.

Late one early June evening in 1963, Wif called from his Air Force base in a remote area of Washington State. After some brief conversation about my upcoming sea voyage to Paris, he asked, "How would you like to come out here instead . . . and be Mrs. Floyd?" I was dumbfounded. Although we'd talked of marriage and had been in love for two years, I felt we'd tacitly agreed to wait until I finished college. I knew he was preparing for an assignment in Southeast Asia and would probably be gone when I returned from France, and he knew that too. Now, after almost a year of letters and phone calls, I think we both feared the upcoming separation. Still, I was surprised at how thrilled I was at the prospect of joining him overseas instead of going off to Paris. Even so, it was a hard decision, and I particularly feared my parents' reaction.

I said "yes" to Wif, but that I needed a couple of days to think and talk to my parents, which I did immediately that night. It was a short conversation. They were in bed, reading, when I tapped on their door and stepped in.

"Mom and Dad, Wif has asked me to marry him, and I've said I need two days to think and talk to you, but I want to do this and hope you'll agree."

"You're crazy!" came my father's voice as he turned his head into his pillow.

"Let's talk it over tomorrow, dear." My mother was already envisioning the wedding.

I was torn, and giving up a year in Paris and a Wellesley degree was not easy. All weekend I wrestled with my decision and with my parents. They actually came around because they really loved Wif and were reassured that we had no intention of starting a family until after I had finished college somewhere. My dad had always told his children that he would pay for our college educations, but if we got married before graduating, the rest would be up to us. He now added that if and when I graduated, he would give me $1000, real money in those days. My mom continued to think about a wonderful wedding a couple of months hence. Wif was my parents' idea of a highly suitable husband. He came from a somewhat wealthy family, had gone to excellent schools, was blond and handsome and charming, and 4½ years older than I. I loved him for all these reasons, but I loved him far more for the interests we shared and the combination of idealism and romanticism with which we viewed our life together. Over the weekend, my parents' initial surprise and dismay turned into hesitant and then full approval, and two days later Wif and I became officially engaged. We set a date to marry in September, just two weeks before my 20th birthday.

When I called the Wellesley dean with whom I'd lobbied so zealously to go to Paris to give her the news, the silence on the other end of the phone was deafening, her shock palpable. But for me, it felt like one dream superseding another. I had no regrets then, only happy anticipation. We married on September 14, 1963, a traditional Presbyterian Church wedding followed by a lovely country club reception.

After a brief honeymoon at Mt. Rainier National Park, our marriage began in the tiny town of Moses Lake, Washington, the home of Larson Air Force Base where a lot of huge B-52s were kept at the ready. Wif was a newly minted lieutenant, guarding the huge black bombers, tending the canine attack dogs trained to detect intruders. We both loved the outdoors, and the wide open plains of central Washington appealed to both of us. Whenever he was off duty, we went hiking, camping, fishing and hunting. It was beautiful country, full of wild fowl, pheasants, quail and chukar partridge.

I would say that my husband and I were pagans. We no longer claimed any particular religion, and were somewhat hedonistic in our embrace of life and all its pleasures. We occasionally talked of feeling God's presence outdoors there, in the world of nature. We felt our walks across huge grasslands, over high bluffs along the Columbia River, up and down forested slopes, were in some way akin to worship, and certainly more meaningful.

3

Laos

In 1965, we left for two years in Laos, part of Agency for International Development relief efforts, tangential to the growing war next door in Viet Nam. Our time in southeast Asia began with a sojourn for me in Bangkok. We were to live in the second largest town in Laos, Savannakhet, but there was no housing available for dependent spouses right away. Instead, half a dozen wives with husbands in various places in upcountry Laos lived in Bangkok, and our husbands came for occasional weekends. This might have been a fine arrangement, but I was really lonely. I had a nice apartment in a little compound around a pool, and I was not far from downtown and the many picturesque, gilded temples and wildly colorful markets of the exotic Thai capital. However, I wanted to do my sightseeing on the weekends when Wif was there, and the long weeks in between weighed heavily. There seemed no point in getting a job as I would be moving up country in a couple of months. The other wives all had young children and Thai amahs to help with them, so that they really had households to manage. Meanwhile, I felt very much at loose ends and kind of resentful of the United States government for spending so much money to sustain me half way around the world simply to be available for the very occasional two-day visit from Wif.

All that changed one morning in October when the phone rang around 7 am. It was Ray Drummond, the personnel officer from the Embassy, wanting to know if I was a friend of "Andy," the wife of another AID officer who had also been stationed in upcountry Laos, in the town of Pakse. I was indeed. Wif and I had been good friends with her and Mike back in DC, and we had arrived in Bangkok within two weeks of each other. Ray, from the embassy, whom I knew slightly, said he needed to go and see Andy and wanted me to accompany him, he'd be over to pick me up in twenty minutes. Brushing my teeth, scurrying to get dressed and ready, I caught a glimpse of my face in the mirror. It was white and scared, and I realized that something terrible must have happened to Mike. As I drove with Ray, he told me that Mike had been killed, along with another American officer and two Thais, in a helicopter crash in the jungle. Mike had died instantly. Even as I was wondering how in the world we could break this news, it was also dawning on me that this accident could have just as easily happened to my husband. He and Mike were sent out at the same time for identical assignments in two different towns; had the assignments been switched, this shocking, sudden widowhood would have been mine.

Andy came to the door, invited us in. Her toddler son was playing happily in the room. As the terrible news was spoken, her face drained of color, and she sank to a chair, stunned. I felt completely helpless, knew of nothing to say. The personnel man began talking about getting her back home to her family in the States and wondered if I would accompany her instead of an embassy official as I was a friend. The next day or so went by in kind of a blur. My husband arrived from up country, and we agreed that I should make the long trip back with Andy to New York where her parents would come in from Connecticut to meet her. Even though the death was an accident, it slammed home to us the reality that we were halfway around the world in a dangerous neighborhood, doing dangerous work. And now someone we'd laughed and partied with and shared the excitement of this assignment with was gone, his wife a widow with one little boy and another on the way. Viet Nam was next door, but until then, we'd felt insulated from the perils of that war.

Andy and I flew out of Bangkok, spent a long, almost sleepless night in the airport hotel in Tokyo, then proceeded on via Seattle to New York. Andy was a devout Roman Catholic, and my skeptical, antireligious self of those days was actually impressed by how her faith seemed to comfort her. She believed she could pray to Mike; she worried about naming the coming baby something he would approve of. In other words, she believed in a real afterlife where Mike now was, and she talked of this faith off and on during our long trip. Finally we landed at Idlewild (now JFK), where Andy was quickly surrounded by her distraught family.

I was to go on to Pittsburgh the next day and spend some time with my family. But before that, another excruciatingly long night began, a night in which I felt as alone and bereft as I ever had, and in part, because of my own sister. Marty, 2½ years younger, lived in New York, and unbeknownst to me, was going through a really hard time of her own. I had called her earlier that day from Seattle:

> "Marty, a friend in Laos was killed in a helicopter crash, and I'm flying back tonight with his wife and young son to New York where she'll meet her family. I need a place to stay one night, can I come to your apartment?"
>
> "Sure," she replied, "but I may be going to a party upstate. It's old friends from Bard, and I don't want to miss it. But I'll let my landlady know. She'll let you in. Sorry, I would like to see you, but it's just not a good time."

So when Andy went off with her family, I was met by another personnel guy who drove me into the city and arranged to get me back to the airport in the morning. I stumbled exhaustedly up the stairs of a brownstone house on Washington Square and into a fairly run-down apartment. It had linoleum floors and smelled of cooked onions and stale coffee, and my sister's room wasn't much more than a narrow cell with a single bed and bureau. The landlady did indeed meet me, and talked, and talked, and smoked, and smoked, and didn't really get why I was there. And I couldn't tell her, really, what had happened. I so much wished Marty had stayed and that she and I could have talked, and talked, and drunk copious amounts of soothing alcohol, and she would have understood. And had I known how much her own life was in turmoil then and how much she needed to be with friends, I would have understood. But no, she was partying upstate, and Mike was dead, and Andy was a widow at 24 and her young son and the baby she carried would never know their father. And what were we doing in Laos anyway? And what comfort could Andy's Roman Catholic God offer? And what God was there for me? The full weight of the tragedy I'd just experienced sank in and left me bereft—feeling God's absence and my own aloneness so deeply that a whole night's tears and wakefulness only drained me further.

The next morning, finally, I called my parents in Pittsburgh, only to discover a final twist in this harrowing journey. The night before, just as I was landing, my father-in-law died of pancreatic cancer. Naturally, my parents figured I had come home for the funeral which was to be in Sewickley. Wif and I had known when we left that Dick had only weeks to live, and we'd sadly said good-bye, knowing it was for the last time. But here I was, and now I would take my place along with Wif's mother and the rest of his family, at Dick's funeral. I wore a borrowed black dress, wept through the service, and tried ineptly to explain how it was that I happened to be there. Again, I felt as though I'd come from another world that people here didn't know about or understand. It was so familiar being back, my hometown, parents, in-laws, the staid Episcopal Church of those days; how was it that the timing had been this way? How was it that one tragic, unexpected death a half-a-world away brought me to what seemed so fitting, my presence at this family funeral? Years later, I would preach about this experience, but then it was just a strange combination of events and a very brief reconnection with life back home before returning, with relief, really, to my new life in Southeast Asia.

A couple of months after I got back, housing was available for us in Savannakhet, and over the New Year's Eve weekend of 1966, we moved into a large stucco house belonging to a Laotian general who was off fighting in the north. Savannakhet had one paved road, electricity on every two out of three days, but also the languorous feel of an old French colonial backwater, which it was. Arcaded buildings and plane trees framed the main street, while water buffalo wandered freely in front of our house, just blocks away. Our neighbors on either side lived in wooden houses on stilts. I soon had an orchid garden—beautiful plants hanging in wooden boxes, living off air and the charcoal in which they were planted. It was almost always very hot, and although we had an air conditioner in our bedroom, it was of no use when the power was off. I remember lying with a wet washcloth draped over my bare back, trying to fall asleep while the cloth was still cool. I remember the French blue-fronted restaurant where, for the equivalent of a dollar, you could have onion soup and beefsteak and salad for dinner. For another dollar, you could have a pretty good bottle of Algerian wine. Or you could eat at the Chinese restaurant where the spicy, exotic food, including fried whole small sparrows was completely different from the American Chinese chop suey we'd had back home. We had a Thai couple, Whett and Taoa, who cleaned and did laundry and some cooking and shopping for us—such a strange feeling for me at age 22 to have servants! It felt odd to be addressed as "madame" and to be expected to manage them. I spoke a bit of Thai and Lao, both of which are fairly simple languages, and my high school and college French came in handy, as all Laotians who had been to high school spoke some French as well.

Our house was only a block from the huge open morning market for the town. The smell of French bread, warm, yeasty and crusty beckoned every morning as I rode my bike there. Mangoes and papayas and all sorts of fruits I'd never seen, lichis and guavas and mangosteens, were piled up in abundant supply. Beyond them, I would enter the meat section, another experience entirely. No neatly packaged and labeled cuts of meat like in supermarkets at home. Instead, whole carcasses of poultry and huge portions of beef and pork were hung on hooks or laid on bloody counters. You had to guess which part you were buying, and then bargain on the price. Various organ meats and entrails were sold right alongside, with their own distinct odors. For me the most astounding of all these delicacies were the live grubs, little squirming worms just waiting to be fried up with garlic and peppers into crispy morsels. I couldn't imagine eating them, but never tired of exploring the many curiosities of that market.

What Savannakhet didn't have was even the slightest trace of Christianity, except perhaps for the lapsed Catholicism of the young French couple who befriended us. In the mix of mostly Thai and Lao people, with a few Chinese and Vietnamese, we were exposed to Buddhism, Confucianism and basically a local animist spirit worship. This latter involved small ornate houses on poles, "pi houses," where rice and other offerings were placed daily in service to the local or family gods. Ancestor worship was important, as were relics, such as, perhaps, the toenail of the Buddha. Shrines for these relics could be anything from an ancient tree to a gilded temple. Funeral processions passed our house almost weekly, on their way to the site of the burning of the body—a very public, smoky, dramatic event on the edge of town.

Laos was a tiny corner of Asia, but it was a microcosm of a vast continent and billions of people who had robust religious traditions that were completely different from Protestant Christianity. Most folks there had never even heard of Jesus Christ. Recognizing this brought up for me one of the biggest stumbling blocks to the Christianity of my background. That is its claim to be the one true religion, that Jesus is the only path to salvation. From then on, I simply could not believe that only Christianity has saving power, even when I went to seminary, even when I became a minister. If there is a power at work in the world that we can call God, that power can not possibly reveal itself to only some of us in only a particular way. I found it impossible then, as now, to reject the validity of other religions. All may not have equal capacity for helping folks to make sense of life and face its tragedies and dilemmas, but that is my own judgment. Certainly Christianity has contributed to evil and violence throughout its history, as have many other religions, and I need to pay attention to how a religion actually functions for good or ill if I am to critique it. But from then on, I have never accepted any exclusive claims of Christianity to be the only means of salvation, the one true religion.

We left Laos in 1967 and returned to Washington where I finished my BA in History of Art at George Washington University in 1968. As promised, right after the graduation ceremony, my dad handed me an envelope with a check for $1000 inside. I had worked as a clerk typist in the Comptroller's office during my time at GW which paid for one course each semester, but still the money was most welcome as we began to establish ourselves financially. Meanwhile, we continued our quasiatheist life in Washington. This was easy to do then, because going to church was no longer the norm for polite society, and attendance had begun the downward slide that continues to this day. Hypocritical church-going was no longer necessary to be a good citizen; so perhaps an advantage was that only people who actually wanted to be there went. I would occasionally go to a church, maybe once a year, to sort of check out whether things had changed. They hadn't. The same boring, stifling, hidebound piety prevailed. My father was concerned and kept urging me to find a church. To appease him, I read C.S. Lewis' *Mere Christianity*, which made the case for the seriousness of religion in an accessible, rational way. I realized I was still caring about God, still wondering about religious questions, still vaguely longing for a sense of faith. But I did little about it.

Once I finished college, we were ready to start a family and went off to see Tom Gresinger, an obstetrician who was an in-law of Wif's. I soon became pregnant and spent much of that time doing volunteer work with Republicans for Nelson Rockefeller. It was a time of happy expectancy and delight at the prospect of becoming a mother. I got my ears pierced, made a lovely green maternity dress and sunbathed by the pool to ensure a nice tan before the May 20 delivery. Christopher McDaniel Floyd was born pretty easily, and after almost six years of marriage, we began the adventure of being parents. It was to take some unexpected and painful twists and turns.

4

Tumult and Coping

I was a young woman who relied on getting things right, being smart, one who counted on achievements for my sense of self-worth. So besides not believing in much of what I heard the Church saying, I didn't have any sense of urgency about God, about being "saved." If that meant going to heaven after I died, well that was a long way off, and I didn't, even then, believe in heaven. It seemed to necessitate a hell, and there was no way I could believe in a God who would send all nonbelievers to eternal torment, or even all sinners, for that matter, since that would condemn us all. Salvation was something I neither understood nor felt I needed.

Maybe none of us does until something brings us to our knees in grief and betrayal and helplessness. In early June of 1969, this happened to me. While our first born son, Christopher, two weeks old, slept in the next room, I guiltily opened a letter to my husband from a Japanese woman he had met on a business trip, right after the baby was born. It was all about their affair in Hong Kong, complete with pictures of her in her stewardess uniform. I sobbed and sobbed, literally on my knees on the brown-carpeted living room floor of our apartment. I realized that this was beyond my control, that I couldn't change it, and that it had changed everything. I couldn't even tell my husband because I felt I shouldn't have opened the letter!

For the first time I realized that I could not count on my own efforts to make my life work out. This affair and my discovery of it felt like an outrageous blow, this transgression, only days after I had born a child. I had little in the way of resources to face this problem, and certainly no sense of how God could help. I didn't even think about God.

Finally, I told Wif about the letter I'd read. Over the next months, we confronted our problems, even as we prepared for another overseas assignment, this time in Japan. I had to acknowledge that I was at fault too. I was needy for acceptance and fearful of criticism. In Laos, whether out of loneliness or simply the compulsions of a young, insecure woman desperately wanting to be appealing to my husband and popular in our social circles, I certainly drank too much on a number of occasions and wrestled with an eating disorder. Back home, in angry reaction to Wif's having cheated, I too committed adultery and let him know about it. It was a one-night, one-time betrayal, but it definitely compounded and deepened our hurts. This chaos within me and within our marriage conflicted with the lovely picture we presented to our families and friends. We were seen as a perfect young couple: Wif headed for big things in the government, "Sue" as his loving and attractive wife. We lived pretty much in denial of the disconnect, hoping that somehow our marriage would work out, but not knowing how to repair it.

In 1971 Wif and I separated. By then we were living in Yokohama, Japan where he was learning Japanese in preparation for an embassy assignment. I was caring for our son and teaching English part-time to Japanese housewives. Despite our hopes for a fresh start in Japan, our marital problems continued there. We hadn't sought counseling; we didn't have much of a community of close friends, and we didn't live near our families. We decided on what we called a trial separation. I would move back to the United States with Chris, and Wif would remain in Japan. Despite vague hopes that we might reconcile, we found that our life in Yokohama, in the small community of the language school and Consulate there had become impossible. This was a terrible wrenching. I didn't want to leave but didn't feel I had a choice. Wif wanted some relief from our tensions and some space away from me, but having me take Chris so far away was a really high price for that young father. One evening we sat in our apartment, talking of our plan and the letter we would write to our parents alerting them of my return. Wif turned to me and choked out the words, "I don't want to lose my little boy!" I held him as he sobbed and sobbed and the sad burden of our problems and where they had brought us sank in. Two weeks later, on July 19, 1971, Wif took us out to Haneda airport and put us on the plane back to Pittsburgh. As I boarded, with Chris in my arms, I realized I was shaking, dizzy, feeling as though lights were swirling around me. My departure was a huge step, and it proved irreversible.

At home, both my parents were at the airport, and I broke down in tears when I saw them. My father never left work early for school plays or games or any children's events, but there he was, early in the afternoon, there to greet his daughter. I walked down the jetway, carrying my son and my failed marriage and a lot of unfulfilled hopes and dreams and worn away youthful optimism. Over the next few days, I stayed at home with my parents and prepared to return to live in Washington. Not surprisingly, Dad reiterated his concern about church and thought if we'd gone, this wouldn't have happened. By then I was tired of hearing about church as a panacea for life's problems. I do think I had made an idol of romantic love, and it had proved false. I returned to Washington with two-year-old Chris and began life in Alexandria, Virginia as a single working mom.

I worked for a travel agency; I kept campaign finance records for a political party; I got my real estate license and occasionally sold something. Wif was highly responsible about paying the alimony and child support we had agreed upon and later, private school tuition for Chris, so I was able to work part-time. I had no real career plans, just chose jobs that suited my schedule and paid enough to make ends meet. Mostly, I tried to be a good mom to Chris and dated somewhat haphazardly. It was the early seventies, and sex and drugs were everywhere, all mixed up with women's lib and anti-Vietnam outrage. Few men I knew had any interest in a committed relationship. The one I loved the best was divorced, had four children already and another girl friend. The one I loved next best was five years younger than I and still in college at 25. Deep down, I knew I wanted to marry again and have at least one more child, but it was as if, in my late twenties, I was making up for the freedom to be young and single that I'd missed by getting married too young. I think if it weren't for little, adorably blond and precocious Chris, my life would have been pretty empty and decadent and rudderless.

5

Going to Church

In 1974 I began dating my obstetrician, Tom Gresinger. This felt safe; we'd known each other since 1967, and he'd delivered Chris in 1969. There wasn't a lot of passion on my side, but there was on Tom's, and he was smart and fun and financially successful and actually wanted to get married and have more children! We married in May of 1975 and celebrated at Tom's house right on the bank of the Potomac River.

It was our marriage that brought me back to organized religion. Tom was a lapsed Episcopalian and lived near St. John's Broad Creek, in Ft. Washington, Maryland. It was a lovely little brick church dating to 1692. We went one Sunday to see about the possibility of being married there and with almost no expectation of anything more. But that morning began for me a discovery of Christianity as I'd never known it, open, nondogmatic, connected to real life. The preacher was wonderfully articulate, presenting the Biblical stories as metaphors conveying truth for our own day. There was a part called "The Peace" where everyone shook hands warmly and greeted each other; some even hugged! I thought this was the end of the service, but it was only a kind of intermission before "The Holy Eucharist." Even that felt new and life-giving—the simple sharing of real bread and real wine around the altar. I loved it, and I wanted more. Tom and I met with the Rector, Bill Opel, for three sessions of counseling before our marriage, and as we got to know him, I began to watch and appreciate all that he did as an Episcopal priest. His sermons always included concrete stories from his own or others' personal experience. The clarity of his teaching and scholarship totally grasped me. He seemed to love what he did, and a big part of that was to bring the religious myths of the Christian tradition alive again for me—no longer as stuffy lore, but as living truths.

During the summer after our marriage, Tom and I worked on Saturdays at a soup kitchen and free clinic in DC that we had heard about at St John's. Zaccheus House had an operating ethos that all human beings deserve to have life's basic necessities and that we should give these with no strings, no attempt to convert or to impose prayers. This open-handed service was new to me, a way of practicing faith in a needy world.

We also took a class for adults wanting to know more about Christianity and the Episcopal Church. From Bill Opel, I began to understand Christianity as if it were a whole new language. I heard about living with power even in the face of difficulty; I learned about following Jesus rather than worshiping him. The dry and pious theology of my girlhood opened up into a vision of a generous and loving God and into a faith that allowed for questions and ambiguity. I began to learn the long, slow lessons of grace, God's unconditional, unsought love. I began to see how this love is not something we earn by "being good" but rather a free gift, that we and the whole creation share. Being good is our response to that love, not our ticket to win it. And when we fail, in big and small ways, the remedy is forgiveness and the opportunity to try again, not ever more dogged striving to achieve some kind of perfection. My youthful rejection of Christianity, my failed marriage, my various irresponsible behaviors did not deny me God's love, or a place in the church. Neither did all my continuing questions and even doubts. These were legitimate ingredients of a healthy faith! The Episcopal Church doesn't talk much about being born again or being saved, but in that small church in those early months, I found two things I realized I'd been missing all along: a faith I could believe in and an acceptance despite my perceived inadequacies. And these have saved me, over and over.

Our church attendance at St. John's continued, and my involvement increased. Because I could play the piano, I was asked to play the small manual organ for one nonchoir service each Sunday. I was not used to being up front or performing in any way and would practice for hours and still be nervous when it came time to play the fairly simple hymns and chanted psalms or canticles. The choir director ordered a black cassock and special organist's white surplice for me, and I felt a delighted awe as I saw a new version of myself in the mirror, vested for worship. This image signified a new role, but at that point, I had absolutely no idea of how that role would unfold.

I continued as a real estate agent, but I grew more and more disillusioned by my own meager selling skills and the business itself. My plan for my life consisted mainly of being married to my doctor husband, doing whatever doctors' wives did and having another child. I was eager to get started on that and forget about real estate or any other career for that matter.

In 1977, after 5½ months of a seemingly normal pregnancy, I miscarried, a tiny baby boy, less than two pounds, who was born way too early and died after twenty minutes. We were away from home, in Florida when it happened, staying with good friends. After the hospital, we mainly went off by ourselves every day, out on a boat, empty-heartedly fishing, drifting, crying, waiting for time to pass. Our attempts to comfort one another were not enough; I felt as though there were a hole inside me. Back home, I dreaded showing up in church as I had been obviously pregnant and now wasn't. I didn't know the term then, but "disenfranchised grieving" is what goes on when you suffer a loss that is not generally recognized as a major tragedy, when many of the societal supports for grief are lacking. I didn't know what to do with this grief, but I knew I couldn't keep going through the motions of being a real estate agent and having no plans except to wait until I could become pregnant again.

I talked to our rector, Bill, hoping for some guidance. I learned that he and his wife Nina had had a still-born baby, and so he knew from experience how I was feeling. He offered to meet with me, or have me meet with his wife a few times, just to talk. My husband and I had gone over and over what happened, wondering why, and I would usually end in tears, feeling stuck in sadness. This offer of counsel from a minister was most welcome and surprising too. It offered to me yet another glimpse of what church is all about, this reaching out to a floundering person.

After a couple of sessions with Bill, I realized that in addition to the loss of the baby, I was bogged down in a vocational crisis; I had no idea what to do with my life, especially if I were to have no more children. He suggested I do some vocational testing and counseling. I didn't know such things existed and eagerly signed up for a summer program. We also talked of my continuing interest in learning more about Christianity, and perhaps taking some courses. He just happened to have a catalogue from Virginia Theological Seminary (VTS) nearby in nearby Alexandria, but he hastened to caution me that it was a place where most were preparing for ordained ministry, and perhaps I'd be happier at one of the downtown universities. I did learn that you could take courses for academic credit at the seminary without being in a degree program, so I decided to visit and find out more.

On a warm sunny day in August, I went to the lovely VTS campus of pre-Civil War buildings, rolling lawns and great soaring shade trees. I can remember the exact spot on the stone steps where I felt my heart leap as I scanned the list of courses. These were what interested me! Basic classes on the Bible and theology, but also seminars on the Resurrection, on the problem of evil, and on great Christian writers whose names were like beacons to me! It was probably on that day that my vocation to the priesthood began, although at the time, it just felt like an academic awakening and a door opening onto a new path into the future. I enrolled for two fall classes.

6

Seminary

Between 1977 and 1985, I went through the long and rigorous process leading to ordination as an Episcopal priest. For several years I was a part-time student. My son Chris was then moving through the elementary grades at the private Potomac School, 25 miles and almost an hour's drive from our house on the river in Ft. Washington. Tom and I loved living there where the Potomac is almost a mile wide, where the sunsets are gorgeous, and where our small brick house under big old trees gave us both a sense of being rooted in a beloved place. However, the Prince George's County Schools were mediocre at best, and so we decided to keep Chris where he had been since prekindergarten when I lived in Alexandria. I had to drive him to his bus stop in Old Town, Alexandria each morning, dreading the frequent lengthy backups on the Wilson Bridge from Maryland to Virginia. Our two sons, Tom and Rob, were born in 1978 and 1979, and I was very much willing to put off full-time seminary until they were at least old enough to go to preschool. These were years of car-pooling and baby-sitters, with classes feeling simply sandwiched in between all these demands. I would lay out a detailed schedule for each semester, complete with all needed driving and child care, and then proceed to see if I could manage the course and church field work requirements that would slowly lead to graduation and, perhaps, ordination.

During those first, part-time years at Virginia Seminary, I was somewhat ambivalent about ordination. I began, intending to complete only the two-year Master of Theological Studies degree. Our friends were almost all nonchurchgoers, and I received more than a few amazed double-takes when I mentioned that I was attending a seminary. Responses were predictable: "You mean we can't swear in front of you any more?" "Will you still be able to drink?" I would usually respond with some demurral, saying I was really just interested in Christianity, not looking for ordination. I was as uncomfortable with their stereotypes of righteous clergy as they were with the idea of my becoming one.

After my initial delight at the prospect of seminary, my sense of actually being called to the priesthood came very gradually. To me, even the words "call" and "vocation" seemed so laden with piety at first. Unlike some of the young men in my class, I had no vision of Jesus in the night, no voice in the darkness beckoning. Instead, I had a growing sense of my own capacity to think theologically. I became aware that my life experience, including the years of doubting and rejection of church, was valuable. I realized that my story needn't be that of a perfect role model, that my divorce and my unimpressive work background did not disqualify me. Rather they equipped me to help others see a way in or a way back to faith. I even began to feel that the church desperately needed me, a woman in her late thirties who had lived much of her adult life outside the church, as a sort of an antidote to the idealistic and virtue-loving young men who had never even thought about faith from the perspective of an outsider. Finally, I admitted to myself that indeed, I was experiencing a call to the priesthood! This call was beyond anything I had ever imagined for myself, but it felt just right for who I was then and where I was in my life.

After four years of part-time work at seminary, I went through the screening process to become a postulant or candidate for ordination. It was rigorous and detailed, and it would take me four more years to complete it. I remember the day the envelope containing the application and all the requirements for becoming a "Candidate for Holy Orders" arrived in the mail. Scanning it as I walked down our long driveway from the mailbox, I realized that there were fully 65 steps to be checked off! How would I ever do this? How could this call to ministry that had felt so much like a surprise and a blessing, now look like an infinite series of barriers to be surmounted, a relentless scrutiny of my worthiness in every respect? It felt like a collision of my hopes with bureaucratic reality, a demand that I conform to the system.

What I began to feel, more than anything about my new vocation, was that it was a gift. It came, really, as a result of the miscarriage. It came to me at a time of great emptiness, literally in my womb, and spiritually in my sense of an unknown future. Had that child been carried to term and lived, I doubt I would have become a priest. But out of that loss, that death, came extraordinary new life for me. When I think about resurrection—new life rising out of death in the most unexpected ways, I sometimes think of that small blue fetus who didn't make it and the call to priesthood that arose in me in his place. I think of him as raised from premature life to new life in me, used not only to heal me but through me to be a blessing to others.

Despite my dismay at the lengthy screening process for ordination, I was accepted first as a postulant, and then, a couple of years later as a candidate for ordination. There was a scary overnight conference at the College of Preachers next to the National Cathedral in Washington. Eight of us were interviewed individually by about a dozen teams on a variety of subjects. We had submitted long written "Spiritual Autobiographies" that included why we wanted to be ordained. With my undistinguished background of housewife and varied part-time worker, I felt a bit overwhelmed by the competition. They all seemed to have credentials, law degrees, Pentagon experience, social worker backgrounds. I also worried that I would seem too suburban "white-bread" and affluent, that I would be seen as out of touch with the problems of the inner city. But one of the interviewers helpfully reminded me that the rich have as many or more spiritual problems as the poor and that they needed ministers too, people who knew and understood what their lives were like. By the end of the conference, I felt reasonably confident, but was still jubilant when the phone call came a few days later, informing me of my acceptance. I would finish my seminary degree (the Master of Divinity) as a full-time student and begin field work in a parish new to me to gain practical experience.

My training at Virginia Theological Seminary consisted of three quite different parts: academic classes, clinical pastoral education and parish field work. During my four years of part-time work, the combination of morning classes and afternoons at home with my children worked well. I had a good local baby-sitter for the two younger boys, and Chris was in school until 3 pm. The juggling was hectic, but it was also exciting and enlivening to be embarking on this great unexpected adventure of becoming a priest. I worked my way through the basic classes on the Old and New Testaments, systematic theology, church history, and such pastoral subjects as marriage preparation, grief counseling and substance abuse. The courses came easily, and it felt good to again distinguish myself with good grades even as I realized they were a small part of what is needed to shape a priest.

Things changed during the summer of 1983 when I did a chaplaincy internship at the Washington Hospital Center and Children's Hospital. This was Clinical Pastoral Education, or CPE and was required for ordination. I found it to be the most valuable part of all my training—the place where theological abstraction met the grueling realities of life and where my identity as a pastor began to emerge. It was full-time work, including one overnight "on-call" at the hospital every week for the Med-Star emergency ward. Little did I know, as I headed out my driveway one warm June morning, waving good-bye to my husband and three young sons, that before I saw them again, I would face tragedy, touch death, and cry as if I would never stop. It was my first night on call.

Sometime after midnight I was summoned to the children's intensive care unit where a very young couple had brought their ten-day-old daughter, Nicoletta. She was near death from an untreated fever and infection. Her parents hadn't realized how ill she was, and now it was too late. The baby died after an hour. The family was Greek Orthodox; the grandparents were there, speaking mostly in Greek and waiting for their own priest who was apparently on the way but never came. As a pastor, I was it, clueless, horrified, trying to somehow provide comfort. I could not in any way accept the grandmother's urging that this was somehow God's will, and, even worse, her expressed hope that God would send another child, next time a boy! But my theological reservations were of no help anyway; these people were in despair, and my role was to be with them, hold them and be a compassionate presence in the face of tragedy. And it was tragedy, because this death needn't have happened; it was anything BUT God's will! It was the result of poor, young, inexperienced parents with no social support. To claim God's will at such times is to abdicate our human responsibilities and make a monster of God. But these were my agonized thoughts in hindsight, looking back on that night.

When the baby had died, the parents wanted to go into the ICU and hold her one last time, which they did with the nurse. Then the grandmother wanted to go too and asked me to go with her to the small crib. After she held the baby, she handed her to me to put back in the crib, and so, for the first time, I encountered death up close, in the flesh, in my arms, this tiny, limp body, a baby, but completely different. It is a feeling I will never forget. When I finally got back to my on-call bedroom, just before dawn, sleep was impossible, only tears and tears, heaving sobs of sadness, for the young parents, for the many other children there in the ICU, for the nurses, who seemed far better pastors than I, and for myself and how helpless I felt, how inadequate my faith or any of the tools of my training seemed.

In the morning, I dragged myself to my chaplaincy support group and poured out my story. They were caring and kind, of course, and we spent time processing what had gone well or could have been handled better, but from that day, my days in the hospital took on a gravitas, a sense of being so close to the heart of life because of having known death there. It was the life outside—the hot sunny parking lot at 4 pm when we got off work, the long commute in traffic to my suburban home on the banks of the Potomac that seemed unreal, almost superficial, compared with the life of that big city hospital. How odd, and troubling, that coming up close to death and loss is sometimes what it takes to truly value the richness and beauty of life!

What proved so helpful over the course of that summer was the opportunity on my own, and in our daily small group meetings, to keep asking the questions that had come up so painfully from the very beginning of CPE. What was I doing there as a pastor? What did I have to offer? I was not a doctor or nurse or social worker, not someone who had answers or cures or painkillers. I wore a cross around my neck in those days, and our supervisor, the Rev. J. Edward Lewis, asked me one day what it meant, how it helped. If I was to be a minister of the Gospel of Jesus Christ, how was I to do that in any meaningful way? It was not about becoming an expert. Becoming a pastor was instead a slow process of insight, guessing, wondering, trying to come alongside others as they faced physical illness and death, and trying to reach for their souls and connect with their longing for a sense of God's presence no matter what. Not that people ever said that explicitly, but in their fear, their questions, sometimes their anger, the question of "where is God in all this?" was very real—for them, and for me. As the summer wore on, I felt myself change from being a woman pretending to be a chaplain to a woman who

actually was a chaplain. I began to trust the importance of simply visiting patients, sitting quietly with them, offering to pray with them but not imposing
my beliefs. I felt the tremors in a delirious woman's hand relax as I recited
the 23rd Psalm—it seemed she knew these words. I found myself visiting a
young man suffering from a then almost unknown disease called AIDs. I'd
been called to come by his sister when one of the other chaplains refused to
go near him, even with gloves, as though he were a leper. I comforted a nurse
who had fled to the restroom in tears after having turned off the respirator
of poor, weary Joe, who had struggled with heart failure all summer until
finally there was nothing more to be done. I think of that summer as rich and
draining. Each day was a contrast between the intensity of living and dying
and healing and struggling and suffering of the hospital world from 8–4 and
during weekly overnights, and the return to my three beautiful sons, blond
and sun-browned from day camp, and to my husband and our home on the
river, a refuge indeed for a fledgling chaplain.

In addition to academics and the summer of chaplaincy training, I faced field
education in a parish setting, the third important part of what is often called
"priestly formation." We were expected to spend 12 hours a week working in
a parish church—for an intern year first before full-time seminary, and then for
two more years during seminary. We were asked to interview at three places at
least and to go to a church that was quite different from our home parishes so
as to experience some of the breadth of the Episcopal Church.

For me this meant urban and big, since my home parish was very small and
suburban. As it turned out, a casual remark in a yacht club bar in New York
City gave me the lead to St. Patrick's church in Washington, DC. We were
having drinks with a sailing friend of Tom's who was also a priest—Jim White-
more, who immediately suggested that St. Patrick's in Washington might
be a good fit. Jim Steen was the new rector, about my age, but he'd been a
priest for years. He had an infectious love for his work along with huge creative energy for keeping church growing and alive. We hit it off immediately,
and soon I was being introduced as the parish intern at St. Patrick's, where
I served for 3½ years while attending seminary and proceeding through the
ordination process in the diocese of Washington.

I began at St. Patrick's 1982, and although the ordination of women in the
Episcopal Church had just been legalized in 1976, I was not much plagued by

the controversies around women priests that so tortured my sisters in ministry in so much of the country. The first generation of ordained women had already done much trailblazing, making it easier for those of us who came later. Washington was a liberal diocese, and several ordained women were already serving in parishes. I was well accepted at St. Patrick's and did not worry in those years about whether my gender would hinder me in my ministry. Back then, I had a rather limited vision of myself as ordained. Perhaps I would do pastoral counseling part-time, thought I, but being a rector or even a preacher seemed remote prospects. Hardly any women priests were actually rectors heading churches back then, and as for preaching, I'd had absolutely no public speaking experience.

However, preaching was definitely part of the deal at St. Patrick's, and so on Dec. 19, 1982, with my heart pounding so hard I thought it might be visible underneath my white robe, I stepped into the pulpit. I had prepared for six weeks! I had had no prior training or experience in public speaking, no training at that point in homiletics (the art of preaching). And all of my young life in the Presbyterian Church had taught me that preaching was the big thing, the sole criterion of a minister's worth! I remembered my parents' critiques of sermons after church, and I remembered the stately bearing and learned scholarship of most preachers I'd heard growing up. All this came with me into the pulpit that morning as I poured myself into trying to deliver something cogent and moving and funny and worth hearing on that fourth Sunday in Advent just before Christmas. I preached about the triumphant song of Mary, called the Magnificat, which the gospel writers have put in her mouth after she hears the news from the angel about Jesus' birth. I talked about how this passage so moved my stern high school English teacher. Her rather formidable name was Miss L. Elizabeth Buckmaster, and it well described her with her manly British accent, her heavy woolen tweeds and sturdy brown oxford shoes. And yet her lined face lit up when she read this passage to us, and for me, back then, it signaled that there was something holy about these words for her. I also remember using an anecdote about my anger at something trivial evaporating one night as I came across a deer, standing alone and beautiful in the moonlight along a road near our house. My sister-in-law Mary has teased me ever since about this: "Was your sermon today about a deer again?"

Well, on that first time at St. Patrick's, they listened, and they laughed; maybe they were moved. And, at the end, they even clapped! Some of that was because they liked me and wanted me to do well, and I understood that, but nonetheless, I loved it. And perhaps even more telling was the reaction of my son Tommy, then four:

"What did you think of Mom giving the sermon today?"
"You were standing where the *man* stands!"

This observation was based on my being the only woman to be in the pulpit at St. Patrick's back then; laywomen who read scriptural passages all stood in the lectern on the other side of the chancel; the male clergy alone used the pulpit. A preacher was born that day, and my work over the years of growing that gift, stretching myself, connecting with folks at the level of their own lives and concerns has been the most rewarding, fulfilling, exciting and sometimes terrifying part of my priesthood.

Along with the opportunity to preach, my years at St. Patrick's began my understanding of how a parish church works, what the role of the rector is, how communities thrive or suffer, and all the myriad elements that go into being a minister: preaching, planning and leading worship, teaching, visiting the sick and dying, preparing folks for marriage and baptism and confirmation, providing pastoral counseling, working with vestries to govern the parish and see to its financial health, overseeing a staff, going to long tedious meetings involving all aspects of parish life, being part of countless social events, going to diocesan gatherings, working with youth groups. The list is endless, yet there are actually people who call and say "Oh, I didn't know you came in on weekdays; I thought you were just there on Sundays! Just the administrative and personnel management expected of a rector are daunting, especially since most seminary training in those days included almost nothing of this.

7

Theology, Worship and Pastoral Work

Along with the practical exposure to parish life, came my inevitable wonderings about where God figured in all this feverish activity. I heard a former Archbishop of Canterbury say that "the word hectic should never be part of a priest's life." Really! Here I was soaking up all this holy activity at St. Patrick's, driving two different carpools to two or three different baby-sitters, cooking and planning and trying to be a decent mom and wife and even have time for some social life that was not parish related. Actually, I did find God in the midst of all this, not set apart in some separate realm, but within the experiences and relationships of my life, within my heart's hunger to do well in this work and in my love for the community I served. I had a prayer life of sorts, mostly the daily chapel worship at seminary, and after that the fairly regular practice of reading Morning Prayer alone, but I did not have a highly developed spiritual discipline, nor do I now, at least in the traditional sense of saying a set series of prayers every day as many priests report that they do.

In those days I was a theist, one who believed in God as a spiritual being who exists both within and beyond the creation, one who is present both in our hearts and beyond all knowing. I believed in a God who is in personal relationship with each of us, who responds to prayers and has a will for us. I believed then that one task of prayer is to intuit God's will and reach in faith for this relationship. I certainly felt that God had guided me onto this path, but my theology was as yet fairly naïve. I had little to say about the problem of evil, and I both loved and struggled with theological and liturgical language. These were whole new ways of expression for me, and I was always trying to find ways of speaking about God that were authentic to my own experience.

It seemed that so many others in church were struggling for the same thing, and yet, when it came to worship, we all read our lines from the 1979 Book of Common Prayer. It included many new forms for the services and was way more inclusive than its 1928 predecessor. I was particularly moved by one small detail in the ordination services for Bishops, Priest and Deacons. In all of them, the pronoun for the ordinand "he" was now in italics *"he,"* meaning, of course, that it could also be *"she."* Just that one change, and the whole world of ordained ministry was thrown open to women! The book contains, in what is called Rite I, almost all of the old Victorian language of the 1928 book, beloved by many then and some even now. There is another option, Rite II, which is increasingly the preferred form used today. The language is far more accessible to contemporary churchgoers while remaining very tied to traditional theology along the following lines: God is still on high in the heavens, and we sinners approach the almighty looking for mercy through the blood of the savior, Jesus. This was my prayer book; I had no old ties to the earlier version as did so many older, more experienced clergy, and back then it fit with my own theological ideas. I loved poring through it, finding prayers for particular occasions, designing services that made use of many options, trying always to use language that best reflected the season or situation of worship and the community in which it took place.

Going to seminary chapel daily, or reading Morning Prayer at home, I usually found that the Biblical readings appointed for each day contained some nugget of interest or inspiration, and the quiet time alone in the mornings, before all the activities described above, fed my spirit. So far, the Episcopal Church, with its openness to reason and ambiguity, combined with a reverence for awe and mystery expressed in worship, suited me. Its Prayer Book was my trusted guide for leading and designing worship services and was a rich resource for pastoral work.

Pastoral visiting and counseling were challenging and exciting for me. With very little experience except the one summer of CPE, I needed to grow into a parish pastor, whether I was visiting sick or lonely people in hospitals or homes, or meeting with people who came to my office, hoping I could help them sort our their problems. I felt God, or sometimes Jesus, because of all the stories about how he encountered folks in pain, to be with me in these encounters, mostly because I seemed to be able to come up with what was needed or helpful, despite my feelings of inadequacy. At first, I went on visits with Jim Steen, my supervisor, and he proved a brilliant model. It was interesting to notice some of the gender dynamics. Sometimes older women, particularly widows, were clearly looking to Jim as the only male with whom they could talk on an intimate level, and since they often had plenty of female friends, they didn't need me. But sometimes, women felt safer with me and freer to confide. With men, the reverse was true. Even from the indignity and vulnerability of a hospital bed, some men were glad to have a woman as a pastor, while others preferred another guy, a man-to-man contact. All this simply affirmed my sense that having both men and women as ministers contributed hugely to the health and well-being of the church.

This recognition also affirmed my ongoing critique of the Roman Catholic Church, especially for its policy of priestly celibacy and of an all-male priesthood. The critique had been with me ever since my parents' prejudices had impressed me in childhood. Their objections had had to do with a hierarchy headed by the Pope, kneeling subserviently in worship, praying to intermediaries such as Mary and the saints. Over the years, however, I became aware of the ways in which Roman Catholic doctrines on birth control and abortion, celibacy and the male priesthood all caused actual hurt and misery among the faithful. One summer during college, I was visiting a friend in Brazil, in Rio. She had been an exchange student in my high school class, and that summer, I got to experience her country and culture which was then totally Roman Catholic. One day we went to the apartment of a friend of hers who was newly married. She was a beautiful young woman, and we were delighted to see her trousseau—all the lovely clothes and lingerie of this new bride. But I was puzzled when, as we admired a really pretty nightgown, she said, disgustedly "de nada," meaning "for nothing." My friend later explained that the woman's husband was in the army and had to travel out of town a lot on a schedule beyond his control. Her doctor had told her she had a health condition that would make it dangerous for her to become pregnant, and, since they were Catholic, they weren't supposed to use birth control. Love-making at "safe" times, using the so-called rhythm method, was almost never possible for this otherwise happy young bride and her husband because of his irregular travel schedule. I saw this as an unreasonable and uncaring demand of an institution, and although I realized that millions of Catholics ignored the rule, that just made it all the more objectionable, an open invitation to hypocrisy.

My problems with the all-male priesthood and the celibacy requirement later became connected to the various revelations of sexual abuse, particularly of young boys, that began to come out in the 1990s. These scandals involved large numbers of cases over decades, and the shameful covering up by the hierarchy exacerbated the crimes. Many bishops allowed accused clergy to continue in their roles and simply moved them from place to place, as if to avoid dealing with the issue. The eventual convictions led to a huge hemorrhaging of money, paid by the faithful to their church, and then spent to cover lawsuits and settlements in the millions of dollars. It certainly caused many Roman Catholics to give up on their church. Some of them came, in pain or disgust, to the Episcopal Church because they felt so betrayed. I continue to feel that any institution that insists that its clergy deny what is for most a normal expression of sexuality in marriage is more likely to attract people with disordered sexuality to begin with, or to eventually distort the sexuality of some of its members because of the deprivations caused by the celibacy mandate. To somehow equate the denial of the life-giving, life-producing instinct prompting sexual desire and relationships with some will of God seems a travesty. No doubt there are some who feel genuinely called to a life of celibacy, but to make this a norm seems an unjust burden and has contributed to the huge decline of priests in the Roman church as well as these many sad cases of abuse.

Finally, in speaking of my objections to parts of Roman Catholicism, I also mention something I value highly, that church's open concern for social justice and the extraordinary contributions of Catholic Charities and other organizations to relieving poverty around the world. Unfortunately, as the leadership in Rome bans all artificial forms of birth control, they cause and contribute to the overpopulation that is so much a part of poverty in the developing world. In doing so they deny women the opportunity for education and freedom from bearing more children than they want or can manage, thus exacerbating the very poverty they claim to deplore. This disconnect is glaring, and, for me, the rules about birth control verge on evil, in the sense of causing unnecessary suffering. The current Pope Francis' gentler, more compassionate stance on some of these matters, especially homosexuality and remarriage after divorce holds out some hope, but he has yet to announce any doctrinal changes in these matters.

8

The Deacon Goes to Israel

Finally, in June of 1985, I had fulfilled all of the requirements to be ordained a deacon in the Episcopal Church and then, six months later, a priest. It had taken me four years of part-time seminary, one year off to test my calling and begin the diocesan screening and intern process, a summer of chaplaincy training, and then two more years of full-time seminary and field work. The normal four-year sequence had lasted almost eight years for me. However, I felt I needed that time. I had been unchurched for over ten years, and I was completely new to the Episcopal Church and the Anglican tradition. I had a lot of theological orientation and spiritual growing to do, and I was grateful for that extended time. It also allowed me to be at home with my children about half the time until the two younger boys were old enough to go to school. But at last ordination day came. I'd finished all the course requirements, narrowly missed graduating with honors, and had gained all the needed approvals from my sponsoring parish and my bishop.

June 8th dawned warm and sunny and beautiful. I got up, put on a clerical collar and black shirt for the first time, and went with my family to the National Cathedral in Washington where Bishop John T. Walker ordained me and four others as deacons in God's "one holy, catholic and apostolic church." I remember standing in the rear of the nave, looking down the long, long aisle to the altar as our procession began, completely awed by the majesty of the setting and the enormity of what was about to happen. I remember moving through the congregation, passing my parents, looking tall, my husband, looking proud, and our small blond younger sons all dressed up, cute and somewhat bemused at all the splendor. I remember the line in the service when the bishop said, "May God, who has given you the will to do these things, grant you the grace and power to perform them." What a wonderful, succinct expression of the understanding of how we collaborate with God! We respond to the things we're inspired or called to do with our best efforts, and we trust that in doing so, we'll be supported by the love that leads us to them.

But before those lines were uttered, there was a shocking disruption. In every ordination service there is a point at which the bishop asks the entire gathering for their consent to the ordination, in this case, "Is it your will that Susan Mann Gresinger be ordained as a deacon?" From the back of the church came a chorus, over 150 voices strong, saying, "We object to the ordination of Susan Mann Gresinger as a deacon." The cathedral fell still.

This objection was not a surprise to me, or to Bishop Walker or the other ordinands; we had known for about a week that it was probably coming. It was based on the objection of a group of Episcopalians from across the river in the diocese of Virginia to my ordination because of my husband's work. Tom was a practicing obstetrician and gynecologist, and he owned a clinic in northern Virginia where he performed first trimester abortions. Although these abortions had been completely legal since the *Roe v. Wade* decision in 1973, this group opposed them and felt that Tom's role rendered me unsuitable for ordained ministry. One of the questions asked of the presenters at ordination is "Do you believe her manner of life to be suitable to the exercise of this ministry?" Another was the bishop's question to all of us, "Will you do your best to pattern your life and that of your family in accordance with the teachings of Christ, so that you may be a wholesome example to all people?" For this group of protesters, the answer was "no" in both cases.

The protesters had already come to me at seminary to raise their objections, and they had warned Bishop Walker of their intention to protest, including marching around the outside of the cathedral before the service with their grisly photos of unborn fetuses. Certainly they were within their rights, both legally and in terms of the opportunity given in the service to object. And so the bishop had worked out a plan in advance with the protesters. Rather than cause a big airing of the issue in the middle of the service, he called spokes-people for the group to meet with him in a private room adjacent to the nave and express their objection which he would hear and then determine whether to move forward. Meanwhile, a very long hymn was to be played and sung by the rest of us. Ironically, it was the stirring, "St. Patrick's Breastplate," almost always played at ordinations, but rejected by Bishop Walker because he had heard it so many times he was tired of it. However, in this instance it was the perfect hymn to cover his absence, and we ordinands were all delighted to have it played after all.

At the end of the hymn, the bishop emerged, stated very briefly that he had heard the objection and was fully confident that I was well prepared and qualified for ordination and that we would proceed. About fifteen minutes later, John Walker, this slight brown man with his own very real history of persecution because of his race, stood before me, laid his hands on my head and said "Therefore, Father, Through Jesus Christ your Son, give your Holy Spirit to Susan; fill her with grace and power, and make her a deacon in your Church." It was a powerful moment, made more so by the tension of the protest and the relief that it had been handled smoothly. Just in case, the ca-thedral had hired security guards inside the building to make sure no physical threats were made. I noticed early in the service that they were actually shad-owing me and realized things could have gotten very ugly. I was also sorry for whatever ways this incident marred the service for the other ordinands, but they were amazingly gracious and understanding. After the service we clustered, each with our family group, for pictures with the Bishop. Because the press had been alerted, my family and I got special attention, a spot on the local evening news and in the next day's paper, describing what had happened and featuring a lovely picture of my husband and me and our two adorable little boys with the bishops arms around us. So much for the evil abortionist!

To explain a bit further, abortion and the controversy around it was not something Tom and I ever took lightly. Once it became legal, Tom felt he should provide abortions safely and affordably as part of being a gynecologist serving women's reproductive health needs. He worked with an experienced Planned Parenthood nurse to open a clinic that consistently earned high marks for patient care, counseling and medical excellence. For me, abortion represented a really tough dilemma, a choice to be made among difficult choices with no clear right answer, only better or worse answers for the particular woman involved. I've never believed that the potential human life that does begin at conception is of equal value with the life of someone already born or with the life of the mother. I do believe that abortion is the ending of that potential life and does have moral valence. I feel strongly that this decision is one that must be made, for good or ill, by the woman who faces the choice and should not be legislated for one and all by the government, at least in the first trimester and sometimes later. For me the argument has always been about who should decide, not about whether abortion is murder. It was never my feeling that abortion or the provision of it was always wrong for Christians or anyone else, just that it was a sad but sometimes best option in very difficult circumstances. I disagreed profoundly with those demonstrators at my ordination and with a group who came years later to St. Mark's Church when I was working there, but I also respected their right to protest. Being connected with the abortion issue was one more continuing reminder to me about how we humans cannot ever live lives of some abstract purity, of how we face difficult moral choices of all sorts. We do need to decide and recognize that these decisions cause harm, but our decisions at these times are not a matter of wrong or right so much as whether they are faithful to the realities that confront us and to what will, we hope, cause the least pain and suffering.

As if my ordination day hadn't already held enough excitement, there was more to come. Later that afternoon Tom and I joined a group from St. Patrick's and flew to Israel for a ten-day pilgrimage! Imagine waking up as a layperson in suburban Washington one day and then, after hours of almost sleepless flight, arriving the next day as The Rev. Susan Gresinger in the Holy Land! For the first and last time on a plane, I wore my clerical collar, savoring the trappings of my new identity. After that, when traveling on trains or planes, I wanted to avoid intrusive questions from strangers, even if well-meant, so the collar stayed in the suitcase.

We were led in Israel by an Episcopal priest and an American Israeli rabbi. I soaked up the history and feasted on the scenery, especially in the places where some of the well-known Bible stories perhaps took place. And "perhaps" was a really important word for this tour, because there is so much hearsay and legend around these ancient sites. As much as I loved the idea of seeing such places as Bethlehem where Jesus was supposedly born, the Upper

Room for the Last Supper, the place where Jesus died on the cross and especially the tomb which was found empty, I realized there was little proof of any of this. Perhaps Jesus was actually born in Nazareth; most scholars believe the birth narratives are later inventions to express certain things about Jesus. Archeologists know a lot about the old city of Jerusalem, even going back to Jesus' time, and there is indeed one flight of large stone steps from a part of the temple that survived various destructions and existed when Jesus lived. He probably walked there. It was thrilling for me to walk these same steps, and I do believe Jesus walked there. As for the tomb, the place of the Resurrection, there are two locations, each of which is claimed to be THE place, and the huge Church of the Resurrection is all divided up between various branches of Christianity and encompasses both tombs. You can buy souvenirs in both. I decided that the tomb with the major claim to authenticity would be a significant place for me to enter and think and pray. Even though I will never know what happened on that first Easter, I felt an extraordinary sense that something had happened right around there that has changed the world and shaped my faith. I had bought a priest's stole earlier that day and brought it with me into the so-called tomb. It meant something to me then, and does today, even if it seems highly superstitious, that I blessed that stole there.

9

Priesthood—First Steps

Once I got back to Washington, I needed to find a job. I was an ordained deacon, in transition towards the priesthood for a six month period. In order for that second ordination to the priesthood to happen, I needed to find employment in a church. Unlike some dioceses where newly ordained clergy are placed in parishes by the bishop, in the Diocese of Washington, you need to find job openings, apply for and receive a call to work in a parish. In 1985, many of the larger parishes with two or more clergy were actually eager to have a woman on the staff, and since almost all the rectors were male then, this meant the associate slots could be for women. I quickly managed to be interviewed by three parishes in the Diocese of Washington, and one in New York. This was heartening, especially when I was one of the last two considered in each place! But after an exciting round of interviews at the prestigious St. James, Madison Avenue in New York City, a nice weekend getaway with my husband, my hopes faded. One by one, all four churches turned me down. The worst news came one July day just before we were leaving for a two-week vacation. This rector came to my office and told me he couldn't hire me because his wife would object. This was probably the one time I really felt that being a woman worked against me and that issues having nothing to do with my qualifications were impacting my employment. I finally made it onto the plane and an opportunity to pour out all my bitter sense of unearned rejection to Tom, and give way to my pent-up tears. Each church had called someone with more experience, raising the tricky "chicken and egg" question of how one ever gets experience if you need it to get a job in the first place. My exhilaration at having made it through the ordination process with top grades and extremely positive evaluations all along the way began to ebb; my hopes for a brilliant career dimmed.

Even so, back at St. Patrick's, I was getting experience, just not getting paid for it. I stayed on there for six months as a nonstipendiary deacon, doing most of the kinds of things that an assistant rector would do. I loved it so much, I barely cared that it wasn't a real job. The rector was generous about letting me preach regularly. As a deacon, I was not yet qualified to celebrate at the altar, but otherwise, I plunged eagerly into my new role and felt myself to be well accepted in that parish that I'd come to love deeply. So much so, that for awhile I happily languished in the comfort of St. Patrick's, reluctant to be drawn into the future and probably another church.

As the months of my diaconate moved along, I grew anxious and a bit embarrassed that I hadn't yet landed a parish job. In an attempt to help me with this, the deployment officer at Church House suggested that I apply for a part-time temporary position at St. John's Norwood, a midsized parish right on the border between Bethesda and Chevy Chase, Maryland. The rector would be on sabbatical from January through May of 1986, and the Associate Rector would need some help. After a brief interview, my job was set up, 10 hours a week for five months. Not an auspicious beginning, but it was enough to get me ordained as a priest.

My ordination to the priesthood took place on a Wednesday evening, December 18, 1985 at St. Patrick's brand new church in Washington. During my time as a seminarian there, the church had raised the money for a handsome new building with high white rafters, clear windows, moveable chairs instead of pews and a spacious altar platform extending out into the worship space. My ordination was the first big event in this building. My parents wondered why they should come back to Washington for yet another church extravaganza, but they did come, as did friends and family from all parts of my life. Bishop Walker presided, and my beloved friend, Bill Opel, who had started me down this path, was the preacher. This time there were no protests, just joy and celebration. The beautiful music and liturgy, the participation of so many dear friends, my young sons and their father carrying the bread and wine up to the altar, Bill's sermon, all these memories still shine in my heart.

The actual moment of this second ordination is very dramatic. All the priests there, usually a dozen or more, cluster around the ordinand. They lay their hands on her shoulders or the shoulders of others who do while the bishop pronounces the words of ordination, holding her head in his hands. I felt so surrounded by loving support, so blessed to be kneeling there on the floor of the church I had watched being built, so fully in that moment! At the end of the service, I gave the final blessing, my first words as a priest. It was a splendid evening, including the catered reception, possibly too splendid. I remember champagne and a raw bar, and pasta and a huge array of other gourmet treats—not exactly your standard church buffet of deviled eggs, cucumber sandwiches and cookies! But it was the culmination of a long journey, a special celebration for St. Patrick's, and a fine time for lavish hospitality.

Two weeks later I began work at St. John's Norwood, and my priesthood began in earnest. St. John's is a large red brick church with a graceful white cupola and a high vaulted nave, built in the mid-twentieth century. It had been founded much earlier, in 1895. It had once boasted over 400 people on a Sunday morning, and one of its former rectors, William Creighton, had become the Bishop of Washington back in the '60s. By the time I got there, it was much smaller, part of a decline in mainstream Protestantism that continues today. Probably due more to the cultural changes that had been going on in the country than to anything else., membership had slowly gone down through the sixties and seventies. Conflicts over the Viet Nam War, women's roles and rights, student protests, drug use and then Watergate raised huge questions and doubts, especially for young people. Folks became skeptical about the institutions that had for so long guided and governed our society. Traditional church teachings began to lose their authority as people more and more began to question the Bible and the belief system based on it. No wonder then, that congregations shrank and churches scrambled to orient themselves in a new environment, to the chagrin of many in the church, and, I suppose, to the satisfaction of those who feel that organized religion has run its course.

Despite this decline, when I arrived at St. John's, the congregation was still healthy, hopeful and good-willed. They welcomed me with great warmth and patient kindness in the face of my inexperience. I remember processing down the aisle on my first Sunday, grandly arrayed in red and gold vestments belonging to their rector and feeling somewhat of an impostor. This was especially so when I mounted the steps into the elevated pulpit where a bronze plaque commemorated the former rector who had become a bishop. The plaque read: "In appreciation of a loving, personally close and challenging God who is revealing himself through the mind, soul and achievements of William F. Creighton—December, 1950." Two weeks after my ordination to the priesthood, here I was, preaching in that pulpit and celebrating at the altar, meeting and greeting my new flock—at least in their eyes, I was a minister!

Five months at St. John's flew by. David Rider, the Associate Rector and Priest-in-Charge while the Rector was away, was a great mentor and friend. He was younger than I, but far more experienced, with a great sense of humor and fine pastoral instincts. Besides Sunday morning duties, which David and I shared, I was supposed to sort out some problems they were having with the Youth Group, something I really failed to figure out or manage. In my naivete, I wasn't prepared for the kinds of power struggles and difficult people that you meet in every church; I foundered on those shoals early on at St. John's.

I also led a women's reading group, and that was a much better experience. The members of this Wednesday morning group were older, bright, interested, and very open to my approach which was a bit new for them. Instead of preparing learned classes on the books of the Bible or some other "churchy" topic, I asked them to read and discuss the work of Frederic Buechner. He had had a formative influence on me during the ordination process and had given me a model for the kind of theology I was growing into and then developing for myself. His several autobiographical books were extremely important to me during those years. Buechner's theology is incarnational, in the sense that his experiences of God's presence come through the events and relationships of our lives. His sense of the divine as being embodied in the creation, in us, in all the mystery and joy and agony of living is one that I share, so that reading him was like communing with a kindred soul. Buechner taught me to reflect on my own life, including all the years away from church and to find God's presence, often hidden, there—in the ordinary as well as the special times. My little group of women were unused to opening their lives up to theological reflection in this way, but together we did this, and as we shared what was real in our lives, we grew close. It was a sweet time, and when it was time for me to leave, they remembered that I'd said my favorite flower was the lilac, and they gave me a small bush. It is huge now, and it blooms in a former garden, but that time at St. John's was indeed a time when seeds were planted that later blossomed magnificently, and I am grateful for the tender guidance those dear people gave to that very new and unsure priest.

10

St. Mark's Capitol Hill

Finally, in March of 1986, I received a real job offer. St. Mark's, Capitol Hill in Washington needed a full-time Associate Rector; they wanted a woman, and they wanted someone right out of seminary so they could mold that person into their somewhat unusual ways.

St. Mark's is a church with a reputation. It is seen by some as being wonderfully open and progressive, by others as scandalously heretical and self-involved. This notoriety is rooted in St. Mark's recent history. It was founded back in 1867, and has been housed in a large neo-gothic brick building on Capitol Hill since 1889. But as the neighborhood around it fell into decline in the mid-twentieth century and the big old Victorian townhouses became rooming houses, the church dwindled and was on the point of being closed. However, in 1954, a small group of committed members found a rector who could turn things around. Bill Baxter, handsome and smart and irreverent and arrogant, was just the ticket. He was also charming, impatient, full of ideas and an unconventional man of God for his day. To attract folks to St. Mark's, he began to tout it as a church for skeptics. He realized that there were by then a number of young couples and singles who were moving back into the run-down townhouses in the neighborhood and fixing them up. Most had moved to Washington from other parts of the country and were in need of a church or at least a community. Bill went door to door with pamphlets advertising St. Mark's as a place for "Interested Pagans, Bored Christians and Others." He staged chancel dramas which were at first theological but soon included secular dramas, such as "Antigone" by Jean Anouilh and "Cat on a Hot Tin Roof" by Tennessee Williams. These plays, and the leaflets, began to draw people to St. Mark's, most of them these young single or married people who were far from their home churches and wanting to try something new.

Baxter also offered a new kind of Christian Education, called "functional education," so named by its originator back in the 1950s, the Rev. Charles Penniman. He was an Episcopal priest who felt that traditional Christianity no longer spoke to people, especially to those who had been to war and back and who found nothing in the dry dogmas of the church to help them with their anguish and doubt in the face of the very real horrors they had endured. Penniman was steeped in the theology of Paul Tillich, which would inform the wildly popular mid-century book *Honest to God by* John A. T. Robinson. This was a time when the traditional ways of believing, including accepting supernatural events and taking the Bible literally were coming under fire. People who could no longer accept this kind of faith were searching for new theologians and new ways of being believers, and the "God is Dead" surge in popular culture was only a few years off.

Penniman was also a student of Kierkegaard and felt that authentic religion springs from those places where we meet despair, or from the shaking of the ground of our being, which is at the core of that Danish theologian's work. Unlike the usual Christian education of the day which began with the Bible and theological doctrines and moral teaching, functional education was experiential. It began with the pressures and tensions of the real lives of people. Through role plays, skits, small group work and discussion, plus occasional theological presentations, students were guided in their search for meaning and for a religion that actually could function for them—hence the name. With Bill Baxter's enthusiasm and leadership, functional education caught on quickly with the young people coming to St. Mark's who were sick of old pious religious jargon and eager to examine their own lives and values for meaning. Penniman, took theological categories such as sin, justification, despair, saviors, and Christ and presented them in ways that connected with the lived experience of the students, helping them to find a more authentic grounding in Christianity. This challenging form of Christian Education grasped people, kept them coming and grew the membership. Amazingly, it still flourishes at St. Mark's today.

One of Baxter's greatest gifts to St. Mark's was to remove the pews and set up an altar on a platform in the middle of the nave, with chairs on all four sides. He sold the old pews to a Mennonite church, and from then on, worship became an entirely different experience. Church in the round was almost nonexistent then (although there is certainly early church and colonial American precedent, among others). Baxter also welcomed the first black member, a school teacher and Biblical scholar, Verna Dozier, who later became a noted author, lecturer and preacher. During the early 1960s Lady Bird Johnson came to St. Mark's. She was an Episcopalian, and although her husband was not, he did come to St. Mark's occasionally. Most notably, he was there on the first Sunday of his presidency, Nov. 24, 1963 just two days after President Kennedy was shot. Undaunted, Baxter stepped into the pulpit and gave a sermon that has been remembered, framed and passed down ever since.

In 1966, Bill Baxter moved on to the Peace Corps, and Jim Adams became the Rector. He was to remain in this post until 1996, when he retired, and his years at St. Mark's were probably the most fruitful of its recent history. He built on many of Baxter's innovations, especially in functional education and innovative liturgy, both of which included strong, creative and dedicated lay leadership. He instituted the Sermon Seminar in which people respond to the Sunday sermon for about 20 minutes each week. This began with a very small cluster of attendees, but soon grew to over a hundred folks, many of whom quite freely offer their comments, criticisms, questions and sometimes off-the-wall musings. Only a very few other Episcopal churches have anything like this, and for many people, it is one of the main reasons they come to St. Mark's.

When Rector Jim Adams offered me a position at St. Mark's, I wasn't immediately thrilled. Even though many of the aspects described above appealed to me, I worried that St. Mark's was somehow a bit eccentric, a bit bohemian. I remained attached to St. Patrick's where I'd done my seminary training, and at that point they were dangling the possibility of my becoming Associate Rector there. I had a hard time deciding. It would have been so comfortable to just remain in that warm and lively community. St. Mark's would be very different, and I wasn't sure how I'd get along with all these lay people who were so confident about their leadership that there barely seemed to be a need for clergy! Skepticism was so highly prized as the hallmark of their theology,

that I remembered wondering if people there, including the rector, even believed in God! Finally I decided to meet one more time with Jim Adams to
discuss my hesitations. On a whim, I asked if we could go over to the church
and just walk around in it. The room was aglow with spring afternoon sun
shining through the stained glass onto the warm brick and wood surfaces. Jim
kept silent for awhile. Then he mentioned that the Bishop would be coming
in a few weeks and would be able to install me then as the Associate. A picture
formed in my mind of that event, of Bishop Walker, whom I so admired, and
me, kneeling at the altar for his blessing, and I knew that the turmoil I'd felt
for days was over. Perhaps that choice had been made almost unconsciously
in the days of indecision leading up to it, but it was that moment in which St.
Mark's first claimed me. I said "yes" to Jim and to the search committee and
began an incredibly rich journey with a parish that became the center of my
life for eleven years.

It might seem that St. Mark's was too much the center of my life. After all,
I had a husband and three young sons, two of them still in elementary school.
The same balancing and car-pooling and multitasking that got me through
seminary continued through my years at St. Mark's, but this was not without
cost. I was faithful about soccer games, school events, birthday parties and
overnights; I cooked dinner regularly; I loved spending time with my boys.
Tom and I managed late night dinners after I would finally get home from
work. But during these years, various seeds of discord between Tom and me
began to grow more troublesome, and I think St Mark's had a role in this. My
work kept me engrossed, involved with many people on a fairly intense level.
I became close friends with my colleague, Jim, with whom I shared a deep
love of theology and Biblical study as well as the many aspects of our ministry
in the parish. Even though I could meet school buses and be home in the
late afternoon for a couple of hours, most days I had to return to St. Mark's
for an evening meeting or class, leaving Tom to supervise homework and
tend the boys. It sometimes felt like having two jobs, as so many professional
women who have gone through this can attest. I actually didn't begrudge it;
it was just demanding. And at St. Mark's I got an enormous amount of affirmation and affection, a sense of being in on a very exciting venture with this
unique church. Looking back, I am still unsure about the effects of my St.
Mark's commitment on the rest of my life. Perhaps it ate away at my marriage

because so much of me was invested there. But perhaps it was actually St. Mark's that gave me things I missed in my marriage and allowed me to focus elsewhere and thus not really deal with my problems at home, enabling me to continue on in a family that might have otherwise come apart.

In any case, I loved my time at St. Mark's, and I loved being a priest. Sometimes I could hardly believe I was getting paid to do this work! St. Mark's was then at the height of its growth, known far and wide for its classes and worship in the round, for its theater and dance groups, both of whom performed in church occasionally, for its pub right in the building with beer on tap, wine and soft drinks. We were attracting new members weekly, many of them young singles or couples, many of the single ones finding and marrying partners at St. Mark's. I became sought-after to officiate at these weddings and loved the time I spent talking with couples as they prepared for marriage. And then, usually a couple of years later, I would baptize their babies. It was almost like a crop with a harvest, these beautiful babies coming along as the fruition of love born right there in the parish.

There were a few rocky passages with the rector early on at St. Mark's. Jim Adams was a very disciplined, organized man, and punctuality was one of his favorite virtues. Beginning with our very first staff meeting, when I showed up ten minutes late in his office, thinking I should wait until he summoned me from my office one floor up, I realized this would never do. Further, Jim was like my father in this, so his criticism triggered childhood memories of being late. I struggled always to fit the messy combined demands of motherhood and commuting, along with my job, into Jim's expectations of me as an associate.

Another issue for me and Jim was much more fraught with emotion and conflict. I had learned at St. Patrick's, following the example of Jim Steen, to say a person's name as I administered the communion bread: "Sally, the body of Christ, the bread of heaven." People had told me they loved this, that it gave them a sense of being addressed personally in what for many was an encounter with God, a sacramental moment of real importance. I remember names easily and was able to call each person by name unless they were new, and I loved the more intimate contact with each person, however fleeting. And so, at St. Mark's, I continued the practice, again with much favorable comment. Except for Jim. One morning after I'd been there a few months, he confronted me:

"Susan, I don't think it's appropriate for you to say people's names when you pass them communion bread. We've had a problem when the lay servers do this with the wine because people think they play favorites since they only know their friends' names."

"But" I rejoined, "I know everyone's name except for the newcomers, and then I try to not use names of people right next to them so they won't feel left out. People really respond to this." Meanwhile I was wondering if Jim was jealous as he didn't have that capacity for remembering names, but I didn't venture with that! He continued:

"You realize that the Worship Committee has a policy on this; we're not supposed to use names at communion. I want you to observe this."

I was just outraged and horrified, stomped across the office and began to cry—angry at him and angry at myself for losing it.

"Are you just forbidding me to do this? You know, I came here to this place where the lay people try to run everything and they have all these policies and practices and now you're insisting that I stop doing something that seems to really touch people just because of one of these rules!" Still standing in the corner with arms crossed angrily, I saw Jim struggling—hugely uncomfortable with my tears. I waited through his silence. Finally, Jim spoke:

"I think I'm beginning to understand something here. For you, this isn't about the worship committee policy. For you, saying the names is part of who you are as a priest, part of the way you inhabit your role."

"That's exactly right! Thank you. I know that's why I'm so adamant about not giving it up."

"Well, all right then; I'll let you continue, and the worship committee can make an exception."

I was so grateful that Jim found his way to understanding me, had allowed his basic kindness to try to figure out what this meant and thus avoided a real battle of wills. I continued to address people by name at the altar at St. Mark's and every other church I have served; it is indeed part of who I am as a priest.

I remain thankful for that difficult morning as it helped me to clarify why saying each person's first name and looking into each face as I place bread from my hands into theirs is a true moment of feeding, for me and for those who come to the altar.

Fortunately, real conflicts with Jim were rare, and I settled in happily at St. Mark's, feeling appreciated and supported by him and the congregation as well. What I began to understand and savor about church ministry is the way that all the various parts of it feed one another and help one to grow as a minister. The rhythms of planning and leading worship connect you with the life of the whole community and with the liturgical traditions of the wider Episcopal Church. The pastoring of people going through joyous life passages such as those weddings and baptisms is tempered by grief counseling and all the dark times when despairing people come to you for counsel and support. At such times, particularly in the beginning, I was fearful that I would have nothing to offer. What can a minister say to someone who is severely clinically depressed, or who feels she has no faith, or has lost a child and finds no reason, no answers that can help? I had a kind of interior prayer I would turn to before such encounters. It was just an acknowledgment of my inadequacy along with an expression of trust that somehow God would be present to us and I would be given what I needed. There was no way to check this out objectively, but it often seemed that in fact some solace did come in such meetings, and I know I gradually became more compassionate to so many who sought my help, even those who initially put me off. In listening to story after story, I would be drawn in and see another's world, see my own world in a different way, and thus gain perspective. To use theological language, I came to see these wounded souls as beloved children of God, hurting, sometimes through their own misguided actions, sometimes due to outside afflictions, but always worthy of comfort and the hope of things getting better.

11

Preaching

The preacher pulls the little cord that turns on the lectern light and deals out his notecards like a riverboat gambler. The stakes have never been higher. Two minutes from now he may have lost his listeners completely to their own thoughts, but at this minute he has them in the palm of his hand . . . Drawing on nothing fancier than the poetry of his own life, let him use words and images that help make the surface of our lives transparent to the truth that lies deep within them, which is the wordless truth of who we are and who God is and the Gospel of our meeting . . . because to dismiss it as untrue is to dismiss along with it that catch of the breath, that beat and lifting of the heart near to or even accompanied by tears, which I believe is the deepest intuition of truth that we have.

Telling the Truth: The Gospel as Tragedy, Comedy and Fairy Tale
—Frederick Buechner

These words are from Frederick Buechner's extraordinary book on preaching. Reading them for the first time, back when I was in seminary, I was moved to tears; reading them to my husband just after quoting them here, I wept again. He asked,

"What is that about? Do you miss preaching so much?"

"No, it's that this is so beautiful and true for me. I know that moment when you step into the pulpit. I know that silence, as they, and you, wait for something, something that will touch and melt and change hearts."

"Well yes, Buechner writes beautifully, but there's more to it for you . . ."

"OK, yes, I do miss preaching. I love the challenge and the struggle of the task, and I so much want a sermon to be good, to mean something."

This exchange brought back all my childhood memories of how much stock my parents placed in good Presbyterian preaching, about how they judged pastors almost entirely on their sermons. It brought back my longings for sermons, my own and others, to be powerful, to move people. It brought back my laments about how few sermons actually do this, about how people caricature preaching as verbose and boring or as fire and brimstone rantings. Most of all, it reminded me of how much I have loved preaching and still do.

Preaching is a unique form of expression, probably more like a spoken op-ed column than anything else. You get to speak, uninterrupted, for usually ten to twenty minutes, and it is your job to bring ancient scripture alive in all its veiled, puzzling and even sometimes obnoxious voices. In the Episcopal and many other Christian denominations, there is a lectionary or schedule of selected Bible readings in a three-year cycle. Each Sunday has its suggested texts, and you are to connect these readings with your own life and that of your hearers in a way that matters. A preacher must always face the "So what?" question about her work: why do people need to hear this? And finally, a sermon is supposed to be "good news" or Gospel in Christian terms. Underneath all that, at its best, our preaching should tell the truth about the way life really is, and where we all get caught, and how and why we need saving help. The task is daunting, and I love its fierce demands.

However, the challenge often looks like this. You're scheduled to preach on Sunday and it is the Tuesday of a very busy week. You decide to stay home and get a start on the sermon before heading to the office. You make a pot of coffee, have some breakfast, look at the paper, maybe do the crossword. Finally you settle in, yellow-lined pad and about four pencils, sharpened and in a row. Your Bible, and a couple of other books you've been reading that may have some good quotes, are spread about. You read over the appointed readings for Sunday. Sometimes your heart just sinks, "not the Beatitudes again!" you say to yourself. "Blessed are the poor, the meek, etc. etc. who will all inherit the Kingdom of Heaven, whatever that is!" You've preached on this so often you've run out of things to say. Or perhaps the readings include the horrifying story of Abraham's almost sacrifice of his son, Isaac. He is prepared to stab him to death and then burn him to prove his faith to God! Oh, I know there is more to it than that, and it has been interpreted by all kinds of scholars to seem less cruel. I've actually managed one sermon on this text which I think deals with it adequately, and when I can pull this off, I'm well pleased (Appendix A).

Sometimes, the readings are so rich in language and spirit and power that you feel a sermon can barely do them justice, but it's a privilege to try. Sometimes you wonder at the effrontery of it all, of thinking you can convey something of how God is with us, if even God there is, and asking why in the world you've chosen to walk this scary plank into the pulpit Sunday after Sunday. At such a time, doing the laundry, or the welcome ringing of the phone affords a break. Finally you begin to write, starting sentence after crossed-out sentence. Sometimes you are three pages in and crumple the whole mess, who wants to hear this? Sometimes you delve so deeply into your own inner story it feels too naked to preach. Crying while you write is OK; crying while you preach is not. You learn after a year or two how to write for the spoken, not read word. You learn about the cadences of your voice and how the words you write will sound out loud. No more are you preparing learned papers for seminary classes. Finally you begin to find your voice as a preacher; and when you do, and a sermon goes well, there is no better feeling.

During my years at St. Mark's, I had good help with my preaching. Part of that was a system they had there of involving lay people in the preliminary preparation of sermons. The preacher for each week would meet with a "sermon planning task force" about ten days before the service for an hour in the evening. This group of about five would go over the assigned readings for that Sunday and discuss their questions and where they found connections with their lives or the life of the St. Mark's community. Often they could offer examples or stories from their experience that might prove helpful in developing the sermon. If nothing else, these meetings got the preacher's mind in gear, opened it up to some themes and alerted her to what was of interest to her hearers. I found these meetings to range from extremely helpful to a complete waste of time except to let others drone on about their pet concerns. Horrified clergy colleagues said, "You mean you let them tell you what to preach?" That was never the aim or the result. The idea was that preaching was a community event and should originate not only in the heart and mind of the preacher, but in the shared thoughts of others in the community. People volunteered for these task forces, a season at a time, so the membership changed from say, Lent, to the season after Easter, and so on throughout the church year. Eventually new leadership at St. Mark's did away with these planning groups, but in my early days there as a preacher, I found them more helpful than not.

Another and much greater help with preaching at St. Mark's was the Sermon Seminar which I mentioned above as an innovation begun by Jim Adams. It continues today as part of the 9 o'clock service, but after the regular hymns, readings, prayers and communion. There is a coffee break, and the children go off to Sunday School while the adults regather in the church at 10. The sermon is given, followed by about twenty minutes for people in the congregation to respond. They go to one of two microphones and offer praise, questions, criticisms, arguments, observations, stories from their own lives—whatever is stirred up in them by the sermon. The preacher generally does not engage in discussion during this time, just listens to the comments.

At first, this was a daunting prospect. Open, honest feedback is highly valued at St. Mark's, and they were known for pressing inexperienced preachers. I could count on negative as well as positive feedback, and in those early days, there was plenty of the former. The hardest moments were just after the sermon ended. I would sit down and wait for someone to speak. This silence could feel like an eternity, even if it lasted less than a minute. I knew folks had to collect their thoughts, but still, I wondered, in agony "what if they have found absolutely nothing to say about this?" But always people did speak, and usually it was helpful, adding nuance and example and depth to whatever I'd said, pushing me to grow as a preacher. Again, my clergy colleagues were dubious. They seemed to feel that preaching had to be inspired by the Holy Spirit and was some kind of private transaction between me and God that should not be questioned. I never felt this way because my belief in the power of Holy Spirit to inspire any of us in any creative endeavor allows for all sorts of channels for this inspiration. Not only books and music and nature and my own experiences of God and of faith, but also the testimony of my community shaped my sermons, and I found Sermon Seminar to be a wonderful, regular way of staying in touch with how well I was getting through as a preacher. And, as after my very first sermon, sometimes they would clap.

Other people helped me become a competent preacher. Betsy, who was well-versed in the functional education program at St. Mark's, took the trouble to request a meeting with me so that she could tell me that my sermons were not "functional" enough. I bristled to hear this as it suggested a kind of formula tied to this particular way of examining faith, a view I found too narrow. She wanted every sermon to illustrate "living in the tension" a favorite slogan from "func ed," as it was informally dubbed. She wanted me to raise questions but not provide answers; she felt I should present faith as the product of despair, the place we come to when all else has been swept away. My own experience is that faith arises in all sorts of ways, sometimes out of times of great joy and gladness, and I also do find answers along the way, not to every question, and not always permanent, but answers even so. I believe a sermon should go beyond questions and offer insights at least into how the preacher has wrestled with the issues raised, and where she has come out, not as a definitive solution, but as guidance for hearers in their own wrestling. Despite my reluctance to follow Betsy's suggestions, I respected her for taking the initiative to come and talk to me, and I did become more adept at incorporating the functional education approach into my preaching.

Another parishioner, Karen, came to me several years later. This time it was about my delivery. She felt I was not being as dramatic as I might be in the pulpit. She referenced a particular passage in a recent sermon where I had talked of Mary's visit with her newborn Jesus to an old man in the temple who warned her "and a sword will pierce your own soul too." Why hadn't I given that a much more forceful expression? Why hadn't I pointed out towards the congregation as I quoted these words? Where was my sense of theater? This criticism hit home. It freed me, in a way, to experiment with being a lot more expansive in tone and gesture. It was part of my transition from a preacher who is delivering a written text to a preacher who is speaking from her heart and trying with all her might to convey the meaning and power of her words.

More than anyone, Jim Adams shaped my preaching the most. People at St. Mark's loved his preaching, and I strove to attain his standard. He was admired for preaching without notes and for combining very keen insights on the real lives of his listeners with well-grounded Biblical scholarship. His sermons had a clear structure and usually only one main point. He was great at finding new questions or new ways of interpreting familiar passages, and he wasn't afraid to provoke people into thinking again about stuff they thought they already knew. He is famously known for a sermon in which he suggested that "God is a jerk." The full context of this utterance reduces the shock, but all that has long since been forgotten, and only that line remains in the collective memory and lore of St. Mark's. It was even mentioned at his memorial service in 2011. Jim and I would have lunch together in my office on Thursdays and proofread the bulletin. We would also often talk about the upcoming sermon for whoever was on. We pretty much took turns, except for special times like Easter and Christmas Eve which were always the Rector's domain. We would discuss the Biblical passages and what our thinking was, critiquing back and forth as to how the sermon might be most effective. But it was after the sermon, on the following Monday morning, during our one-on-one staff time, that I really learned from Jim, sometimes painfully. I would ask, "How did you like the sermon?"

"Which one? You preached three."

Or "I have no idea what it was about."

Or once, "With sermons like that, you'll never become a rector."

My response was usually tears, but over the years I began to skip that part and ask him questions about how to achieve more clarity, less clutter, more fluency of language. And, I got better as a preacher, so these sessions weren't so grueling, and at times I could criticize him back. Jim was a stickler for correct grammar and for proper definitions of words. He kept the Oxford English Dictionary right behind his desk, ready for consultation at any time, and each of us delighted in correcting the other, especially when, (heaven forbid!) some kind of grammatical or vocabulary mistake was made in the pulpit. I came to appreciate Jim's honesty, including his criticisms, as a tribute of respect, and I know he listened in turn to my take on his preaching and teaching. He changed me, and I felt myself to be part of changes in him as I heard, every so often, an idea or phrase from him that I knew had come from me.

One sermon in particular stands out for me from those days at St. Mark's. It was a Palm Sunday sermon, probably 1988. This is the Sunday just before Easter when the services begin with great fanfare and end in dark tragedy. We would rearrange the church with a huge center aisle, chairs facing it, and the whole congregation would walk in carrying palm branches and singing "All glory, laud and honor" in commemoration of Jesus' triumphal entry into

Jerusalem. But then the Passion Gospel, the story of Jesus' arrest, trial, crucifixion and death is read. The music turns somber, and the reality of failure
and betrayal and grief, not only in Jesus' story, but in our own lives takes
over. On that Sunday, the sermon was to be preached from the chancel steps,
facing out into the nave, with no pulpit or place to hold a manuscript, and
so I prepared to do this without notes of any kind, just standing alone there
in my white robe and red stole, speaking words about a time when betrayal
had been very real for me, and there had seemed no hope, no consolation.
I preached about my trip home from Laos when the friend had been killed,
and my sister's absence, and my friend's grief, and my own loneliness, and
how none of it made sense, and how any notion of God having the power
to bring some kind of redemption or fulfillment into the story had seemed
utterly lacking to me at the time. The room got really quiet as I spoke. It's a
quiet I've come to know as a preacher, and it happens infrequently, but when
it does, it feels as though you are part of something more, that something is
happening through you. Perhaps because I had no notes, perhaps because I
was scared standing up there so exposed, perhaps because of the power of the
story, I just felt the words pour out with a passion and a conviction I'd never
before known. At the end, there was dead silence, and a few people were
crying. Instead of the usual sermon seminar, folks seemed content to just
sit quietly and then move to leave. I felt drained and exhilarated at the same
time, and I'll hang onto that feeling forever.

There have been so many sermons, and many others that I know have had
power, or have moved people profoundly. There have been others where I've
had no idea of their impact except for what people have told me, even about
sermons I thought were mediocre. But that Palm Sunday stays with me as a
day when I truly felt that God was speaking through me, that my words had
led us into the heart of the Passion story and left us all, like Jesus' frightened disciples, wondering where and how God could bring saving help. The
sermon ended on that wondering, and with these words, "That's a story for
another Sunday. Amen."

12

Sabbatical

In 1992, I took a six-month sabbatical, a fairly common practice for Episcopal clergy and part of my agreement with St. Mark's. There were really no strings attached; the time was for rest and renewal. I was fully compensated and also received an extra stipend to help cover travel expenses. What a blessing! I divided the sabbatical into three sections: time at home doing cleanup and neglected household projects, travel, with family and alone, and finally two months of solitude in Nantucket, doing a guided reading project with a mentor. I looked forward with both curiosity and trepidation to what it would be like to be out of my role as a priest for an extended period. I had so far not felt that being a priest made up my identity or that without it I'd be bereft, but I did look forward to a sense of relief, an anonymity for which the black shirt and white collar never allow.

For years I'd dreamed of flying to Paris with all three sons, and in 1992, they were just the right ages. Chris was 22, finished with college and getting ready to go to culinary school. He was eager to sample French cuisine and probably even more so to drive a car at European speed limits! Tom and Rob were 14 and 12 and old enough to be interested in such travel, just as long as museums and cathedrals didn't take all of our time. The younger boys had never been out of the country and were unsure about what to expect but eager to go. When the big silver bird raced down the runway at Dulles airport and soared off towards Paris, my own heart soared with it, full of hope and the sheer joy of this big adventure.

In Paris, we walked for miles, seeing all the favorite tourist places. Despite the many interjections of "Look at that cool car!" as we passed so many glittering sports cars, the boys did actually respond to at least one sacred space in Paris. This was our visit to La Sainte Chapelle, the beautiful small Gothic church whose walls are almost entirely of stained glass. You have to enter underground, into the crypt, and then go up a narrow winding stairway opening suddenly into a space filled with streaming light and color. So I didn't warn the boys, just said there was a chapel I wanted them to see. I went first up the stairs so I could see their faces when they reached the top, and it was so worth it. Just as I'd thought that perhaps sports cars might be the only objects of true awe for them, I saw wonder and delight on each of their young and vulnerable faces. The beauty of that jewel-lit space was not lost on them; it was this mother's treasured moment.

My boys were not particularly religious, even though they'd been to Sunday School and church through grade school. By the time of this trip, their interest had waned, and their questions had formed, and they mostly tolerated my interest in visiting churches, a sort of humoring of Mom, because she was, after all, a priest! As for Notre Dame Cathedral, or the much older church of St. Germain de Pres, they were underwhelmed and preferred to sip wildly overpriced cokes in cafes while I lost myself in the cool dark interiors of these age-worn temples of the spirit. To me, these ancient churches spoke of an all encompassing love for God, a desire to reach for the realm of heaven through architecture and art and stained glass. The peasant souls who labored and the craftsmen who designed and fashioned these buildings created something transcendent, a realm that feels sacred even today. To enter them reignited my own longings for a sense of the holy, rekindled my sense of the human response to God throughout the ages.

Another treasured Paris memory is of the three boys ahead of me, walking down along one of the quays just next to the Seine in the late June twilight. They were young, exuberant, so fresh and alive to new experiences; I simply loved them and the beauty surrounding us.

After four days in Paris, we headed south to Chartres where we had a very special and unexpected treat. Back at home, I had become friends with Bill Flanders and his wife, Claire, who was French. Bill is an Episcopal priest and served as an adjunct clergyman at St. Mark's. This meant he helped out in the

Sunday services on a regular basis, while working as a composer and music teacher during the week. Claire was a photographer, and it happened that that summer she was launching her first professional show in her small home town of Lèves, just outside of Chartres. Since she would be there when we visited Chartres, she generously invited us to meet her there for lunch, and then back to her sister's house where family members were picking cherries in the large back yard. We shared them fresh from the tree for dessert. We spent a long sunny afternoon, then stayed on for supper with Claire, her sister and husband and a niece. While Claire and the niece and I took a long walk through high green wheat fields looking across to Chartres Cathedral, her brother in law, Pierre taught my boys to play boules. This French game was perfect for them, as you didn't really need words, although Chris bravely ventured what school French he had, and they got along happily. This visit to the home of a French family was a highlight for us all, and for me, it later became the beginning of a real and important history with that family.

The rest of our time in France flew by. We spent five days at a rented old house in a tiny village called Huisnes-sur-Mer, and from there we discovered the charming walled town of St. Malo, where the boys got me to spring for a sailboat rental one morning. I gladly accepted as it freed me to walk the city walls with their gorgeous views out over the ocean and then to spend quiet time in the cathedral there, perusing the French Catholic prayer book and noticing how similar their mass was to my own Episcopal liturgy. I bought a rosary there. I'd never prayed with one and am not sure why I bought it except that its dark wooden beads were lovely, but I still have it in my bedside drawer.

From our rental we could see the famous Mont St. Michel in the distance, rising out of the water like a fairytale castle. We found several stumps just the right size to sit on in a vacant field not far from the house, and each evening, around 10:30 when the late June summer sunset turned the sky pink and gold, we'd gather there to admire the monastery. We'd actually spent a night there earlier, and again, I was awed by the incredible construction of this abbey, high on an island, jutting out of the water and surrounded by the sea at high tide. That people had built and lived and prayed there for so many centuries reminded me again of the variety and sweep of Christian belief and practice over the ages. I was part of all of this, even though my beliefs came nowhere close to the devotion to Mary or the literal belief in the Bible or the stern doctrines of damnation and salvation of those twelfth century monks. I live in a different world, but it would be a poorer one without these weathered, cherished shrines of Christians gone before. I love being part of this heritage, this glorious and flawed history.

Our last day in France included a visit to the Bayeux tapestry in the town of Caen, on our way to the ferry at Cherbourg which would carry us across the channel to England that night. Rob loved this as he had been studying William the Conqueror in school and so could recognize and identify the story depicted on the tapestry. It would also give him something to brag about to his classmates when he got home. He and Chris began an argument that day about whether moats surrounding castles had existed in England before the arrival of William in 1066. Each was totally sure of his position, willing to bet money, and determined to prove himself right. It was during that time, one day in the car, that the Experts on Everything, or EOE Club, was born, with the four of us as charter members. It arose naturally from the trip together as our various certainties about everything from directions to history to culinary details would clash and erupt in only half-serious arguments. If anything, the recognition of our shared desire to be right drew us closer than our differences of opinion, and so this "club" has endured until now. It is mentioned and laughed about at most family gatherings; each of us has presided over the club, and now a new generation is about to be ushered in as Emma, Chris' twelve-year-old daughter, shows all the appropriate qualifications for membership. Precocious, smart, highly verbal and sure of herself, she is a natural.

Once in London, we met up with Tom and began the second phase of our trip. We spent four days in London, churches and museums for me and Tom, and Madam Tussaud's Wax Museum and the Hard Rock Café as highlights for the boys. In fact we made a deal on Sunday morning. If the boys would go to church at Westminster Abbey with us, they could go with Chris to said Hard Rock Café that night. It was thrilling to worship at the renowned Abbey, but for me the most compelling moment was when, at the end of his sermon, the priest simply stood in silence for perhaps a whole minute before quietly saying "Amen." Usually, before you have even a moment to reflect on what you've heard in a sermon, the service rushes ahead into the recitation of the Nicene Creed which is an expression of Christian orthodoxy dating to the fifth century. It can be about the driest, most incomprehensible and unbelievable utterance of the entire liturgy. I understand the theology behind it and how it came to be, but for me and countless others, it is a stumbling block, a cross-your-fingers-behind-your-back moment in the service. Following immediately upon a provocative sermon, it is a distraction.

From London we traveled to the north and west to visit friends in the small cathedral city of Lichfield. There, I actually became a minor visiting dignitary. Two years earlier, on a trip with a group from St. Mark's, I had met and become friends with Tony Barnard, one of the Canons at the cathedral there. This time he invited me to give a talk as part of a special all-day education program at their newly renovated Visitors' Center, actually an old stone medieval building, visited the year before by the Queen Mother, then 91. I was asked to speak about being a female priest, as this was still several years off in England. So there I was, in this ancient space graced by royalty, dressed in a tailored suit, black shirt, clerical collar and high-heeled pumps, a sight never yet seen in that august setting. I held forth on my own journey and realized this was something very new, and that people were more curious than opposed. They had many questions, but basically, I felt I had advanced the cause of women priests at least a bit by presenting a positive image.

Finally, back in London, I said good-bye to my family as they headed for the airport and home, and I headed off by train. I had arranged to spend a week in Lincoln, another small cathedral city. I was to live in an apartment right on the cathedral close. It was a sabbatical center, and I was expected to take part in the worship life of the cathedral, but was otherwise free to read, write and explore.

I remember arriving in the tiny exquisite apartment—a fold-down bed, fresh lilies in a vase and a stunning view of the cathedral façade just across the way from my window. I felt giddy with the thrill of finally being on my own, tired from the long train ride and dragging my excessive luggage, and I had no idea of what to do next. The prospect of this whole week of rare unstructured time was an amazing gift, and I hoped to make the most of it.

To start, I went each morning to the brief service of Morning Prayer in one of the small chapels inside the cathedral. There were usually only three or four or us—the dean and bishop and another priest or two, and me. Sometimes

I was asked to read a scripture passage or a prayer; mostly I remained silent, letting the old traditional language wash over me. That felt different in England, because I was not at work, not in my role of trying to make sure liturgy was accessible, new, open and creative in order to attract others. Here I could relax back into the Victorian language of the British prayer book and the passive role of a worshiper. I could muse on a phrase from a psalm or reading, savor the cadences and search the meaning of these archaic words. I could reach towards God; I could feel a sense of holiness in the place and the rhythms of this worship. It renewed my soul. The week turned out to be a mixture of spiritual nourishment through the daily prayer cycles in the cathedral, social and political contacts with the various clergy living and working on the close, and long walks and runs all around the beautiful hillside town. Lincoln's cathedral and castle sit on a hill with the old part of town sloping steeply down from it on narrow winding streets. Wandering through the cavernous church, not unlike our National Cathedral in its design, I remembered that the wonderful novel *Catherine* by Anya Seton, which I'd loved as a teenager, was set mostly around Lincoln, and the title character on which it is based is buried in the cathedral. This is the highly romantic story of a young woman whose long-term affair in the 14th century with John, Duke of Lancaster, was a huge scandal but which eventually resulted in the legitimization of the four children she bore him out of wedlock, one of whom became an ancestor of England's Queen Elizabeth II. I believe my attraction to this story has to do with how a person who did not follow the expected norms but who did follow her own passions both suffered for those choices and also found a sure redemption. It was poignant to stroll through Lincoln Cathedral where so much of this saga had unfolded. I felt drawn back into the history of my church and ever more solidly grounded in my own faith, evolving as it was from those age-old roots.

For the last part of my trip, I joined a group from the Cathedral College in Washington who were part of a week-long course on Anglicanism based at Canterbury Cathedral. There too, I lived on the cathedral grounds or precincts, as they were called, of the King's School. We were a group of about twenty who met with the dean and other clergy for seminars, daily worship and evening fellowship, always enlivened by plenty of good red wine, or claret, as the British call it. Canterbury Cathedral is the scene of the famous murder of Thomas Beckett in 1170 by the followers of King Henry II, and the actual place of the horrific murder is shocking to see. I felt in that space, as I did in various places in Jerusalem, a sacred grandeur, a sense of connection with the long and tortured history of my faith, including this grisly martyrdom, all because of a misunderstanding of the king's intent. Henry had expressed his frustration about Thomas, then Archbishop of Canterbury, who was standing up for the authority of the church against the crown. The king had said aloud, in front of courtiers, "Who will rid me of this meddlesome priest?," and they took him at these words. Added to my conviction that Christianity is not the only valid religion was a growing sense of how deeply ensnared it has been in the vicissitudes of history over time, how much connected with the ways of the world. Thomas' blood and brains had been scattered over the very floor I looked upon, some 850 years later, and it was because of that that Canterbury became the great pilgrimage shrine that it remains today. A religion that was born in the aftermath of a bloody cross has never been pure and removed from human strivings and sins, deepest aspirations and worst depravities. It is a religion about life, all of life, and of a God imbedded in our human souls, a presence, rather than a being, not removed, but close, embodied in all of creation. The dramatic history and the various talks and classes we attended in Canterbury did much to educate me about the richness of the Church of England and its traditions and liturgies and how all of that came into the Episcopal Church, and I very much loved embracing these roots. Paradoxically, the roots have been important to me over the years, even as I have sought to push the church beyond them. I never want to sever myself, I just want my church to evolve and grow into new life.

The last part of my sabbatical was time alone. More time alone than I'd ever had in my life. I spent all of September and October of 1992 on Nantucket, in a house my brother and his wife generously let me use. By this time, my oldest son, Chris, was away at the Culinary Institute of America in Hyde Park, New York, and our son, Tom, was beginning his first year at St. George's School in Newport, Rhode Island. That left youngest son, Rob, and Tom at home together, but both seemed agreeable to my absence. The reactions of some of my women friends were interesting. To some, the idea of leaving one's husband and children and going off alone for two months was unimaginable—how could I? To others, it was nirvana, they'd give anything!

I was definitely in the latter category, but when parents' weekend at St. George's came around about halfway through, it was wonderful to take that ferry and meet Tom and Rob and then young Tom for a fine family weekend. But my absence during those months did create some distance between my husband and me, something I wasn't willing to look at then. I just wanted time to myself.

On Nantucket, I soon developed a routine for my solitary days. I biked or walked everywhere, using my car only rarely. Most mornings I went to the 8 am communion service at St. Paul's Episcopal church, usually a very small gathering of about 6. They were between rectors, and an older retired cleric shared the priestly duties with a young woman who flew over from Boston during the week. Once they realized I was available to help out with these tiny services, they were happy to let me cover occasionally, and I enjoyed keeping my churchly hand in. I even began thinking, for the first time, that I might look for another church, perhaps even a rector's position. St. Paul's was vacant, and I realized I was in no way prepared to move there, but I did at least make inquiries about their search.

After church, I would work on my guided reading project. I had planned this with my old mentor from my earliest days in the church, Bill Opel, who was now retired and living on Cape Cod. We agreed on a reading list of about eight books which we would both read and then meet to discuss every two weeks. This held me accountable to get the reading done and gave me a way of reflecting on it. It also afforded an opportunity to take the ferry and leave the island for twenty-four hours and visit with Bill and his wife Nina. I remember sitting before their warming fire on cold autumn days, debating the merits and import of our various books with Bill, and then gathering around their big kitchen table for Chinese food, cooked by Bill while Nina and I caught up. I have lost that reading list, but in general the books were a varied assortment of heavy and light reading. We read post-modern theology by Stanely Hauerwas and Matthew Fox and the history of particularly American religions by cultural critic Harold Bloom, and most helpfully Brian Wren's *What Language Shall I Borrow?* about new forms of liturgical language. I did make careful notes and gave a series of talks when I got back to St. Mark's, but the time in Nantucket wasn't really about the reading. Sure, I got to stretch my brain and indulge in the luxury of reading daily for several hours at a stretch, which I never got to do while I was working, and I could expose myself to new theological ideas. But my time in Nantucket felt more like a test of who I was and what kind of life I would make for myself should I ever be on my own.

Routine was valuable and developed quickly and naturally. After a morning of reading, I would spend the middle hours of the day on errands, post office, bank, grocery store. Most afternoons I napped, and then later I would go to the beach, or take a long walk or bike ride, often out to Madaket at the west end of the island for spectacular sunsets. I can remember stopping on those golden late afternoons just to listen to the silence and drink in the beauty around me and literally hug myself with the delight of it all. The ocean stayed warm into October, enough for an occasional swim. Even the rainy days had a gray mystery, a gloomy, brooding feeling, especially if there was fog. Things would loom up, an old house, or the memorial marker for Benjamin Franklin's mother, who lived out on this "faraway island," which is what the Indian name Nantucket means. Most evenings, I mixed a drink, watched the news and then cooked my dinner, read some more and went to bed early. A few times, because I adore good restaurants, and because Nantucket has many, I took myself out for dinner, overcoming my anxiety about eating alone. After all, men away on business do it all the time, why not me? I'd always call ahead, asking if they minded reserving a table for one, and then off I'd go, armed with a book and a keen appetite for some fine food and wine. It worked well; I was never uncomfortable, and I actually liked being alone and simply enjoying the meal without the added stimulus of conversation.

I stayed in touch with Tom and son Rob through occasional phone calls, and they seemed to manage well on their own. Rob called once, asking me for a chili recipe as he was cooking dinner that night, and I loved going over it with him step by step, long before electronic communications did away with such exchanges.

During this time I deliberately avoided developing social contacts. There was something very important to me about seeing what it was like to live alone, to manage my finances and a household on my own and to learn about myself in this different mode. I was even reluctant, at the end, to have my husband arrive to share my last weekend there before we headed home. The time and the place had been so much mine, I was selfishly wanting to keep it to myself, with no intrusion, even from Tom. As the early morning ferry rounded Brant Point and headed out of the harbor, I stayed on deck. As I looked back at the beautiful dawn-lit town, tears misting my eyes, I knew Nantucket would always be a special place for me and that no return visit would ever be the same.

13

Washington Interfaith Network

Social outreach was never a big thing at St. Mark's during my years there, and that bothered me. There was a tiny committee of about three stalwart souls who tried to drum up interest in working at the local soup kitchen and on occasion other projects, but most people were more interested in reflecting on their own issues, spiritual and otherwise, through the many functional education classes. Jim didn't show much interest, and people took their cue from him. But I had a theological problem with this stance. The Church has always called itself "the Body of Christ," meaning that the members, individually and together, represent Christ in this world, here and now. Our central symbols of bread and wine at communion are called the body and blood of Christ. We take them into ourselves as a ritual way of claiming this role as the body of Christ. To me, this meant that churches ought to behave in the world as this body of Christ we called ourselves. And that meant, unmistakably, in my eyes, that churches ought to do things that Jesus did, feed the hungry, reach out to the poor, work for social justice, care about outcasts. I didn't do any of this except for some charitable giving; I was too busy inside the church to do more outside, or so I thought.

But then one day our bishop invited all clergy to a meeting at a major downtown church to hear about the Washington Interfaith Network, or W.I.N. The network operated under the aegis of the Industrial Areas Foundation (IAF) which was founded back in the 1940s by the noted Saul Alinsky who wanted to improve the lot of the poor in Chicago by organizing local neighborhoods to work on their own behalf. The underlying principle is that organized people and organized money can wield power of their own. They can confront political power and hold elected officials accountable on issues that actual citizens, especially the disadvantaged, care about: affordable housing, better education, and jobs being some of them.

At the well-attended meeting, a slight Jewish man with dark hair, blue eyes and a soft voice talked to us, and I felt a door open in my heart and my work. Arnie Graf was the lead organizer for W.I.N. which was just getting started in Washington with a handful of churches of various denominations. Arnie talked about power, and politicians and corporate money and how they worked together to further their own interests while ordinary voters, especially the poor, stood by helpless, with no seat at the table, no power of their own, except votes. Community organizing could bring people together in large enough groups to get the attention of politicians and the press, and gradually, over time, a network like W.I.N. could bring about change. Not only that, the organizing process itself, with meetings at different churches all over the city, would build a sense of community and empower the faith communities to speak with conviction on problems afflicting our citizens. While politicians could care less about what parish x, y, or z was for in terms of social action, they would sit up and take notice of a group of a thousand or more church members from all over the city, people who would vote based on the issues they identified. Similar networks all over the country were already working with IAF, and it was time we did this in Washington. That was why our bishop had brought the clergy together, hoping that we in the Episcopal Church would become part of W.I.N. I was sold; this initiative roused some youthful idealism in me; it answered my frustration about there being so little involvement at St. Mark's in the problems of the city.

Two weeks later, there was a meeting for clergy of all the denominations who were already part of W.I.N. I walked in and saw . . . not ONE other Episcopalian! Had I come to the wrong meeting? Where were my colleagues? Had no one else listened to Arnie Graf and been inspired as I had? I began to see a role for myself anyway, not only at St. Mark's, but in our whole diocese. I would launch a campaign to get our churches involved! I began at St. Mark's, with sermons and newsletter articles about IAF and W.I.N., with informational meetings and invitations to W.I.N.training and orientation meetings. At the same time, I began contacting all the local Episcopal rectors, urging them to at least explore this venture.

As I saw it, W.I.N. offered an additional, crucial process for addressing the needs of the underprivileged; it tried to get at the institutional and structural causes of injustice and bring about widespread change. Individual people and individual churches could certainly reach out with feeding programs and support for shelters and tutoring for kids and used clothing and toys, but these efforts did nothing to actually reduce poverty or provide more affordable housing and better schools. Jesus reached out to individuals to help and heal and comfort, but he also taught his followers to address the causes of poverty and the institutions that favored the rich and ignored the poor. It seemed to me that we Christians, and all people of faith, for that matter, had an obligation to do both the individual outreach and the social justice work as well. W.I.N. offered one way to work for institutional change, not perfect, perhaps not even very effective. I didn't know at that point how or whether it would work at all in the District of Columbia, but I was determined to get involved and give it a try. I felt a passion for this effort, a sense that I was living into a neglected part of myself and doing something that would liven up St. Mark's and be good for our city.

My efforts paid off. St. Mark's people eagerly turned out for big W.I.N. rallies, and slowly other Episcopal churches joined us. I even talked the bishop into guaranteeing a million dollar loan for an affordable housing project on a site that would otherwise have gone to high end developers. I soon had help, especially from Luis Leon, the newly arrived rector of St. John's Lafayette Square, the famous church right across from the White House. Luis had been active in the IAF affiliated network in Wilmington, Delaware, where he had led a church, and he was more than willing to support W.I.N. and to lend his prestige as a rector of a major church to my efforts to coax people along. Soon a dozen or so Episcopal churches had joined W.I.N., and St. Mark's would reliably turn out as many as 80 folks for a major W.I.N. action, such as a panel of City Council members to be queried on their positions on various W.I.N. initiatives. It was important that these initiatives had the support of the entire network. Anything particularly controversial would not be pushed by W.I.N., so things like abortion rights or a minimum wage were out. Only those things identified in hundreds of grassroots meetings in churches around the city as having widespread support would be part of our agenda.

I got myself on the steering committee of clergy to plan our strategies, probably because I was a white woman minister and most of the other leaders were black clergy from inner city churches. I learned so much from them! I loved their roaring impassioned preaching at our events, their humor, camaraderie and easy acceptance of me at meetings and sharing the dais at events. At one huge event, they even let me introduce our keynote speaker, then first lady Hilary Clinton. I looked out at the huge crowd, over 1800 people, with a large contingent of St. Mark's people right down front, including my husband and sons. I also spotted in the crowd two Wellesley roommates and thought to myself as Hilary spoke that we Wellesley girls, even a dropout like me, could be proud of this night. It was a high point, but the work and growth of W.I.N. continued, and the network remains active in Washington today, recognized as one force to be reckoned with that represents the ordinary citizens and their well-being. I had long felt that faith communities should have a stronger voice in the public square, and W.I.N. gave us that. It gave me a role beyond my assisting clergy role at St. Mark's and taught me about leadership and how political power is gained and managed. More than anything, I was awakened to social justice and discovered how strongly I felt that churches could and should make a difference. To this day, I detest the question "Where are the churches?" in the face of struggles over poverty or inequality or war. Churches have legitimate voices about such matters and should use them.

14

Into the Wilderness

Except for the newness and excitement of the W.I.N. project, life back at St. Mark's after my sabbatical went along much as it had before. I considered looking for another position and actually applied for one in Alexandria, Virginia. I was one of the last two candidates, which was heartening, but when I wasn't chosen, I wasn't especially disappointed. I realized I didn't want to leave St. Mark's. I loved working with Jim Adams; the church continued to grow and flourish, and my own place in it seemed secure. There was even beginning to be some talk about my becoming the rector after Jim's retirement which was expected in 1999 when he would turn 65.

Meanwhile, my marriage was becoming shaky and uncertain, and I was fearful about making any changes in my work or personal life. Tom and I were seeing a marriage counselor, which felt fruitful, but I didn't know how much we could break out of some entrenched old patterns. I had always felt very torn about how to deal with our marital difficulties. Having been divorced once, I felt as if I didn't get another chance—I had to somehow make this work. There were good reasons for me to stick with Tom and wrestle with our problems. I felt there were things I needed to learn in this troubled marriage about compassion and forgiveness and judgment and patience. I had kept a journal since 1984, and it was in this that I poured out, year after year, my misgivings, my anger, my guilt at my anger, my sadness and fears and disappointment, and yet, through all this, I felt that I owed it to Tom and to our children to stay married and to keep trying. I also learned the hard, sternly powerful lessons about how God can work through our failures and flaws, about how God can use us as healers out of our own wounds. Over and over, through my years as a minister, I would be surprised by how my own imperfections and vulnerabilities, my own fears and even doubts about God would actually help me to connect with others in pain. Someone would sit across from me on the small couch in my office and pour out her deep despair. Often I didn't have any answers, but what I did have were my own failures and losses and a life that was more complicated and sad in ways that she would ever know. It was not some kind of priestly purity or special knowledge of God's ways, learned in seminary, that helped. It was simply my own life, my own dark places that allowed me to feel compassion and to be a healing presence. I would sit and counsel others with troubled marriages, realizing my own was in even more trouble, and I would know where they were, what they were going through, and I could speak to them in ways that went far beyond moralizing or offering pat answers. Even though most people were unaware of my own problems, I carried with me always the knowledge of this area of failure in my personal life. Even if it all looked really together from the outside, I knew I was hurting in this one part of my life, and I was scared of where that would lead.

I was scared of the personal consequences of divorce to me and Tom and our sons, but there were also professional consequences I was soon to confront. Although divorce and remarriage are permissible in the Episcopal Church, second divorces and subsequent remarriage are looked on with much more scrutiny, particularly in the case of clergy. Further, clergy are not assigned positions, they must seek vacancies and apply for jobs. There is no guaranteed tenure, but rectors tend to be able to remain in place until retirement if they are in a good relationship with their parishes and if they are not looking to move to a bigger parish or get elected bishop. However, for me, as an associate rector, there were no guarantees. When Jim's retirement came, my future at St. Mark's would become a big question. Once a new rector was called, I might or might not be asked to remain in place. Furthermore, associates were generally not allowed to become the rector or to even apply for the job if they stayed on during the search process. I knew all this and felt that if I were to divorce, I would stand almost no chance of being considered anywhere else as rector—just seeing that second divorce on my application information would deter most search committees from even interviewing me. I also knew that even if folks at St. Mark's wanted to consider me as their next rector, they would be up against our bishop's policies about associates and might not be willing to challenge them. I drifted along, thinking Jim would retire in 1999 and hoping that somehow things would work out with the marriage and my career prospects. I now realize how frightened I was back then, how unsure about how my life would unfold.

One September morning in 1995 my drifting and denial all changed. Jim arrived at work full of energy and excitement. He swore me to secrecy until he would announce this to the parish: He was going to take early retirement to continue his writing and work on a progressive Christianity network. He would depart in April of 1996. He had been at St. Mark's for 30 years and was ready to move from parish ministry to these new pursuits, and he'd figured out how to make it work financially for him and his wife.

I was completely shocked! I had never expected this, and all the ramifications for me, personal and professional, tumbled through my mind like a kaleidoscope. I knew for certain that any possibility of divorce would have to be postponed until the question of where I could continue my ministry was settled, a couple of years at least. In a way, this was a relief. I still had so little heart for splitting up our family and for whatever pain it would undoubtedly cause Tom and the three boys. A part of me still hoped we could rebuild our strained relationship, that continued counseling would help us to change. I felt that if a separation were to come, it would be better later than sooner, when the younger boys were off to college and perhaps better able to understand. If nothing else, I was determined to navigate carefully and to make no impulsive moves that would make us all more miserable.

Meanwhile, St. Mark's would also be shocked at Jim's early retirement and would probably go through a lot of uncertainty about how to proceed, as they had not had a rector vacancy for 30 years. Back when Jim had been called, rectors were usually brought in on the recommendation of an outgoing rector or powerful lay people in the parish who knew of so and so who might be just right. Often the associate would become the rector. But the lengthy search process in place since the 1970's involved up to two years, an interim rector, a consultant, a parish profile committee and a search committee. It was cumbersome, expensive and time-consuming, and many felt it was no better than the old system in terms of results. This new process was based on an assumption that all parishes needed this long period of time between rectors to either "heal," if the pastoral relationship had been difficult, or to open up to change and new ways if the pastorate had been very long. The idea of a qualified and well-loved associate being promoted to the top spot was just not acceptable to our bishop and nearly all of the Episcopal Church.

I was aware of all of this, but still, I had high hopes of being called as St. Mark's rector anyway. In private, Jim supported me in this but felt it unwise to do so publicly lest people saw him as interfering. He did feel that St. Mark's, with its history of independence and progressive ways, would not hesitate to challenge the bishop's authority if they wanted to proceed differently in calling a new rector. There was also a group of diocesan clergy who were discussing the impact of the current deployment policy. They felt that by denying associates the option to be called as rectors, or even to apply, unless they first left and found an interim job somewhere else, was having the unintended effect of keeping women and people of color or gay clergy from moving into the very rector positions they had the most likelihood of filling. In other words, in the places where they were already known and had proved their mettle, they could not be considered. However the group was never heard on this point, or else the bishop was unconvinced; his policy remained unchanged. I would have to be patient and let the process play out.

Jim announced his retirement in November, and a huge outpouring of energy, questioning, planning and general excitement ensued. Many were devastated to see him go, but there was also a feeling that 30 years had been a long time and that this was a good decision for him. People began speculating about the possibility of my becoming rector, and I couldn't help but be thrilled as this support seemed widespread. I saw myself as quite different from Jim Adams, someone who would bring different strengths and new ideas but was also very much a part of St. Mark's and well understood its unique character and history. But soon the bishop sent an emissary to talk to the vestry about "The Process" that was to be followed. It was laid out step-by-step, and questions about deviations were deflected with a sort of "we know best" condescension by the diocesan agent.

I had an advisory committee with whom I met monthly, and they proved amazingly helpful during this time. We hashed over all the possibilities and whether or not St. Mark's should or would disregard the process and try to either call me as rector directly or at least allow me to be a candidate without having to resign as Associate. It felt so unfair to me that after 10 years of work, during the years of the most growth in St. Mark's history, a hugely successful capital campaign and widespread popularity in the parish, I would have to give up my job and therefore my income and set out to find interim work while the search process at St. Mark's played out. But by staying on and competing in place, it would not be a level playing field for other candidates, or so the thinking went. Obviously, because of my long term work at St. Mark's, I would not be in the same category with other folks, whether I was in place or not. I was known at St. Mark's in ways that no other candidate could be, for good or ill. In any case, none of this was to be decided until Jim actually left in April of 1996, and I was happy to stay on at least until then. I wanted to be part of his retirement celebration, and I wanted to provide continuity when the interim came on board; after that, hard decisions would have to be made by me and by the vestry.

Jim left amid wonderful outpourings of gratitude and love during a festive weekend which climaxed with his last powerful sermon. He spoke about Jesus as the gateway for the sheep, not as the shepherd, but as the one who provides an entrance to the sheepfold. He saw St. Mark's as one gateway into Christianity and Christianity as one gateway, but not the only one, to connection with God. I was reminded of my conviction, going back to the days in Laos, that Christianity's claim to be the one true religion would never be true for me. I was further reminded that no minister is the perfect shepherd, but rather each serves as a gateway through which people may seek for a sense of God's presence and love. Finally Jim's last morning was over, and I left to drive to Connecticut for a five-day conference on church leadership. It was good to be on the road; it was good to be away from St. Mark's. I missed Jim already. He had been my mentor and friend and colleague for eleven years; in some ways he resembled my father. My tumult of emotions along the way north were of sadness and the lonely realization that my future was very much unsure.

The next step, back at St. Mark's, was the calling of an interim rector. The diocesan deployment officer gave some names to a committee of the vestry, but none proved appealing. It then occurred to me that my old friend and mentor from St. Patrick's, Jim Steen, might be interested. He had left

St. Patrick's after coming out as a gay man several years before that and was doing consulting work. I called him up, and to my delight he said yes, for St. Mark's, he would consider it. It took only a couple of days for him to meet with the committee and be invited to serve. They found him to be charming, full of energy, funny and wise, and at St. Mark's, his sexuality was no issue. His partner, Tom, would come with him and share in the life of St. Mark's. For many parishioners this choice was a plus, a confirmation of their full acceptance of gay people into the life of the community. For the few who were not ready for this, Jim Steen's presence brought an opportunity to experience the ministry of a gay man, and in many cases, their minds and hearts were changed. More than anything, Jim Steen's arrival as the interim was a blessing for the several dozen gay and lesbian people at St. Mark's. One gay man who was on the vestry choked up during the first meeting with Jim, saying "I can't tell you how much it means to see someone like me at the altar." His words reminded me of my own feelings as a woman, standing at altars and in pulpits where for centuries, only men had stood and where no one had looked like me.

15

The Process Plays Out

Once Jim Steen was on board as Interim Rector, decisions about calling a new rector came to the fore. Early in June of 1996, much of the parish went off for its annual retreat weekend at Shrinemont, in the mountains of southwest Virginia. Every year they had a lively program of meetings in which the general state of the parish and upcoming projects were debated. This year, the topic was to be the process by which a new rector was to be chosen. Fortunately, my son Tom was graduating from St. George's School up in Rhode Island that same weekend, so I had a good excuse not to be at Shrinemont. The parishioners would have the freedom to be candid with one another about how they felt about either calling me as rector or allowing me to be a candidate and whether I would have to leave to do this.

After watching young Tom receive his diploma on a bright sunny lawn overlooking the Newport beaches and then all the attendant festivities, I stopped by at St. Mark's once I got back on Sunday afternoon. A close friend and supporter happened to be in the parking lot, and when I asked how Shrinemont had gone, his words were chilling. "The knives are out," he said. He didn't elaborate much, just said that there were a growing number of folks who wanted to see who else was out there as a possible rector and were very likely to insist that St. Mark's follow the diocesan process to the letter. My cloak of denial and optimism began to fray.

Over the summer, wrangling continued. I met with the bishop who lectured me about how I had to go along with the process. The parish hired a consultant who told them I needed to go, and that they probably shouldn't call me back; they needed new blood. I kept wanting to both keep my job and apply for the rector's position.

During this time, Jim Steen was a good friend and great advisor. We also enormously enjoyed working together, as we had back in my seminary years at St. Patrick's. In fact, parishioners began to see and enjoy our camaraderie, and some even wondered if we couldn't both stay on, as Co-Rectors! I had actually heard of such arrangements in a few churches, although usually the two priests were married to each other. But Jim and I talked about it a lot, especially after one parishioner wrote to the Vestry suggesting this idea. However, we felt it could only happen if it came from the St. Mark's lay leadership and not from us, and we realized the bishop would probably hate the idea as it was so not in keeping with "The Process." I was becoming extremely disillusioned about St. Mark's. They prided themselves on being so independent and progressive, and yet now they seemed fearful about deviating from standard practices. Perhaps Jim Steen and I should have pushed harder for an idea that would have been a new model for ministry, but here I think my own inhibitions kept me back. Ever since childhood, my mother had cautioned me about being "too forward." She was always urging me to be polite and not rock the boat, and so here I was, so much wanting to be the next rector, but still holding back from pushing aggressively, still wanting to be the good girl. If I was to leave St. Mark's, I certainly didn't want to leave in bitterness and conflict. So I gamely continued to explore what might be possible.

In this endeavor, my advisory committee made all the difference. They were a group of eight, and although there was some turnover, most of the members had been serving for a number of years and knew me and my ministry well. By our September meeting, we knew that a decision by the Vestry was imminent, and that I needed to decide what I was willing to do and what would be best in terms of my long-term career prospects. As we saw it, many at St. Mark's favored having me as rector, probably more than half, but many wanted to go through a search and compare me with other candidates. I called this the allure of the "glamorous stranger." So my choices boiled down to these: 1) Staying on as Associate and not being a candidate, perfectly permissible, but then I would only be able to continue in that role at the pleasure of the new rector. And since I would have been there for 12 years, a new rector might feel that my experience and place in the emotional life of the parish might threaten or overshadow him, and he well might prefer to choose his own associate. 2) Staying on as Associate but defying the Bishop and some of the St. Mark's leadership by becoming a candidate anyway, probably a foolish option that would lead to my not being chosen, and to my not staying on once the new person came, both for the reasons noted above and because folks might be annoyed that I'd bucked the system. 3) Resigning as Associate Rector and entering the search process as a candidate.

It seems pretty clear now that number 3 was really the only viable option, or at least the only one that could lead to my becoming rector of St. Mark's. But I had the hardest time seeing this. I think I was so fearful about not getting an interim position, of being unemployed, so offended that this path was my reward for 11 years of faithful service, I just couldn't choose. Most of my advisory committee were trying so hard to root for me, even to the point of defying the system, but finally, one member pointed out the truth I hadn't been willing to face. He simply said that if I wanted to be the next rector, the only way that offered a chance to do this would be to leave and find an interim job somewhere else and then apply to St. Mark's. Even then, the odds were not great. Not because of my qualifications or because many were opposed, but because of the process and the feelings that had built up in the parish that somehow my presence was interfering. I needed to get out of the way. As he spoke, quietly and lovingly, I finally realized that he was right, and that it was I who needed to take the initiative and resign and not force the vestry to ask me to leave. It was a very tough moment, for me and for the whole committee, this telling of a hard truth to someone in a loving way so that she could hear it.

Exhausted after the long meeting, I got into my car and began the drive home, down along Route 295 on a cloudless moonlit night. As I drove, a remarkable feeling washed over me, and I said to myself, out loud, "Now I get to have a whole new life!" I felt astonishing relief! After all my waverings and reluctance to move, I had made a decision that would lead to changes not only in my work, but probably in my marriage as well. I was free to embark, out into a wider world and a larger life.

16

Good-bye to St. Mark's

My resignation was gratefully accepted by the Vestry in late September, and we agreed that my last day at St. Mark's would be Sunday, January 19, 1997. In the meantime, I would continue with my usual responsibilities, finish up leading a long adult confirmation class, make opportunities to say good-bye to groups and individuals, and at the same time, look for an interim position that would leave me free to apply for the St. Mark's job.

Interim positions open up almost every time there is a clergy change in the Episcopal church, and there are two categories of interim priests. There are those who feel especially called to this ministry and have special training in dealing with parishes in transition. They may serve in a long series of interim positions and don't mind changing parishes every year or two. In fact many relish this opportunity to move in and out of parishes and play the role of healer, change agent, new role model, whatever is needed. The second category are people in my situation in 1997, those who for whatever reason, do not have a long-term position and need gainful employment as a priest while they are seeking it. In my case, I needed interim employment because of the diocesan process, a place to be while the St. Mark's search process played out. I was certainly willing to serve as an interim, but I definitely did not want to become a long-term interim, or be perceived as on the "interim track" which seemed to me to be where some clergy who never got called as associates or rectors ended up. So I found it humbling to put myself forth as an interim after my great long run at St. Mark's.

Given this somewhat snobbish attitude about interim work, I began by calling the rector of probably the leading Episcopal church in Washington. I knew he had a vacancy for an assistant or associate, and I'd worked with him on a diocesan project and liked and respected him. I was sorting laundry at home when he returned my call, and to my delight, was interested in talking to me and setting up some interviews. Wow! My first shot at this seemed promising; I was already envisioning myself metaphorically waving across town from this new and lofty perch to St. Mark's. This was the shot of energy that I needed, just a positive response from one good place allowed me to feel charged up with what I had to offer and with the possibilities out there for me.

As it turned out, this church did not offer me the job, but I was buoyed enough from their interest to forge on, exploring a variety of other openings around the diocese. But then came the windfall. My husband and I and a few others were at dinner with my good friends Rebecca and Steve who were entertaining Alan Jones, then Dean of Grace Cathedral in San Francisco. Alan was tall, white-haired, British and extremely attractive. His accent definitely helped. He was a great mimic and wit, and his dinner table stories kept us all laughing and urging him on. I had met Alan the summer before when I was in San Francisco, visiting my oldest son who was there training to be a chef. I was immediately drawn to him then and was glad to see him again. I was also glad to pour out my tale of woe about St. Mark's and ask if he knew of any possibilities for interim work in San Francisco. I figured with my son out there, it would be fine to take a temporary job there if nothing came up around here. To my surprise, Alan said, "As a matter of fact, I have an opening on my staff at the Cathedral. It's not much pay, and it's only for three months, but you're welcome to come and interview. We need someone to plan and lead adult education for the spring semester while we look for a long-term person. I'll have Fran, my Vice-Dean call you and set up a visit." I was ecstatic! If nothing else, I'd get a trip to San Francisco to see Chris, and, from what Alan said, they really didn't have anyone else on deck. The Vice-Dean did finally call, just as I'd about given up, and it was arranged that I would fly out just before the New Year for two days of interviews.

I had fallen in love with San Francisco back in 1994 when Chris first went there as part of his chef's training. He was working at Aqua, an upscale seafood restaurant downtown in the financial district, expensive, elegant, reviewed in "Gourmet Magazine." I had flown out for a visit during the spring and was utterly captivated by that city of hills and vistas, ocean and bay, a patchwork quilt of neighborhoods and ethnic groups, gingerbread Victorian houses perched in steep rows, all of it enchanting, new and exciting to this East coast girl who'd never been to California before. But what was most captivating was my young son. Chris and I had arranged to meet at the restaurant just before he got off work, around 10:30. I stationed myself at the long sleek bar and treated myself to a glass of some wonderful California chardonnay, the kind they don't ship back east. I sipped slowly, savoring the serene ambiance of Aqua, and then I looked up and saw Chris. Tall, blonde, handsome and dressed in blazing white from his toque to his feet, he was dazzling! My mother's heart just swelled up with pride and love at the sight of this young man, now on the way to living his dream, proud and happy to be doing what he was doing. That first visit in 1994 was the beginning of many as Chris worked his way up through several restaurants from lowly "garde-manger" to line cook to sous-chef and finally chef at the Mandarin Oriental Hotel and then at a French restaurant in Menlo Park before he returned east in 2003.

So by the time I arrived for interviews at Grace Cathedral at the end of 1996, the possibility of a job there was pure gold to me, especially after the rejection and discouragement I'd felt at St. Mark's and in my failed attempts to find interim work back home. After a happy reunion the night I got in with Chris and his girlfriend Felicia, who would become his wife three years later, I was up early Sunday morning and dressed for the Cathedral. I was to meet at the 8:30 service with Fran Tornquist, the Vice Dean and Canon Chancellor, spend the morning with her and then meet with my friend Alan, the Dean, over lunch.

Grace Cathedral is an imposing place. It sits atop Nob Hill, overlooking the city and bridges and bay. A huge broad staircase leads up to the façade— two tall square towers with a gorgeous stained glass rose window in the center over massive bronze doors. Inside, there is a labyrinth on the floor where you enter, an enormous baptismal font full of water, and then the long nave with its center aisle leading up to the altar. Stained glass windows filter in hazy light, and murals depicting the history of San Francisco line the walls. The smell of incense tinges the air but doesn't overwhelm. It feels somehow more holy, more spirit-filled than the much larger Washington Cathedral.

Fran Tornquist was a warm, no-nonsense woman with a job to fill. She was about my age, sure of herself and well suited to the task of overseeing the cathedral congregation while the Dean managed the role of spiritual leader, chief preacher and fund raiser, the visible figurehead of Grace Cathedral in the city and the world. Our meetings went very well. I was introduced around to all the other cathedral clergy and staff; we talked about the pay package, and we had a deal. I would start February first as an Assistant Pastor for Education. As all this proceeded I could barely contain my excitement! This would be such a feather in my cap, such a prestigious position even if only for a few months! And I would get to live in San Francisco, really get to know it, and on top of all that, have time with my son after having him a continent away for the past few years.

One part of the San Francisco interview trip had been hard and scary. I needed to find some rental housing, something furnished, close to the cathedral and affordable on a month-to-month basis. I turned to the classified ads and found just a few apartments that qualified. I set out on Monday morning, the day after the interviews, in a cold rain, slogging along up and down the steep hills from one place to the next, feeling like some sort of homeless person. As I traipsed through a couple of dreary places, blocks from Nob Hill in cheesily decorated modern buildings, my spirits drooped. I just felt like crying, and did, as what seemed then the enormity of the step sank in. I would need to make all the arrangements to move and start a temporary life on my own, going to work, supporting myself, being away from husband, two younger sons, siblings and friends, all back east. What had seemed so glamorous just the day before now loomed as drudgery, foisted upon me by the process that had led to my leaving St. Mark's where I'd been so happy and comfortable.

Eventually, I stumbled across a building, just two blocks down the hill from Grace Cathedral on Bush Street. Renovations were in progress, but the landlord was on site and assured me that the apartments would be ready by February 1. He showed me a charming efficiency, just a convertible futon couch/bed sharing a room with a table and chairs and a large armoire. But there was a separate kitchen, a well-appointed bathroom and a small alcove with a desk and shelves and a huge closet. I liked the Victorian furniture, liked that it was on the ground floor, that it had a communal open garden area and laundry room. I didn't like the price, more than half my monthly paycheck, but for three months, I could do it. I walked away with a signed lease, no longer homeless and sad and sorry for myself, but a woman with a plan!

I flew home, triumphant, just in time to celebrate New Year's Eve with my husband and friends. I had secured what I needed to move forward with my work and my life, and I could worry about long term plans later.

I did, however need to say good-bye to St. Mark's, a bittersweet experience filled with uncertainty. The reason I was leaving was to be a candidate for rector, and I believed I had a good chance and lots of support in the parish, so my good-bye felt conditional; maybe I'd be back! Even so, a celebration was in order. The plan was for a gala party on Saturday, January 18th and then my last sermon and last Sunday services on January 19th. When folks asked what kind of party, I quickly replied that a dinner dance would be my first choice. Dinner dances were special at St. Mark's because they could happen right in the nave, in the same space where we prayed and worshipped and celebrated baptisms, weddings and funerals, plus classes, meeting and plays. As former Rector Bill Baxter commented "all of our life is laid out before the Lord here." Because there were no pews, all the chairs, and the altar and pulpit could be moved out, and tables set up all around with a large dance floor in the middle. It was always lovely to see new brides and grooms dancing in the very space where only an hour or so before they had made their vows. The party for me would be in a space where I had learned to preach, become a worship leader, and prayed and sung and joined in celebrations of ten years of Christmases, Easters, Good Fridays and all the other services of the church year. As an enthusiastic committee labored to make it the best party ever, I labored to make my last sermon the best I could do. I felt so much love and gratitude for my time at St. Mark's. It was there that I truly became a priest and gained a sense that I could be a leader in a church of my own. Jim Adams and the congregation had accepted me right out of seminary, and had mentored, criticized, challenged and supported me. Despite all the machinations of the "process" that led to my departure, I felt truly beloved as I left to go out into a wider world and see where my ministry would take me.

The night of the great party was truly splendid! It was a black tie event, with a seated dinner before the dancing and toasts. I wore a favorite dress, long black chiffon with a brilliant sequined jacket sparkling in blues and greens and golds. The first time I wore it, several years before, my son Tommy, probably around 10 at the time, exclaimed "Wow, Mom, that looks just like Michael Jackson!" I added my highest black suede heels, which I loved. High heels were kind of a trademark of mine at St. Mark's. Parishioners loved it that their priest wore these instead of the usual low-heeled sensible shoes favored by most of my female colleagues. When dinner was finished, I was seated in a chair as the entire congregation moved into the nave for the dancing. The room was decorated with flowers and lights, and a live band played as folks streamed in. I remember thinking to myself that no matter how this all played out, this would be one of the best nights of my life. Here I was, a 53-year-old woman, a relative late-comer to serious religion. I was an irreverent, skeptical Christian who loved dancing and good food and wine but who also loved theology, the struggle to make sense of how God is in the world. And more than anything that night, I loved those hundreds of people there who had loved me back. All of that was right there in that chair, in that room with me, a beloved freeze frame I'll carry always. The festivities continued with dancing. I was actually given a dance card which about ten of the men in the parish, all friends and fans of mine, had signed. After a dance with my husband, these men all cut in , one after another to give me a whirl. What was especially fun was about half way through, unexpectedly and spontaneously, Karen Getman, a good friend, just came out and cut in too! Later, Art Siebens, with his guitar, sang a song whose words he had written himself to a medley of my favorite folk tunes; "Leaving on a Jet Plane," "The Circle Game," "Four Strong Winds," and "Little Deuce Coupe" by The Beach Boys. The words were all about ten great years and whether this would be a final good-bye. This was a sweet, loving gift, and the CD he gave me was one I played many times in San Francisco, especially when I was feeling homesick for St. Mark's.

The next morning I took my place in the pulpit and then at the altar, maybe for the last time, maybe not. I preached about how things we can not even imagine do really come to pass, such as my own priesthood, not even allowed when I was a girl, and certainly totally beyond anything my parents or I ever dreamed of. But then I moved to the future, and where it might lead them and me. I based this part of the sermon on the gospel reading for that Sunday which was about Jesus noticing a man named Nathanael sitting comfortably under a fig tree, and Jesus' calling him out from there to follow him. In the Biblical times, a fig tree was a symbol of peace and prosperity. There are many passages in the Bible about people sitting under their own vines, and their own fig trees, contented, satisfied. And for good reason. Fig trees have broad flat leaves, and their branches spread out like umbrellas. They would keep a person cool in blazing sun and dry in a sudden shower. I was delighted to uncover this imagery connected with fig trees as it led me to consider just how much St. Mark's had been a place of safety and comfort for me even as I learned and grew there as well. My desire to stay on bespoke a timidity about testing myself in the larger church, a lack of confidence, or of faith. If I were to be called back, I would be better qualified after a time away with new congregations and new challenges. St. Mark's too, I felt, as much as it hurt, probably needed to get out from under the comfortable fig tree that thirty years of Jim Adams' leadership and ten years of mine had afforded. They needed to at least consider new models for their clergy, fend for themselves during an interim time. Jesus had made a promise to Nathanael along with his call to him. He had told him "You will see greater things than these . . . you will see heaven opened and the angels of God ascending and descending upon the Son of Man." (*John 1:50-51*) I puzzled over that promise, a vision I couldn't take literally. But symbolically, it seemed to me that Jesus was promising Nathanael that in following him, his world would be opened up and that his sense of connection with God would be hugely enlarged—like a great ladder stretching between heaven and earth, bringing them together in a new reality. For me, and for St. Mark's, it was time to leave the fig tree and venture forth into whatever new reality and new sense of God's purpose was going to unfold for us. I ended the sermon saying "This is a time of rediscovery for all of us. May we live it with faith and guts and lasting affection for one another, through our savior, Jesus Christ. Amen."

17

Grace Cathedral

And then I flew off to the West Coast, relieved, finally to put a continent between me and all the upheaval of that past year. Tom seemed to understand how important this interim opportunity was for me and raised no objection to my going away to San Francisco for what was at first to be only three months. Welcomed by Chris and Felicia who helped me get settled into my tiny digs on Bush Street, I eagerly made my way two days later up a dauntingly steep two blocks of Taylor Street to Grace Cathedral to begin my work. I was expected to design and lead an adult forum on Wednesday evenings during Lent, which began the first week I was there. I was also scheduled to preach every few weeks at the 8:30 am service in one of the chapels, holding about 120 people. And there were staff meetings and pastoral visiting responsibilities and much to learn about how a large cathedral operated. I loved it all. I loved having the time to carefully plan out my Lenten forums. I used material from the functional education curriculum at St. Mark's, drawing on some theological constructs by the founder, Charles Penniman. I enjoyed experimenting with this material and using it somewhat differently than I had before, testing it for its durability in another setting. I would introduce abstract theological formulations of categories such as sin or saviors to stimulate new ways of thinking about the old church dogma. Then I would ask folks to work in small groups to connect what I had presented to their own life experience. It worked. Folks were intrigued, provoked into useful theological reflection, and encouraged to be honest about their doubts and questions. I was beginning to find out which parts of my training at St. Mark's would convey successfully into other church venues.

I loved the daily rhythm of the cathedral. Morning prayer at 8 am, preceded by Holy Communion at 7:30 in the tiny Chapel of the Good Shepherd on the days I was to preside. Working alone in my office on various adult education proposals to come after Lent. Getting to know fellow workers, clergy and lay. Fellow priest Chip Barker was right next door and gave me all the tips I needed to fit in with the staff. Mary Wood was across the hall, working with untiring energy and charm to figure out how best to welcome and include newcomers in the cathedral community. She became a close confidant, always available for a coffee or a chat or a quick lunch. Alan Jones welcomed me warmly onto the clergy staff, listened to my ideas and made me feel I had a theology worth promoting. He was progressive in his thinking, far more well-read than I, and with an incredibly well-furnished mind. He was able to come up with quotes and ideas from a huge range of thinkers and writers and was an author himself. He treasured the mystical strain of Christianity along with the Buddhist tradition and had a healthy skepticism about the institutional church. I loved sparring with him about churchmanship and theology in clergy staff meetings, something my male colleagues seemed reluctant to do. I began to realize how fruitful this time was in San Francisco. I gained a sense of how much I had to offer as a priest and educator whether at St. Mark's or elsewhere. I became a lot more confident about my future prospects. One of those was staying on at Grace Cathedral. It was now early June, and I'd already been there a month longer than the original three-month interim. They were not getting very far with a search for my replacement and began hinting to me that I might be their best choice if I were open to staying. Finally they made an actual offer, put this way by Mary Wood, reporting on the committee's decision, "It just felt like the Holy Spirit came roaring through the room on a bull-dozer, telling us you should stay." Inelegant as this sounded, it was thrilling. Just to be wanted somewhere during this time of uncertainty was a huge boost to my spirit. Heady as the offer was, I knew practical wisdom and the demands of the rest of my life were against saying yes. I asked for a long weekend back home to talk it over with my husband and children and really to distance myself from the seductive environment of San Francisco that I'd come to love so much.

By that June of 1997 I was pretty certain that my marriage to Tom was no longer viable and that when circumstances permitted, I would probably ask for a divorce. We had grown far apart over time, although we had invested in marriage counseling on a regular basis for over twelve years, going all the way back to seminary. I know that my journey into ministry and my life in church had changed me in ways that made me feel that continuing in our marriage was betraying what marriage is intended to be. We were two very different people, and Tom's heavy drinking and serious financial problems had taken a toll, not helped by my own anger and judgmentalism. I had tried and tried to change Tom, change me, change us, but only the second of these was the slightest bit successful. After years of vacillating between pushing for change and stifling my discomfort, which felt like capitulation to the status quo, I knew I would need to make a decision. But I also knew, as I flew back across the continent to consider what a move to San Francisco would mean, that it would be a very stupid, cowardly way to end a marriage. I knew well that I was in no way prepared to leave Tom unless I could support myself financially and unless I had a more or less tenured job. Grace Cathedral's offer provided neither of these. And although one son lived in San Francisco, my other two sons lived in Maryland, and I had no desire to bow out of their lives, even though they were by then in college. The emotional impact of what such a move would mean hit me that late afternoon as the plane began its descent into Dulles Airport. It was a beautiful sun-gilded June day, and the plane circled over it all as we made our descent. As if by special instruction, just for me, the plane came up the Potomac, past our house in Fort Washington, over the city with its monuments, the churches where I'd served, the cathedral where I'd been ordained, out over Virginia and Potomac School where my children had gone, showing me, all spread out below, the landscape of my entire adult life. I burst into tears, pressing my face against the window, knowing beyond all doubt that this was home, that this was where I lived. No matter what happened with Tom, I could never desert this place where my sons, my sister and brother and most of my friends lived. I had loved the pilgrimage to San Francisco, but I knew in that landing that here was home soil.

I called Fran before going back to California, and she was very understanding and not actually surprised by my refusal of their offer. I think she realized that my personal situation was complicated and that I wasn't really in a position to relocate at that time. They still needed me to work through July, which was fine with me. I did want the opportunity to say a proper good-bye to the people and place that had nourished this fledgling as I left the nest of St. Mark's to try my wings in the larger church. It was a loving good-bye with gifts and good wishes, some time with close friends, and a couple of last restaurant treats with Chris and Felicia. One of the best parts of that so-journ in San Francisco was spending time with them, even the last month in their apartment, where I got to know Felicia well and to realize what a well matched couple she and Chris made.

18

St. John's Broad Creek

The fall and winter of 1997 and 1998 were the next phase of my slow process back to full-time, long-term employment. Soon after returning to Washington, I learned that my home parish, the little church of St. John's, Broad Creek, in Fort Washington, where I had first rediscovered Christianity and where Tom and I had married, was seeking a new rector. They needed an interim while they finished their search. I of course had my name in at St. Mark's and a couple of other places, but none of these were close to deciding. So an interim stint at St. John's seemed like it would work well. The church was just three miles from our home, quite small compared to St. Mark's, and, because I'd gone there as a parishioner before seminary, I knew most of the people. The work would not be too demanding, but it would give me the experience of being the priest-in-charge, i.e. the rector's role. I began as interim priest in mid-September.

During this whole time I grappled with how to think about God. I had never embraced the notion of a God who has a mapped-out plan for any of our lives and that our job is to figure out what that is. In fact I was grossly turned off by a couple of parish profiles I read from churches who were seeking rectors. They actually said "God has already chosen our new rector, and our work is to discover who that person is." I just don't buy that kind of determinism. Our human freedom is one of the greatest gifts we have, and although we often misuse it to cause great harm, I don't believe it is shackled by some divine being plotting out the twists and turns of our lives. I did, however, pray and look to God as a sustaining power, and I sought for authentic guidance from within myself and from trusted others. I felt I needed to be open to the future, true to my own best instincts, and patient as things played out in which I had only limited control. There was one prayer, from the Book of Common Prayer, that became a mainstay for me during this time. It goes like this:

O God, by whom the meek are guided in judgment, and light rises up in darkness for the godly; grant us, in all our doubts and uncertainties, the grace to ask what you would have us to do, that the Spirit of wisdom may save us from all false choices, and that in your light we may see light, and in your straight path may not stumble; through Jesus Christ our Lord. Amen. (The Book of Common Prayer, p. 832)

St. John's, Broad Creek is one of the earliest parishes in the diocese of Washington, built on the banks of Broad Creek, close to where it enters the Potomac, in Fort Washington, Maryland. Historians believe George Washington occasionally worshipped there, arriving by boat from his plantation just down the river at Mount Vernon. His box pew is still in the church. The church itself is a lovely brick building in spare Georgian style, with just a small bell tower over the entrance. A renovation in the 1980s restored clear glass windows after decades of Victorian stained glass, and some original roof beams still exist, standing out against the oyster-colored white-washed plaster of the interior. The very old cemetery surrounds one side of the church, and it includes a section for burials in simple pine boxes, as they would have had in the early days. Also on the property is Bayne Hall, housing a large events room and kitchen, Sunday School rooms and offices. It was a treat to settle into my own office, walls lined with bookshelves, big wooden desk and upholstered chairs, an oriental rug. It was a luxury after years of commuting to Capitol Hill, to drive only five minutes from our house to work. It was exciting to at last be the priest-in-charge of a congregation, free to exercise leadership in whatever ways I felt would be most life-giving for that community.

The people of St. John's were a strong, rugged lot, probably only about 100 families, many of them elderly and very long-time members. They had seen clergy come and go, many of them either with limited gifts or on their way to bigger and better pulpits. Fort Washington is about twelve miles south of Washington in Prince Georges County, which, until recently was seen by many as the sort of neglected poor sister of the larger booming metropolitan area. The schools were notoriously bad, zoning laws allowed for a lot of un-attractive and haphazard development, and quality retail, entertainment and dining options were scarce. A lot of this has changed in recent years, and the county today is clearly thriving. But most folks come from very different reli-gious traditions, such as Baptist or evangelical, and when I got there, old St. John's held little appeal for either newcomers or new rectors. Large African American churches were flourishing, with praise bands, charismatic preachers and a wide variety of programs, but St. John's limped along, supported by its faithful core. They prided themselves on "The St. John's Way," which was the name of their newsletter as well as a kind of rueful motto. It seemed to me to mean "We have our own tried and true ways of getting along and get-ting by, and no matter whether other folks are interested, we'll maintain our church, keep the faith, and keep pumping out the basement after every storm that makes the river rise." Indeed, soon after I got there, dear old Jim Titus, probably in his 80s by then, showed up after a storm wearing overalls and hip boots and carrying all his equipment for fixing the sump pump and otherwise attending to the flooding. High water downstairs was clearly not new!

Despite its traditions, there were some real spiritual seekers at St. John's as well, and I always loved it when someone came forth who really wanted to talk seriously about their faith. One member was Cathy who was a true skeptic about literal truth claims based on the Bible and about traditional orthodoxy. We had several conversations in which I recommended such writers as Marcus Borg and Frederick Buechner. She would come back after reading, filled with excitement at these new possibilities for faith. It was as if I'd given her permis-sion to explore her doubts and to turn away from what she could no longer accept towards a whole new way of believing. Her response, however, stung me. "Why don't preachers say these things from the pulpit? You learn all this stuff in seminary, but you stick to the old orthodoxy—you don't let us in on what you know or are thinking about!" She was partially right. Although I had tried to be open about my own skepticism and to introduce new theo-logical insights in my preaching, I had held back, not wanting to offend, or else not being willing to get too far out ahead in my thinking, especially while I was still seeking a long-term rector's position. I knew many of my clergy colleagues were the same way, as if we had special in-group knowledge that we weren't willing to share with our flocks. Based on my conversations with Cathy, I began to see that as condescending, and I began to be more open in preaching and teaching about who I was reading and what I found valuable in all the progressive theology that attracted me. It took years for me to really become bold in these efforts, but I credit Cathy with getting me started.

For the first time, I had a staff to manage—a secretary who came only in the mornings, a music director who worked ten hours a week, a part-time sexton, and volunteer Sunday School teachers. So not much management was needed. I could organize my own time without all the coordination and planning I'd been used to in bigger churches. Such freedom was also a temptation as I could so easily head on home early after a pastoral call or two in an afternoon. There were far fewer night meetings and classes than at St. Mark's, hardly any weddings to prepare for. However, I had to preach every Sunday, something completely new, but a rewarding discipline. It allowed me to preach in sequence on a series of readings or on a particular theme such as discipleship. And because I was in the pulpit every Sunday, it felt as though there wasn't so much at stake each time. If I bombed one week, I'd be back the next to do better! And because I had more time, I could really enjoy sermon preparation and not have to sandwich it in amongst all sorts of other demands.

The extra freedom also allowed me to pursue what was sort of a part-time job on its own, my continuing search for a call to be rector somewhere. At any given time, I had various irons in the fire, applications in to several churches. Each of these involved long written answers to all sorts of queries about my spiritual journey, my theology, my ideas for ministry and church growth, my style of preaching and worship leadership, my pastoral skills, my "growing edges" (the common euphemism at the time for areas of weakness). No two churches asked the for the same material in the same way, so major rewriting had to go on for each application, all in the hopes that the written presentation would be sufficiently appealing that I'd make the list of people a church wanted to meet in person. It worried me that in a profession where one's actual presence, appearance, sound of voice, and manner of interacting is absolutely key to how one comes across as a minister, one must first make it through a highly competitive writing contest. The way I thought of it was that I needed to "get off the paper and into the room." I needed to get to the interview stage. But for most of the fall and winter of 1997–98, I was in the early stages of application processes while very much enjoying my role as a kind of country parson in this small backwater of a church community.

The people of St. John's welcomed me extremely warmly. Many of them already knew me from when I'd been a member there between 1975 and 1982 before heading off to St. Patrick's for seminary field work. The lay leadership were smart and fun and committed, eager to get their church moving again, and the more conservative old timers seemed to trust me not to push them beyond their comfort zones in terms of theology and liturgy. The congregation was racially mixed, reflecting the majority African American population of Fort Washington, and this mixture existed as graciously and cooperatively as I've ever seen in any church. The vestry and other committees were naturally integrated; I never noticed any overt attempts at creating a racial balance; it just existed. Differences in theology and worship style, even differences in behavior around death and dying were accepted with respect, sometimes a kind of wry recognition of these differences as just part of who they were, part of "The St. John's Way."

I fondly remember Sunday mornings when I could stand outside in my white priest's vestments and greet worshippers as they headed up the gravel walkway that led from the parking lot to the church. Clear autumn mornings were the best, but even on snowy Sundays, I loved being out there as folks arrived. It was easy to learn everyone's names as the usual attendance at worship was around 60–75. I felt like the mother of a little flock, a pastor in simpler times, and sometimes I even wondered what it would be like to stay on there, as rector, even though the same diocesan rules that prevented that at St. Mark's forbade it at St. John's as well.

My interim time there was certainly not completely easy, despite what felt like a very good temporary fit. One thing I missed a lot was the collegiality of working in a multistaff church, which I'd had up until then. I missed having a clergy partner such as Jim Adams or Alan Jones, someone to engage with theologically, someone to compare notes with on books, someone to share the pastoral burdens.

I also missed good music. The all-volunteer choir at St. John's actually made me cry one Sunday. They were practicing before a service as I was setting things up, and they were so off-tune, so quavering in their aging voices, struggling along with the small electronic organ. After seven months listening to the glorious men and boys' choir and great organ of Grace Cathedral, the contrast was just too much. I wasn't sure I could stand long-term service in a church where the music couldn't be part of what fed my spirit. But I knew these singers, and I knew their good hearts, and I knew they loved their church and their choir. Weren't their offerings just as valuable as service to God as those of the paid professionals in the lofty shrines of Christendom? I knew they were, but they were still hard to hear, even as I was touched by their devotion.

The frequency of funerals was another new and sometimes difficult aspect of my work. I conducted more funerals at St. John's than in all my time at St. Mark's. People were older, and being with people at the time of death and presiding over their funerals were a part of my ministry in a way they'd never been before. The restrained way of mourning typical of many white members contrasted with the unabashed weeping and moaning and caressing of the body that I saw in black families, whether in their homes or in hospitals. It seemed the outrage of death was tempered only by a much more overt hope, at least for many, in a very real afterlife. Open caskets were common—again, more of a southern and/or African American tradition than I was used to. Here I began to hone my ideas about how to preach a funeral homily. I felt myself to be in a bind here, because people have very different beliefs about what happens when we die. I do not, cannot, believe in some kind of literal heaven, the pearly gates, streets of gold and all that. Orthodox Christian faith points to life after death that is spiritual but in which we do not lose our identities and during which God can still work with us. We have prayers about being reunited with others who have gone before us, seeing those we love in the next world. The Book of Common Prayer actually has this to say in its section on Burial Services:

> *The liturgy for the dead is an Easter liturgy. It finds all its meaning in the resurrection. Because Jesus was raised from the dead, we, too, shall be raised. The liturgy, therefore, is characterized by joy . . . [that nothing] in*

all creation, will be able to separate us from the love of God in Christ Jesus our Lord. This joy, however, does not make human grief unchristian . . . So, while we rejoice that one we love has entered into the nearer presence of our Lord, we sorrow in sympathy with those who mourn. (from The Book of Common Prayer, p. 507)

That's the Prayer Book take, and in many ways, I suppose it offers comfort. Certainly the idea that nothing can separate us from the love of God is one I embrace. Still, I feel dubious about this counsel of joy, especially when a death has been particularly tragic, such as that of a child, or one born of violence or war or suicide. I do not believe in a bodily resurrection, not even for Jesus, and so when these words promise that we too shall be raised, I need to imagine something quite different than a heavenly idyll where we'll happily rejoin loved ones. And if that is "nearer presence of our Lord" then, I reject that as downgrading this world, this amazing creation as only a foreshadowing of something more to come. None of us can prove an afterlife, and near-death experiences notwithstanding, I find it difficult to go along with explicit beliefs in such a place. And yet, as a minister, my job is to offer comfort and hope at the time of death. It is often hard to find the line between saying what you think folks would like to hear and sticking with what you yourself believe. Here is an example of the last part of a funeral homily I offered for a woman named Victorie several years ago. It illustrates my tendency to minimize talk of heaven but at the same time try to give voice to a sense of spirit that encompasses all life and death always.

"And the soul of Victorie, in all the years I knew her, was strong and warm and beautiful. We've lost the near presence of that soul, but we hold her in our hearts and take comfort that she is held in the embrace of the larger Love that holds us all. Amen."

Despite my uncertainty, or agnosticism about what happens after we die, I do reject the notion of hell as either a place or a state of eternal torment. Certainly we can and do create our own hells here on earth, for ourselves, and for others, but I can't believe in a God who would punish any part of creation in this way. Such beliefs about hellfire and damnation turn Christianity into a religion of fear; they hold out a God of wrath rather than of love. Such beliefs are part of what has turned so many away from the church, and such beliefs have been used over the centuries to manipulate and control folks, to make this life irrelevant and a life to come the main arena.

19

Agonies of Transition

By the spring of 1998, I was in the final stages of several search processes including St. Mark's. I had been turned down back in the fall of 1977 by St. Margaret's Church in Washington after making it to the final short list of candidates, and that had hurt, but what I really wanted was St. Mark's, and so I was also relieved to be still available. As the St. Mark's process unfolded, it felt strange. They wanted to create a level playing field for me and their other candidates, but because of my eleven years of working there, that was really impossible. Still, we persisted through interviews, an awkward dinner with my husband and me and the search committee, all of whom knew each other well. They came to visit at St. John's to hear me preach—something they'd done for years. Finally, they gave me a tour of the Rectory on Capitol Hill, a house in which I'd spent hours over the years at various parish gatherings. I began to realize that it would have been better if St. Mark's had simply made a decision one way or another about calling me as rector, and then embarked on their search for someone else if they felt I wasn't the best choice. But that was history, and I was now one of four remaining candidates, and then one of just two, as two of the other priests withdrew at the last moment. I did know who the one other candidate was, a colleague and friend from the diocese whom I had always liked and respected, and I felt him to be real competition.

Finally the phone rang at home one Monday morning—my day off. Rob and Winnie, the senior and junior wardens from St. Mark's wanted to come and see me. Deep down, I knew from the serious, caring sound of their voices that this would not be good news, but I remained full of suspense during the half hour it took them to get to Ft. Washington. In they came, all dressed up, both looking as if they were about to cry. Both were people who had loved me as Associate Rector, and now their job was to tell me they'd called the other person, Paul Abernathy, the rector of a mostly African American parish in Washington, DC. They felt St. Mark's needed real change, that I would be somehow a continuation of Jim Adams' leadership. Paul was black, came from a different liturgical and preaching tradition and was also highly intelligent, theologically sophisticated, and he had totally won them over. As they dabbed at their eyes and made sympathetic sounds, patting me gently and voicing their concern, I managed to remain cool and dry-eyed. They would not see me dissolve in tears. I had taken the risk, left St. Mark's to play by the rules of their process, gone off and found other places to serve, and I was unwilling to play the victim of defeat at their hands.

I waited until they left, then cried my heart out for a dream which had probably been dying for many months. I just hadn't let myself give up hope that I would be called back as rector of St. Mark's, and I hadn't been able to really imagine another scenario that would make as good a use of my gifts as a priest. Now the answer had come, and besides grieving, I needed to assess my remaining options. Right around that time I'd been turned down for an associate's job in a large parish in Northwest Washington. I'd also been turned down after being one of the last two candidates at a suburban Montgomery County church which I'd actually hoped wouldn't call me, because I didn't want to work there or live there. I'd put my name in only to assure the Bishop that I was serious about getting a rector's job and wasn't placing all my hopes with St. Mark's. Even so, it was another rejection, and it hurt. All these months of submitting applications, going to interviews, waiting for processes to play out had been draining and demoralizing. I had felt so beloved at St. Mark's, so eagerly accepted and affirmed at Grace Cathedral, so appreciated at St. John's, and yet it seemed there was no viable call for me to continue in the work that meant so much to me.

I was dependent on whatever vacancies existed in the greater Washington area. Despite my time on the West coast, I realized I was not prepared to move far from Washington, and to do so would be to abandon Tom and the boys. At that point, I'd put the idea of divorce on long term hold. For all of us, the DC area was home, so I really didn't explore job possibilities elsewhere, and of course that limited my options. There were, by that spring of 1998, only two that I knew of.

One, ironically, after all I'd been through, was St. John's, Broad Creek, where I was serving as interim. With me in that role, the church was flourishing, growing, and feeling hopeful about their future. They wondered if I could stay on, since things were going so well, and their protracted search had not turned up equally appealing candidates. Once again, I went over the process which did not allow for clergy already serving in the parish to be considered in a rector search. Just like at St. Mark's! I'd have to go away, be unemployed, all that nonsense all over again, so disruptive to my life and theirs, just so we could comply with our bishop's seemingly iron-clad, one size fits all policy. The leadership was incredulous and insisted on going to the bishop and asking for an exception, which he wouldn't make.

Meanwhile, one other parish was of great interest to me, but I figured it was a huge long shot. That was St. John's Norwood in Chevy Chase where I'd served part-time very briefly way back in 1986. It was a big church, about the size of St. Mark's, but more conservative theologically, socially and politically. While people at St. Mark's were mostly Democrats, and many worked for the federal government, folks at St. John's were more divided, with plenty of Republicans, private sector business people and professionals, and an older group of retired, high-ranking military men. Although they'd had women clergy as associates, I doubted they were ready for a female rector, especially one who had never been a rector before. So I dallied around and waited until the very last date when applications could be sent in. It was as if I didn't have the heart or the energy to get myself all revved up about yet another church that would probably turn me down. But, having no other inviting options, I finally called Earle O'Donnell, the head of the search committee, and a friend from my time back there in 1986.

"Hi Earle, it's Susan Gresinger, and I'm wondering if the deadline has passed for sending in an application." There was a long pause.

"The deadline is actually tomorrow, Friday, but, for you, we can extend it a couple of days. When could you have it in?"

Good sign, I thought—they remember and like me, or they're pretty hard up for good candidates.

"Thanks so much—I'll get it to you by Monday."

And so back to work I went on yet another long series of questions about myself, my spiritual journey, my areas of strength, experience with fund-raising, ideas about how to grow their church. However, maybe because I'd done it so many times before, maybe because I didn't think I had much of a chance, I was pretty relaxed and quite open and honest about why I thought churches were in trouble and what was needed and what I could offer. I didn't think much about what they wanted to hear; I just gave them who I was. I hand delivered it and settled back to wait. An excerpt from my written application follows:

"The church is in a new world, like it or not. A whole generation re-belled against the church beginning in the sixties; their children are reaching adulthood without having had religious education of any kind. Churches seeking new members face the dual task of re-explaining Christianity to those who were turned off a long time ago and, at the same time, presenting Christianity for the first time to people who may be Biblically and theologically illiterate. Churches can address this dual task, or they can give up on both groups and just minister in the familiar old ways to their shrinking congregations. I want to address this task. I want to bring back people who have left, bring in new folks, and figure out how we can articulate why we come to church so that the curious, the skeptical and the turned-off will be interested in giving Christianity a try. How does the church provide spiritual nour-ishment" How can we be more effective in connecting our Christian beliefs with the way we live our lives? We have a liturgy to give struc-ture to our deepest longings, fears, hopes and gladness. We have parish communities to support each other in the joys and struggles of life, including the spiritual quest. I want to help people appreciate what the Episcopal Church has to offer! I want to be in a position to make Christianity come alive for people. We have a Gospel story that can heal the wounds of existence and enable people to be strong and free, and I want to help the church tell that story effectively!

"As a rector, I would see myself as the spiritual guide, pastor and administrative leader for a community of seekers in which both skepticism and belief are challenged and where faith really functions in people's lives in the wider world. I would want to serve a parish that is diverse in its membership and that takes outreach seriously. In a broader arena, I would want to develop and implement programs to assist clergy in enlivening their own churches and in shaping ministry for this new world."

Meanwhile, St. John's Broad Creek had come up with a loophole by which they could call me as rector with the bishop's permission. If I left for just three months, and they completed a full search and wanted to call me back, they could. Three months was less than the usual six-month minimum, and my guess is that the bishop was tired of their long search and of my continuing unrest about this process and decided to give us all a break. Further, to spare me the loss of income over three months, the leadership at St. John's offered to pay me the money they would not be spending on me during that time, kind of like a signing bonus, if I ended up going there. During the three months, I would be free to pursue other calls, and they too were free to call someone else. I still much preferred being called to St. John's Norwood, but I felt they were not as far along in their search, and probably St. John's Broad Creek would call me before they decided. In that case, I would have to accept; I couldn't pass up a call to a real rector's position just in the hopes that the other, bigger, more challenging and interesting parish would choose me. In early June, we all said tentative farewells at St. John's, and I began another several months of down time, a kind of enforced sabbatical—not unwelcome after all this maneuvering and disappointment and uncertainty.

As I've said before, I'm not one who believes God has a plan all mapped out for my life. I also don't believe in bargaining with God, either in prayer or otherwise. I did pray and yearn and try to figure out during that time, what path would be best for me and my family, and how I could help to make that happen. I found myself wondering, as I always had in such matters, about the difference between what might be seen as God's will and my own self-will. It is an unanswerable question, but I think it is useful and necessary all the same.

So much of these clergy search processes are out of the priest's control, subject to vacancies, how one comes across on paper, the biases and expectations of committees who never see you until they have a short list. But once the arrangement with St. John's Broad Creek was in place, I grew fatalistic. If I ended up there, I would need to commit to staying there in that community where Tom and I already lived, just three miles from the church. It seemed to me that if that happened, I should see it as somehow God's will and do my best to make my marriage work, to fix up our dilapidated house on the beautiful river bank and live out my ministry in the parish where it all began. I felt I would need to accept our marriage problems and do the best I could in this small historic parish. Certainly our boys would love for mom to be working locally, although by that time, Chris was well launched in San Francisco, and Tom and Rob were away at college. For me, there was an emptiness at the heart of this plan, personally and professionally, but if nothing else came through, this would be the plan.

Meanwhile, much to my surprise, in late June, St. John's Norwood called me for two days of interviews. They were down to three candidates and planned to call a rector by the end of July. I was amazed. I'd never thought they would move this fast, and as far as I knew, folks at St. John's Broad Creek were kind of coasting through the summer. Off I went to a full day, evening and the next morning out in Bethesda-Chevy Chase, interviews, social time, tours of the parish and rectory. By now this was a familiar drill, and again, as with the written part, I felt relaxed, at ease with the committee which actually included two members who used to go to St. Mark's and knew me from there! In order for me to have the same experience as the other out-of-town candidates and not have to commute home, they reserved a room for me at the College of Preachers, a handsome stone building on the cathedral grounds. My quarters were a bit monastic, but that seemed appropriate for a night when I felt my fate was being determined. I wrote in my journal, as I had almost daily since 1982. Here were my thoughts from that evening:

Journal Entry—Friday, July 17, 1998

Today has been special. I think I'm finally experiencing that magical chemistry when a call starts to feel right for both sides . . . but this time did feel different and better! Informal brunch, free-ranging conversation, a lot on outreach, then free time. Much fine tuning of my sermon at the College of Preachers, then back to St. John's for the service in the Chapel. It went really well. I began to get that good feeling early on after only brief nervousness. I was really *in* my preaching and saw nods and smiles and people being moved. I had us all up around the altar, brought real bread. People's comments as they left seemed genuinely favorable. A nice high, then dinner and the interview. Well-timed, not confrontational, much give and take. I didn't feel interrogated. As we closed, several told me how well it had gone and were very warm.

I've allowed myself to really want this now. And tonight really has felt like those wonderful meetings other priests have told me about when things clicked. So, I'll trust my instincts and go to bed happy. Tomorrow is breakfast and "next steps." Coming back from the interview—full moon over St. John's and the cathedral and this College of Preachers where I was screened for ordination years ago. Can it be that what I have longed for for so long—a real call to be rector in a place I want to be . . . will actually come about? I know, don't get hopes too high—but, they are!

I had told the search committee that I would be leaving for vacation on July 26, the day they said they expected to decide. I carefully gave them the number of the friends where I would be staying in Connecticut that night and then the number in Tenants Harbor, Maine where I had been renting a house every year since 1994. In Connecticut, I was in agony. I hadn't told anyone but my family that I was moving through this search process, so I tried to hide my suspense and anxiety every time the phone rang. My family weren't with me; they would be joining me later in the week when work and summer jobs would permit. No one called for me, and I went off to bed to imagine that St. John's had either called someone else and were waiting for him/her to accept before letting me know, or simply hadn't decided, but they had seemed adamant that July 26 was their deadline. I then dreamed that they actually did call me, only to awaken and realize they hadn't. The next morning I headed on up to Maine, dejected and so tired of waiting. Monday, Tuesday and Wednesday went by with no call. I was glad of the solitude there in my little house on the harbor, and I prepared myself for disappointment again. On Thursday evening, around 8, I was doing some ironing when the phone rang. It was Earle O'Donnell, and I knew by his voice, it was good news.

"Susan, I'm calling on behalf of the Search Committee of St. John's Norwood to ask your permission for us to submit your name to the Vestry as our first and unanimous choice to be our next Rector."

"Oh, my God!" I almost exclaimed, but was able to slow it down and substitute "goodness." And then, "Yes, yes—you have my permission!"

"We want you to know that although the Vestry needs to make the official call, and they'll want to interview you, it is really our decision, and there would have to be very serious reservations for there to be any problem. But we would like you to come down next weekend for a quick visit."

And then: "The Committee is all here, and we want to sing something" And they did! All together at the other end of the phone, I heard:

"Praise God from whom all blessings flow.
Praise him all creatures here below.
Praise him above ye heavenly hosts.
Praise Father, Son and Holy Ghost."

It was corny and sentimental and so sweet I wanted to laugh and cry at the same time. And I was utterly exultant. When the call was over, I poured myself a stiff bourbon, turned on music from Grace Cathedral at top volume, actually ran to the bathroom to look in the mirror just to see how wide and happy my smile was. The Rector of St. John's Norwood! I danced around the house, finally settled in on the porch to look out over the harbor as darkness fell, taking in this unexpected turn that would change my life.

And here is the journal entry for that glorious night:

Journal Entry—Thursday, July 30, 1998

St. John's Norwood has picked me! Earle called this evening to say they were submitting my name to the Vestry! They popped corks; they sang the Doxology! And I did too—Amen! It's just staggering, this delight, this joy, this relief. Even the happiness I'd imagined wasn't this sweet . . . later sitting on the porch, I wept with relief that this waiting and self-doubt and uncertainty are over. And it's not a sense that I've earned it, so much as sheer gratitude. I've tried not to lose heart during this harrowing time, and now it's come together—my story has a new, welcome and fitting chapter. And there's something coming *back* from the committee—their joy, relief too, and so, (barring some hitch with the Vestry, and I know it could happen) I have a future, a job. How great to have the whole rest of vacation suffused with this wonderful promise! I'm full of plans and dreams and hopes and energy—thanks be to God!

20

St. John's Norwood Parish

My life began to accelerate. I flew down to Washington for a brief overnight visit with the St. John's Vestry. It felt like a love fest, and my call as rector was officially completed with a Letter of Agreement spelling out my job description and the salary and benefits package I would receive. A very painful next step was to call St. John's Broad Creek and let them know I had received this other call. Their own search had been lagging over the summer, and they were saddened to lose me but also very kind about wishing me well. They realized I had wanted a bigger church and could understand how exciting this new challenge was for me. We were grateful on both sides for the time we'd had together, and I will always have fond thoughts of that small struggling church on the edge of Broad Creek and of the many good people who supported me there.

Once things were settled with St. John's I felt free to announce this triumphantly to friends and colleagues. One of the first calls was to Jim Adams. He knew of my interim situation and probably thought that's where I'd end up, so when I said, "Jim, I'm calling to tell you that I've been called as the Rector of St. John's . . . Norwood," he responded after only a slight surprised pause, "Norwood—that's a real church!" For him, that was pretty high praise. I had learned from the search committee that he had assured them that I was capable of being a rector even though I'd not been one before, so I thanked him for that—it had probably made a real difference.

Tom and all three sons seemed thrilled. They knew I'd wanted this and were glad to have my long journey through self-doubt and rancor and even desperation about my prospects over with. There had been times when I'd actually envisioned myself checking groceries, and there was at least one well-meaning soul at St. Mark's who suggested I look for some other kind of work than parish priesthood and suggested a few government agencies! It's difficult to describe how much being a priest becomes part of who you are, perhaps more so than with many other vocations. Once you're ordained, the priesthood is yours, whether or not you work in a church, but for me, it was parish ministry that I loved and wanted to continue. More than anything, I had wanted a faith community to lead and help shape into a lively, flourishing church, and now that opportunity had finally come.

Still, there was uncertainty about details. For one, we lived too far away from St. John's for commuting to be a reasonable option. The drive from Ft. Washington to Chevy Chase was forty minutes in ideal circumstances, such as early Sunday morning, but usually it was an hour to an hour-and-a-half. The church owned a lovely brick colonial house in Chevy Chase, just blocks from the church, and I could live there or else receive a housing allowance and live somewhere else. The house was rented at that time and wouldn't be available to me until early in 1999, but that would give us time to figure out what to do. I had been thinking about renting a small apartment near the church with the allowance and then going back and forth to our riverbank home as time permitted. But then I saw the rectory! Tom and I were given a tour of the inside, and, for me, that was decisive. I wanted to live in that house! It reminded me of the houses I'd grown up in, the tree-shaded neighborhoods, dark hardwood floors, a dining room with coral red walls! Tom seemed to like it as well, but at that point we didn't really talk very specifically about what living there would mean and whether we'd maintain two houses. That conversation risked leading us into more fundamental differences that I still felt unready to address directly.

I was to start work at St. John's on October 1st. But first I got to savor a couple of months of free time during which I could do some of the things a parish priest never gets to do. I could actually go to my mother's 80th birthday party on a Saturday night in Sewickley. She managed to gather all of her five children, the spouses, and nine grandchildren for a festive dinner and dancing party at the local country club. Even budding chef Chris was able to take an overnight flight from San Francisco after a full day of work on Friday and arrive on Saturday morning. He then spent the whole day and night catching up with brothers especially and family in general and was back on a plane on Sunday in time to show up for work that evening! The party was really fun, with champagne toasts, much dancing and mingling of family and friends of several generations. I noticed that night that Dad was beginning to show a kind of vagueness, but this was easy to ignore. About a year later, when he was diagnosed with Alzheimer's, I would remember that party as the last time I saw my parents dance together. It was wonderful to be able to enjoy an entire weekend with no concerns about getting back for Sunday morning church or worrying about how things would go in my absence. "Normal" weekend getaways, especially for special milestones or weddings are so often impossible for clergy, so I lived into that special family time with great gusto and appreciation.

I also managed a six-day trip to England in late September to visit the friends in Lichfield and then to go off to Lincoln, Norwalk and Cambridge for some cathedral touring before a final night in London with a couple of friends from St. Mark's. It had been five years since I'd been there, and I loved renewing those ties and also enjoying traveling on my own, savoring my new prospects as a rector even as I enjoyed that last month of free time.

Back at home there was lots of preparation as October 1st neared. As it happened, my first Sunday would be October 4th, my 55th birthday. What a present! I worked for hours on my first sermon, wanting it to be just right as it would be the first impression of me for most people in the parish. I carefully reviewed the three morning services I was to lead, one at 8 in the small chapel, the others at 9 and 11 in the main church. October 4th was a beautiful clear early fall morning, and my heart just swelled as I walked into the chapel in my white robe and green stole. I preached without notes, a practice I'd developed at St. Mark's and one that delighted the folks at that small service. Then came the big, more formal services with curious crowds all wanting to meet their new rector. The Sunday School kids sang to me; a huge banner was hung outside the church with my name in big red letters. There were wonderful refreshments. I loved every minute of it, even though I knew I was playing a role I would need to learn how to fill over time.

Part of this was getting to know the lay leadership and staff. I got close to the senior warden, Wilson Krahnke, right away, through the negotiations about a Letter of Agreement between me and the vestry. Wilson was direct, funny, perhaps a bit unsure of what it would be like to have this woman rector. I also learned that Wilson's wife had recently received a tragic diagnosis of ALS, or Lou Gehrig's Disease. Betty Ann had been a prominent and beloved Montgomery County Councilwoman, and her gradual decline had already begun. At Wilson's behest, I not only had lunch with him periodically but began visiting Betty Ann every two weeks for the last couple of years before she died in 2003. These visits made for a close, important pastoral tie for me, and it added an element of personal caring to my ongoing relationship with Wilson as he moved from Senior Warden to parish Treasurer. In that role, he needed to be something of a curmudgeon, but because of Betty Ann, I knew the warm and vulnerable and deeply caring side of Wilson, and we never had serious conflict.

I also met Harrison West, the Associate Rector. He had already been there for three years, and even though he was younger and much more recently or-dained than I, his experience at St. John's was invaluable in helping me to get to know the place. Although new rectors have the option of letting all staff go and choosing their own teams, I never considered asking Harrison to go. He was a good complement to me, a fine and caring pastor, a little more "old school" in terms of reverence about the Prayer Book and church customs. These traits gave me the freedom to take more risks with liberal theology and changes in procedure, such as real bread at communion instead of the dry round wafers still common in many churches. I think Harrison's presence reassured people, especially older folks, that I was not going to take their be-loved church into some wild new realm. It was wonderful to have a close col-league again, and we soon became dear friends, a bond that continues today.

Also on staff was Joan Pirie, who had been the front office administrator back when I'd worked there in 1986! We'd gotten along splendidly then, and having her still there also provided vitally important continuity. She was great at telling me what I needed to know about how the former rector had operated, about the many pastoral issues amongst the older set, and about what she thought people expected of me. There was the wonderful Nancy Derr, recently recruited as the Church School Director. She was about my age, had a PhD and worked as a portrait painter in addition to her part-time work at St. John's and was raising a young daughter as a single mom. Nancy would become an incredibly valuable staff member at St. John's during my whole time there. She had the ability to connect with young families, draw in newcomers and bring an energy and imagination to the programs for young people that was better than anything I'd seen elsewhere. I would have Nancy to thank for much of the church growth that happened while I was there, and over the years we would become close friends. There was also the Music Director, grumpy and churlish, a youth group leader, a live-in sexton and his wife and a part-time administrator. It was a big staff for me as a new rector, and I had a lot to learn about personnel management, but I was not eager to make any changes until I saw how we would work together.

21

The Rector

My first year at St. John's was a wonderful kaleidoscope of learning, getting to know people, trying to get programs started or energized and feeling my way into this new role. It was easy, because people wanted to like me and support me and were eager for their church to come alive. It was hard, because I'd never been a rector, and despite my long experience assisting in various places, being a rector is different. The burden of overall responsibility can be heavy; the hours can get very long, and it can be lonely. Sunday mornings are festive and celebratory, the payoff for the week of work preceding. It is always a moment of elation when the church is full, things are going well, and the procession heads down the nave at the beginning of the service with me bringing up the rear, singing the hymn and smiling to folks as I pass by, feeling both anxious and excited about the sermon to be delivered. That has always been a rush for me, and it wonderfully leavens the slow day to day work of building a community and becoming an effective leader that is so complicated and demanding.

My memories of early staff meetings, always held at 1:30 on Tuesday afternoons, are like this: The staff gathers in my large office, sitting in a circle, usually in the same places each week as groups tend to do. I take my place—the others look expectantly at me. "Aren't you going to pray?" someone asks, usually Joan or Harrison. This flusters me, because although I'm completely comfortable coming up with a prayer at any time, I'm not someone who feels that a prayer is a necessary introduction to any gathering just because we happen to be in a church. I realize opening prayers play a role—they offer a moment to shift gears; they remind us to be grateful, especially before meals; they can pull a group together. But it was the idea that the rector needed to offer the prayer, that I was the expert that gave me pause. Over time I would ask others to open our staff meetings with a prayer, and over time they would, at least some of them, but from the start, there was this expectation that I was in charge, especially of everything religious, and it took some getting used to.

We would work our way through the agenda, reviewing first how everything had gone on Sunday and what newcomers had appeared. We'd move to pastoral concerns—who was sick, needed a visit or other attention. The previous rector had sent birthday cards to every single parishioner, and when I expressed doubt that this was time effective or meaningful since all he did was sign his name, like when you get a birthday card from your dentist, there was tension in the room. Was I going to change this? People expected it; they'd always done it, and the whole system of addressing the envelopes and preparing a list for me each week was in place. OK, I decided I would do it, but I would make a change. I would write a short note on each card and try to personalize it if I could. Personalizing the cards turned out to be a great decision, even though it was time consuming. It meant that every year, every single member of the parish from newborns to very old people would get a personal message from me. In that first year, I used the notes to let folks I hadn't met yet know that I hoped they'd introduce themselves in church or let me know if they would like a call or a visit. For people I knew, I used the cards to thank them for ways they'd helped or to mention things I did know were of concern to them. I found that if I did these cards every single day, it would take about twenty minutes. If I let them pile up, not only would they go out late, but I would be facing an hour or so of tedious catch-up. Other clergy were aghast that I would do this in a fairly large parish, between 300–400 households translating into 800–900 people. However, especially for older members, this small note every year meant so much. "I got your note, thank-you" some would say as they greeted me after church, sometimes with tears in their eyes! I came to believe that these notes carried a symbolic value. They were a way of letting people know that I, on behalf of the church, but more importantly, I, on behalf of God, no less, cared about and remembered them.

And that's part of the honor and the burden of pastoring. You actually stand as one who mediates God's love to people. At the altar, the priest leads the people in offering their prayers to God and in turn offers God's forgiveness and blessing to the people; she stands, symbolically, in an in-between place. At the bedside, or at the tea table or funeral or wedding or office counseling session, the priest is herself, gifts and flaws and feet of clay, but she is also representing the church community and God as well, and it's a tall and laden order. My birthday cards were just a small part of that, but by at least writing a brief note in each card, I felt it was worth the time.

Back in staff meeting, we would discuss upcoming programs and events and who was coordinating what, and who might be recruited to do various jobs. In the beginning, it seemed they wanted me to do all the recruiting, all the inviting of volunteers to do anything! Joan would point out that the former rector had gotten new volunteers for the Altar Guild by sending written invitations. Back at St. Mark's, outgoing leaders of committees found their own replacements and turned to the rector only when all else failed. At St. John's the culture was much more centered on the rector. Inevitably, in staff they would turn to me for a decision or an idea, wanting to know what I proposed. "You're the rector" they would say, looking expectantly at me, and I would kind of shrink up inside, because simply declaring a course of action was still foreign to me. I'd been an associate so long, had worked collaboratively with other clergy and lay people for so long that an authoritative style of leadership came very slowly. I was used to St. Mark's, where lay people shared much more of the leadership and where most programs were initiated and run by volunteers, not the clergy. It seemed as though the expectation at St. John's was that they had called a rector to come there and put forth my ideas and programs and that they were to sign on and carry them out, as long as they approved. My expectation was that I would come there bringing ideas and approaches but that together we would come up with a vision and plan for our community life that would involve the efforts of a wide spectrum of parishioners, not just the clergy and staff. The profile developed by St. John's for their search process had said, memorably, that they wanted for St. John's "to become a happening place." Over the years before I got there, St. John's had become a bit flat in membership and a bit stale in its worship and programs. The same people kept running and doing the same things, and new families, especially those with young children, found little to engage them. It was up to me to get things going, but I soon realized I needed to enlist the energies and imagination of lots of others and give them permission to stop asking me for permission to do anything! Early on, I had a message from someone who wanted to know if it was all right with me for her to use name tags at a meeting she was chairing! People wanted me to make all the announcements in church on Sunday. They would come up to me with scribbled notes at the last minute, or call on Saturday night or early Sunday morning to ask me to announce this or that, and it was quite the struggle to gradually get these folks to make their own announcements for their own meetings and programs. These were not powerless, shy or incapable people. Many were highly effective professionals or government employees, teachers, health care workers. Why were they so reluctant to stand up in church, especially in front of a mike on Sunday morning? It may sound like a small thing, but in most churches, announcements are considered boring by many, and there are often arguments about what time in the service is appropriate for them, the middle, end or nowhere. In my view, these announcements communicate the life of the parish and not only let people know what's going on, but when made by parishioners, they let people know who does what and that the work of the parish is so much more than a performance of worship put on by the rector on Sunday morning.

Slowly, over time, things really began to come alive at St. John's, and it did indeed become "a happening place." But all along, I was growing into the new role. There were times I felt as though I were simply pretending to be the rector. I remembered the slogan "Fake it 'til you make it." Was that me? I was wearing the clothes, saying the words, bearing the authority, but I hadn't really yet claimed that role from the inside.

That would come eventually, but not at the beginning, not even at the great event called "The Celebration of a New Ministry" when a rector is formally instituted in her new parish by the bishop. For me that was planned for the evening of December 3rd, 1998, just two months after I'd begun. We all needed that time to plan, not only for the elaborate liturgy, but for an all-parish party to follow. Soon after I received the call to St. John's I telephoned Alan Jones, still Dean of Grace Cathedral in San Francisco to see if he would preach at this service. I knew he was to be in town around then for an appearance at the cathedral in Washington, and I was thrilled when he quickly accepted. A well-known preacher and author such as Alan would lend some real cachet to the event. I was also aware, in my less than fully Christian lack of charity, that I wanted to upstage the bishop who had given me so much trouble with his process and who would have otherwise preached, and I further wanted the people of St. Mark's to be impressed with my new status and connections. Unbecoming spitefulness, I'm sure, but it's the way I felt.

St. John's was still finishing a renovation of most of its interior space except for the church itself, so getting it looking elegant for the upcoming reception was a challenge. But a wonderful group of young women took this on, and with the aid of lots of garlands of seasonal greenery and white roses galore, it was beautiful. My associate Harrison completely organized the service, helped me choose readers and other participants as I hadn't been around long enough to really know who all the players were.

The service began with my favorite hymn for any great processional, "Christ is made the sure foundation," with its wonderful Henry Purcell tune. Moving down the aisle on that special evening, I saw not only all the St. John's parishioners, but my whole family and also many beloved friends from St. Mark's and even St. John's Broad Creek. My friends Nita and Cliff Vawda had come all the way from Lichfield, England, and Bill and Nina Opel, from way back at the very beginning at St. John's, Broad Creek, made the trip from Cape Cod. Next to them, were Bill and Claire Flanders, he as a colleague from my St. Mark's days, she, a French atheist, deigning to come as a friend, a lovely surprise. Alan preached about Mary, the mother of Jesus, and her role in giving birth to Jesus as God's incarnation in human flesh. He beautifully affirmed my own ministry and that of all women priests in suggesting that Mary, in presenting Jesus to the world, was the very first priest!

After the sermon there were various symbolic gifts of my office: a Bible and a prayer book, water and oil for baptism and healing, a priest's stole, keys to the building, bread and wine. Notably, they added a hard hat and these words: "Susan, receive this hard hat and be among us to raise the money and share the dust and the noise as we renovate and beautify our building for the enhancement of our ministry." Even in the most glorious moments of church life, there lurks the financial burden of supporting a parish and its building and programs, and this burden would be with me throughout my time at St. John's. That night, it was merely a hint.

The service continued with what stood at the absolute heart of it for me. It is a prayer of dedication, a traditional part of the prayer book service. I had read it over the years, wondering if I would ever say it. I'd read it when it looked like the process was going well at St. John's and wept at the prospect of praying it. And now the moment came. I knelt on a small cushion on the top chancel step—the place where the congregation space ends and the altar and sanctuary space begin. Even with a cushion, the stone step was hard, and there, kneeling, my heart pounding, I felt my small female frame and the immensity of this role. I heard my voice going out into the nave over the microphone, clear and low, and I felt as if the floor trembled under me as I began:

O Lord my God, I am not worthy to have you come under my roof; yet you have called your servant to stand in your house, and to serve at your altar. To you and to your service I devote myself, body, soul and spirit. Fill my memory with the record of your mighty works; enlighten my understanding with the light of your Holy Spirit; and may all the desires of my heart and will center in what you would have me do. Make me an instrument of your salvation for the people entrusted to my care, and grant that I may faithfully administer your holy Sacraments, and by my life and teaching set forth your true and living Word. Be always with me in carrying out the duties of my ministry. In prayer quicken my devotion; in praises, heighten my love and gratitude; in preaching, give me readiness of thought and expression; and grant that, by the clearness and brightness of your holy Word, all the world may be drawn into your blessed kingdom. All this I ask for the sake of your Son our Savior Jesus Christ. Amen. (The Book of Common Prayer, p. 562)

The rest of the service and the reception following were a heady blur, and I felt myself surrounded by good will and fond hopes and heartfelt love and prayers. It was a great official beginning to my tenure, and a solid foundation for some difficult decisions I soon faced.

22

Tearing Apart

As Christmas approached, serious personal concerns were beginning to demand some resolution. Throughout the whole time of my getting started at St. John's, Tom and I continued to have various strains between us, although we kept them pretty much in the background as we waited for me to settle in. St. John's had not included spouses in their search process. This was forward-thinking and rare at the time, but they had not called me with any particular expectations about my marriage, had never even asked about it. Tom began coming to St. John's on most Sundays and was getting to know folks there, but was certainly not a part of the community yet as he'd been at St. Mark's. Meanwhile, we needed to decide about housing. Because the Rectory wouldn't be available until February, I had figured out a temporary plan. Wonderful, generous St. Mark's friends who lived just a few blocks from St. John's had offered me a room and bath in their large Chevy Chase house, rent free. This allowed me a place to stay three or four nights a week, and then I went home to Fort Washington on the other nights. This offer kept the commuting at a manageable level, especially when I had early morning or evening commitments at church, and I loved this easy arrangement, even as I put off a more permanent one. Tom and I couldn't seem to come to an understanding about whether or not to rent our house in Fort Washington or keep using it, even if we moved to the rectory. I know Tom didn't want to lose access to our beautiful perch on the Potomac. He had bought it in 1968, long before he married me, and it was truly part of who he was. I felt we needed to rent it for the income. We had some hefty federal income tax obligations, and renting the house would allow us to pay them off. I realize that what seemed a simple practical matter to me was an emotionally fraught one for Tom. He was not charmed in the way I was with the rectory, and I think he just wanted to be able to use our house at least occasionally, perhaps spending more time there than I, still having his place on the water.

One Sunday afternoon in a Toyota dealership in Alexandria, these concerns all collided. After a good morning in church, I headed over to see about leasing a small, affordable Corolla to replace the old and ailing Chrysler I'd inherited from one of Tom's nurses. I'm sitting in the showroom, still dressed in my suit, black shirt and clerical collar. Things start off well, and the lease seems all worked out. $310 a month is easily affordable, given my new rector's salary. I've picked a lovely dark green model, just right for me, nothing flashy, appropriate for a minister, and all mine, something I'd picked and paid for.

But then, a problem! The somewhat flustered man who had been steering me through settlement and loan papers came out of his office, clearly embarrassed at having to have this conversation with a lady minister all dressed up in her Sunday garb. Did I realize that there was an IRS lien on our house? Oh no, I cringed, inwardly. "Yes," I replied. "It is a tax lien and my husband is working with the IRS to take care of that. However, you can see from my salary that I am fully capable of taking on this lease, and the tax lien should make no difference." The man retreated to his office where he conferred with a couple of other men, looking over their shoulders through the cubicle window at me surreptitiously as though I were some sort of unusual specimen, which I suppose I was, a female priest with a tax lien trying to lease a car in her own right. The men came out; now they wanted my husband to co-sign the lease! Why? Hadn't we agreed that this was affordable for me based on my own income? More conferring, leaving me sitting alone and embarrassed, but increasingly angry, in their cheesy showroom. Slowly, a conviction arose and took its place at the core of my being. I'd had enough. Enough of Tom's IRS debts and problems and liens which were not of my making and which had survived all of my attempts to get them worked out. Enough of never knowing if any of our credit cards were paid up, or when, if ever, we'd get out from under. Enough of this secret financial shame, of fear about the future, of rage at Tom's seeming inability or lack of concern about getting this taken care of.

It was time for me to leave the marriage. I'd reached this conclusion many times before, but this time, unbidden, a plan emerged, a concrete scenario that would begin my departure. It was a scenario that would leave a door open for us to work things out, good for our sons and for the parish and a way of separating from Tom that would not immediately dictate the final outcome. I was due to move into the St. John's rectory in February, and I would tell Tom I didn't want him to move with me except under certain set conditions. I felt we had already agreed that we needed to rent our house in Fort Washington in order to generate an income stream to pay off our IRS obligation. In order to rent at an optimal rate, we needed to do a great deal of renovation. In a sense, I came up with an ultimatum: I would not agree to have Tom move into the rectory with me until these renovations were finished and the house was ready to rent; it would be too difficult to supervise such a project from the distance of the rectory in Chevy Chase, and Tom would need to stay on site to complete this. Further, we needed to have a plan in place including a timetable for paying off the tax debt; I was no longer willing to drift along, always at risk of IRS action to seize assets. I needed us to be in full compliance with the IRS and to make our way out of years of debt. Just there, sitting in that office, this new narrative had emerged. I felt an enormous surge of energy as I returned to the business at hand, that of getting a car. To do that and assuage the salesmen's concerns, I finally agreed to actually buy the Corolla at a somewhat higher but still affordable monthly rate. Grateful to have that settled, and feeling empowered because now I had a plan, I left the office on a high, driving my shiny little green car off into a new future that had just taken a giant leap forward. In hindsight, that afternoon was a God-given moment of fresh perspective and a clearer capacity to face the reality of my life. A new possibility had emerged and become imaginable in very practical ways, not because of my own planning, but because of the fear and vulnerability I realized I would no longer live with.

My new narrative would allow me to move to the rectory by myself and would provide a plausible reason to give the parish, the need to renovate our house for rental, for Tom remaining in Fort Washington. For our sons, my conditions were not impossible; perhaps Tom would actually go along and we could salvage our marriage. Although by that point, I was almost positive he would not or could not meet these conditions, I felt that they were fair. I also knew, deep inside, that as much as I had been increasingly unhappy and wanting to be out of the marriage, that if Tom did do these things, it could have brought about a drastic change of my heart. I knew it would force me to consider again and to respect a depth of commitment to our marriage and a willingness to change that I would not turn my back on. Even as friends and family worried that I would be miserable if Tom accepted these terms, I knew that if he did, I would be open to renegotiating and recommitting to our marriage.

During all the years of troubles in our marriage, I continually wrestled with my own conscience about divorce, and not only because I had already been divorced once. I never felt divorce was to be taken lightly; in fact I felt then and do now, that it is actually a grave sin. It is a sin about breaking solemn promises. One or both people either can not or will not keep the promises they made to each other at marriage, and this is always a betrayal. However, it falls in the moral category of those decisions where sometimes one sinful path is the lesser of two evils. Marriages can and do die, and I came increasingly to feel that God as I understood God, would not condemn people to live in a marriage that was not a true one in any except a legal and superficial sense. The marriage service states up front that marriage is meant for the "mutual joy" of the husband and wife, and after that for "help and support given one another in prosperity and adversity," and finally for procreation. Without going beyond the various problems that I've mentioned so far, suffice it to say that our marriage was devoid of joy and the kind of help and support needed. For myself, I wanted much more than this in a relationship, or else no relationship. I knew Tom would be deeply hurt. He had always maintained that he loved me and wanted to be married to me, and I think he always felt he was doing what he could. The burden of leaving would be on me. The boys would certainly blame me, although I felt that since they were then ages 30, 21 and 20, they were old enough to be aware of our problems and to understand and that this would not be too painful. The younger boys were still in college so not living at home most of the time, and Chris was living with his girlfriend in San Francisco and actually contemplating marriage himself.

I was well aware of the position of the Church on divorce. In my own Episcopal denomination, remarriage in the church had become permissible in the early 1970s. Until then, as still today in Roman Catholicism, it was not. Many, many people in all of the parishes where I'd served had gotten divorced. Many had remarried successfully. Sometimes they asked me what I thought about divorce, what the Bible says, whether it's wrong. The few mentions of divorce in the Bible say it is against God's will, although there are some varying conditions such as adultery or the unbelief of one partner that make allowances. However, I have never seen the Bible as the sole moral arbiter for our behavior today, whether in connection with divorce or many other moral dilemmas that either didn't exist in Biblical times or are so changed by today's circumstances. The Bible's guidance is that it is good for man and woman to be united in a marriage covenant. The Bible's many accounts of multiple wives, siring heirs through servant women, adultery and the general subservience of wives to husbands just don't hold up as useful rules for sorting out the difficulties of marriage in today's world. After years of grappling, listening to other people's marital woes, wondering what to do about my own and torturing myself about whether I could ever bring myself to divorce, I had finally come to a way of thinking about divorce that recognizes the ambiguity of the church on this matter. As a Christian, what I have is a tradition that takes marriage extremely seriously and values lasting unions. What I also have is the story that is at the very heart of Christianity, the Easter story of Resurrection. To me, the story is about God's power to bring about new life out of situations of death. God did this with Jesus, and my belief is that God does this with us in all the dark and dead places of our lives, great and small. We experience losses and deaths of one sort or another, and yet we hope that things can change, that they can get better, that we can be better and live newer, fuller lives. I can't believe that marriage is the one area of our lives that is excluded from this promise. And so I weathered the years of gathering clouds in my own marriage and finally got to the place where I chose to move towards new life. I would have felt unfaithful if I hadn't, if I had been willing to settle for what was then, for me, a dead place.

After that afternoon of clarity and resolve in the Toyota dealer's, I lived with new energy. I had a plan, a way into the future. I also lived with apprehension. I would have to tell Tom and our boys about my decision, and

I would have to let the parish know. I let the holidays pass, feeling full of a secret that could not yet be told. Finally, on January 11th, with Tom and Rob off for dinner at my sister's, I told Tom of my intention to move to the rectory on my own, and of what I felt needed to happen if he were to join me there.

"Does this mean divorce?" was his immediate answer.

"No, no! These are the things you need to do for us to then see whether we have a viable marriage, and if you can do them, I promise I'm open to that possibility." And I meant that despite all my reservations.

"Well, you'll have to tell the boys."

I knew this was coming, and that it was up to me, and so when they arrived home from my sister's, the four of us sat together in our living room. I explained what I was proposing, and immediately both choked up, as if they'd been expecting the worst and now were faced with it. Tearfully, Tom said, "Dad, you can do these things" looking beseechingly at his father. I remember saying I was so sorry and that maybe things would work out, but our sad gathering didn't last long. I went off to bed in despair, feeling as if I'd just destroyed two young lives. After a very disturbed and fitful sleep, I woke early the next morning with that horrible sinking sensation you have when you remember something awful that has just happened. I decided I couldn't go through with it, and I was actually tempted to take it all back, stay together, not divide the family. I couldn't stand seeing our sons so upset, it was way more than I had expected. Many of their friends' parents had divorced, and I thought they were pretty aware of our problems. I had so underestimated their response!

But before I could start backtracking and trying to make everyone feel all right again, my sister called. She had been a sympathetic friend through all the years of my marital woes and had helped me the night before by having Tom and Rob over while I talked to Tom. She asked me how it had gone, and the minute I started to express regrets, she warned me off, telling me to stick to my plans, not to go back to the same old stuck place, not to give in to my guilt and remorse about hurting people. Her call was just enough to strengthen my resolve, and from then on, I persisted. I moved on with the plan I had conceived. Later that week I flew to San Francisco for a weekend to talk to my oldest son Chris about my decision. He was saddened, as he had always cared about Tom, but he was also not at all surprised and had seen this coming. He was supportive and even wrote Tom a loving letter encouraging him to do the things I had asked in the hope that we could keep our family together. In the parish, I told people we were working on renovating our house and that Tom would be staying out there until it was ready to rent, enough information for the time being.

On March 8, 1999, I moved to the St. John's Rectory. The last weeks with Tom had been awkward as we divided up furniture, but he seemed to have no sense of finality about this and actually began making some preparations for clean-up and renovation. On that morning, he left for work as usual, we kissed each other on the cheek as usual, and he was gone. I was shaking. Our separation had really happened. We would now live apart; a season of our lives had ended.

.

23

Building Community at the Crossroads of Faith and Life

Even as my marriage was slowly unraveling, life at St. John's was full of growth and vitality. I was learning how to be a rector and learning how to be my kind of rector. I never wanted to be an authoritarian dictator, and I never wanted to lead from way out ahead, trying to drag reluctant followers along. I wanted to develop strong ties with talented lay leadership; I wanted to be open with the whole parish about my ideas and plans, and I wanted input from others about moving forward. I needed the creativity of others and collaboration from those I served.

The hardest part for me was personnel management. I'd had no prior experience with it except as a spectator in other parishes. Early on, against the urgings of several influential laypeople, I had decided not to fire a very difficult music director—hoping that he and I could work together and wanting to at least give that a try. He was also in quite frail health at the time and backed by a small group of passionate supporters, so I held back, trying to be wise and compassionate, possibly actually being cowardly. Our music program suffered for several years as a result, and when I finally did replace him, the results were just stupendous, with huge growth in the choirs and in the quality of music in our worship. I also had to learn about employee evaluations and how to keep good job descriptions and records, how to push for salary or benefit increases for the staff and even myself. Eventually, we formed a Personnel Committee to provide counsel, and although we didn't always agree, at least I had a forum in which to air concerns about personnel.

More of interest to me, and more in line with the gifts for which St. John's had called me, was the development of an adult Christian education program. People seemed hungry for more theology, more Biblical understanding, more spiritual guidance, not only on Sunday mornings but at other times during the week. I began by trying a number of things I'd done at St. Mark's, but with mixed success. The "sermon seminar," where folks get to discuss the sermon after it is preached at the end of the service pretty much bombed, even though we only held it once a month. Out of a congregation of say, 150, only 20–30 would stay for this. Starbucks was just a couple of blocks up the street and seemed more alluring for the young parents while their children were in Sunday School than reflection on the sermon. Not only that, St. John's was used to having a "Forum" during the Sunday school hour where a variety of speakers from within and outside of the parish presented various topics, everything from political to spiritual issues. These options were apparently preferable, at least based on the numbers, to the sermon seminar, and soon more and more schedule conflicts arose on sermon seminar Sundays and the experiment died.

There was a much better response to the functional education I had soaked up at St. Mark's, and it was an exciting challenge to try to adapt this to the St. John's community. I began by meeting with a couple of people who had actually gone to St. Mark's and knew about this form of education. Then we held a forum about the process and the options for taking courses. Our emphasis was very strongly on how these classes were to help us all make sense of our religion and how it affects the way we live, how we cope and make decisions and deal with tragedy and failure. Finally we launched a short introductory class, one weeknight for each of four weeks, called "The Ties That Bind." The title held dual meaning, those important ties of relationship and devotion that hold us to one another in life-giving ways, and the various ties that come along with them or conflict with them to bind us up and constrain our choices. In each class we presented a situation in which people are torn between conflicting loyalties, between parenting and professional development, between spouses' needs and individual aims, between self-interest and moral integrity. The class was a good start with about 18 attendees. They came willing to enter in, to open up and talk about their own life experience and to think about the role of faith in these issues.

Next, after an entire year of planning, we offered the "Faith and Values" class. It involved ten week night classes, a weekend away at a retreat center and an all-day wrap up session at the rectory. I had two co-teachers, Margaret, who had been at St. Mark's and had taught there, and Anne, a psychiatrist, who was curious to learn about how this process worked and was game to plunge in and help teach. Even though the weekend cost money, and even though parents with young children were unwilling or unable to commit, we managed to recruit a class of thirteen, mostly women, mostly older than the usual class at St. Mark's, but all eager to try this new adventure.

It had been several years since I'd led such a class or such a retreat while I was off chasing jobs, and I loved the exhilaration of launching something I knew well and believed in. The weekend retreat was especially poignant for me. We gathered at the wonderfully home-like blue-shingled Dupont Memorial House in Rehoboth, Delaware, a former Dupont summer residence just two blocks from the beach. I'd been there so many times, taught so many other classes, it was as if the sprawling house was full of the ghosts of all these times gone by. Beloved friends, teaching teammates, annoying pests, all the texture and richness of these many former gatherings filled my heart and memory as we began the weekend. To my huge satisfaction, functional education proved its mettle, and what I had learned and taught and used before succeeded in bringing this new group together. We gathered in front of the fireplace in the living room for each session. Comfortable bamboo furniture, hardwood floors, a gracious country house look. We teachers had worked hard to design the weekend and were thrilled at how fully people were willing to enter in. Together our work led to a deepened understanding of our lives and of our faith, just as it had back at St. Mark's. In one session we asked people to respond to the question "What is faith?" One older man, probably the oldest one there, volunteered to share his response. He simply laid out his long life, his military service, career, lasting marriage and the rearing of four daughters. He did this in a straightforward way, with both pride and humility, and he choked up as he finished, saying, "That's about it." This indeed had been his life of faith, and it was a gift for us to hear it. The telling of stories is really at the heart of this kind of Christian education, just as the telling of stories is really the essence of the Biblical record that has come down to us. In telling our stories, we draw together in our common humanity and in the facing of joys and sorrows which are part of every story. Talk of faith creeps in, not as something presented by the teachers, but in glimpses of what keeps us going in dark times and what leads us to rejoice when life seems better than we ever believed it could be. By the end of the weekend, we were a closely bonded group—all ages, varying life situations, but together in having shared a common quest.

We continued to develop functional education at St. John's in various formats, and both the "Faith and Values" class and a number of other shorter classes continued to draw members for several years. One class continued on as a theological book discussion group. I knew there were people who were hungry for more theological substance, but I also realized that for many, especially parents of young children, church was just not about that. Even though most folks were very open to my preaching and the progressive theology I put forth, additional classes outside of Sunday mornings never really took hold after my early years. My own skeptical, questioning approach to religion prompted me to always want to give others permission to express their doubts and to embrace the inevitable ambiguity that faith has always entailed for me. But after about five years, it seemed that the level of interest in functional education had begun to wane, and my own energies began to focus elsewhere.

As in many parishes undertaking new growth and change, we carried out a strategic planning project. This involved a committee and for awhile, a consultant and took way longer than the nine months intended. However, it was an in depth study of all aspects of our life, and it yielded helpful data about what was working well and where change and improvement were needed. As part of this process, we developed a mission statement, something many churches do, but to my mind, most of these iterations are meaningless church jargon, something one member referred to as "gobbledygook." They are often way too wordy, a paragraph rather than a statement, or way too abstract: "to know Christ and to make Christ known," to cite a common example. What does that mean? How do we do that? On a vestry weekend retreat, we worked with a consultant to come up with a meaningful statement that accurately described what we were up to at St. John's. After several hours of considering what we were doing well and what we cared about, it was clear that we valued a strong sense of community. We loved the many parish events that brought us together to share meals and projects, and we loved our sense of connectedness even though we worshiped at several different services. We also valued making clear connection between our faith and the realities of our daily lives. We didn't keep religion in a special corner; we didn't see spirituality as a separate dimension of existence. And so, finally, thinking about our location at a major crossroads in Bethesda/Chevy Chase, I suggested "Building Community at the Crossroads of Faith and Life." To my delight and satisfaction, they liked it, and we approved this as the St. John's mission statement which it remains to this day. It was remarkable because it contained no mention of God or Jesus, and I was surprised that there were no objections. It was brief, it was honest about who we were, and it was unique. I was proud of our work on that vestry weekend and felt we came away with new energy and clarity about where we were going.

One important new emphasis for us was a greater variety of worship experiences. We had a small 8 am service of around 30 people with a sermon and communion and no music; we had a large family friendly service of 150–200 at 9 with its own choir, fairly informal music and a somewhat contemporary liturgy. At 11:15 we offered a more traditional service which appealed to many of our older members and which included our fine adult choir. That service drew barely 100 people, and it was getting smaller. All three services had the same sermon. What my colleague Harrison and I realized more and more was how little the 9 am service offered for really young children, those not yet able to read or follow the service. They went out for "story time" during the sermon, and there was an occasional children's sermon during the service, but there wasn't much else. We did have a nursery, but that was for children up to three, and some parents were reluctant to leave their children. Harrison had heard someone comment that for very young children, sitting restlessly in pews with their parents, church was like sitting staring straight into a blank wall, hearing "blah, blah, blah, blah, Jesus, blah, blah blah, Jesus, blah blah!" Standard Episcopal worship is just not meant for four year olds!

Thanks largely to a model Harrison encountered during a trip to California, we began a Children's Chapel in 2003. We had a large open room underneath the church, "the undercroft" in church-speak. We furnished this with small chairs, a rug up front and a small altar. We had two wonderful women who helped: Liz who played the piano, and Marnie who was an early childhood specialist in real life. Each Sunday one of us clergy would join them downstairs for the first half-hour of the 9 am service to lead a series of songs and simple prayers and a story, usually connected with the morning's gospel reading or seasonal theme. There were no printed programs; all the songs could be easily taught and memorized, and the children could draw their prayers on little cards to bring forward and show to the group. One distinctive feature was a special confession. Each child was given a fist-sized smooth stone which we would hold up to our hearts as the leader led us in a very short litany saying we were sorry for things we'd done wrong or ways we'd hurt others. We would ask God's forgiveness. Then came the favorite part for all, especially the boys. Everyone would come forward and drop his stone into a bowl, plastic, of course. Then the leader would pour a pitcher of water over the stones, saying something like, "Your sins have all been washed away, you are forgiven." After this brief service, we would all go upstairs and rejoin the congregation for communion. Children's Chapel was a lovely, slightly chaotic, totally kid-friendly scene, and it grew rapidly. Within weeks, this new service was attracting up to 30 people including children and parents, and by the first Easter, there were over 50! It was definitely a way to bring in and hold young families, and I was grateful to Harrison and proud of his initiative and creativity in bringing this new service to St. John's.

That same year, he and I decided we needed yet another service, something in the late afternoon on Sundays. This new service would be informal, experimental and very much open to seekers who didn't particularly feel comfortable with conventional Sunday morning worship. Several other Episcopal churches in Washington had already begun such services, either Saturday or Sunday, and we decided to give it a try. To educate ourselves, Harrison and I and some other lay leaders attended a workshop in New York City at St. Bartholomew's, a huge church on Park Avenue. It was there that I first encountered a "praise band" playing a kind of music many of my colleagues and music directors derided as not dignified or substantive enough for the stately Episcopal worship tradition. But there, up front in the huge chancel of St. Bart's, we found a small orchestra with keyboard, strings, drums and singers, leading the congregation in a sort of soft rock, slightly folky genre of music—loud, rhythmic, full of energy. I absolutely loved it, and when the service ended with the band and about a hundred of us singing "Shine, Jesus, Shine," I was right there, singing out with all my heart, wanting this song, this music to sound forth back at St. John's. The clergy wore street clothes instead of vestments, jeans, even. Communion was passed around informally, and the sermon was given without notes, a sort of review of the morning's presentation. We came away hugely impressed and determined to offer our own service along the same lines.

Finally, by December of 2003, everything was in place. We hired a keyboard player and a song leader who proved a bit too operatic and grandiose for our group but who at least helped get us started. We recruited twenty people to commit to attending this 5 pm Sunday service from December through the following May, just to make sure we had a congregation. We put up signs and publicized our "Come As You Are" service widely, both within and outside the parish. I still remember our opening night with enormous pleasure. We'd planned to hold the service up in the chancel, using the choir pews in front of the altar, but right from the beginning, far more than the 20 who had promised to come showed up. We were more than 30, and the chancel was full. Our opening song was one that began "Let there be peace on earth, and let it begin with me." A bit schmaltzy and sentimental, perhaps, but it moved me to tears as we all sang out together. The late afternoon sun slanted through the windows, casting rosy shadows on the walls; people clustered close together to share the bread and wine, and my heart filled with the sense that something new was being born at St. John's. And so it was, continuing over the years, moving out into the larger space of the nave, bringing people around the altar during communion, offering a place for many different kinds of less traditional music. No organ, no vestments, everyone welcome regardless of what they believed, or didn't.

Welcoming everyone to receive communion, whether or not they were Episcopalian or even baptized was something we'd done at St. John's ever since I'd gotten there. This was not the universal practice in the Episcopal Church, or many others for that matter, not back then, and not even now. Traditionally, communion was intended for baptized Christians only. Even so, more and more churches practice what is called "Open Communion" and during my tenure, no bishops ever questioned our embrace of this. Both Grace Cathedral in San Francisco and Washington National Cathedral welcome all people to communion. Often there is something printed in bulletins such as "All who seek God and are drawn to Christ are welcome to receive Communion," but even these conditions are never actually questioned. I would always offer communion to all, regardless of religious background.

To me, open communion is hugely important. Baptism has been the traditional way into Christian community, going back to the early church, and gradually, infant baptism became the norm in many denominations. Parents made promises on behalf of their children who were expected to have those promises confirmed when they were old enough to decide for themselves. Even then, confirmation took place at an early age, usually 12–13, and communion was withheld until then. The institution set up a series of levels of inclusion bounded by rules and regulations about every step. Meanwhile, the simple receiving of bread and wine at an altar along with one's family and community is at its heart such a basic human act, something which anyone of any culture and any age can do and find meaningful. Restricting access to this sacrament seems the opposite of what Jesus taught and did. He was the one to welcome all people, women, children, sinners of every kind, outcasts and the marginalized to listen to his teachings, receive his healings, eat and travel with him as companions. How odd that the blessing and sharing of bread and wine at his last supper should become a sacred ritual reserved only for those in compliance with church rules!

Especially odd is the expectation that young children who have not yet been baptized for whatever reason, should not take communion. Often parents who have been away from church for years decide to bring their children to Sunday School and church. When it comes time for communion, I've occasionally seen this: a family, all lined up at the altar rail, parents and, say, their children aged 3 and 6. As the priest moves along, passing out the bread, the children hold out their hands, hoping for a little taste of home-baked bread and a sip of grape juice. One of the parents, thinking communion isn't allowed because their children aren't baptized or confirmed, swats their little hands away, sternly warning them they must not receive; they are to meekly fold their arms across their chest and receive a blessing from the priest! It is so distressing to see this, to see the disappointed, wondering look on these children's faces and to realize that some of the first messages they are getting from church are that they are not fully welcome. Communion is the one part of the whole church service that little kids can actually understand, and it is a lovely thing for them to participate with their parents. This is especially true when real bread, and not a dry thin wafer, is offered. A young mother once told me about how they attended another church on their summer vacation where wafers were used. Several days later, when she was doing her little 4-year-old son's laundry, she found one of these wafers in his pocket. He told her that he had no idea these were edible and thought it was something he should take home and keep! Open communion is just as important for adults. Here again, for the increasing numbers of unchurched folks wanting to give Christianity a try, it is important that the central ritual be available to them from the start, that Jesus' radical hospitality is extended by the church. For most seekers who decide to join a church, baptism is a natural follow-up once they have a chance to experience life in a faith community and get familiar with the worship and teachings. Baptism for them is like a formal initiation after a period of exploration. To those who argue that if we offer communion to anyone, regardless of religious background, they will have no incentive to get baptized, I use the analogy my father used to make in his arguments for virginity until marriage. Crudely, in my view, he would argue that if one already could have the milk, why would anyone buy the cow? i.e. if you had sex with someone they'd have no incentive to get married! If communion and full participation in the church are meaningful and life-giving to people, and if they are welcomed into our communities without conditions, it seems to me they will be all the more likely to want to eventually formalize their participation through baptism. Communion thus should function as an incentive to baptism, not as a reward for it.

By 2003, I felt well established at St. John's. The parish was healthy, financially stable; our physical plant was in far better shape than when I had arrived, and the parish had grown somewhat. The lay leadership were people I liked and trusted, and our many programs were lively—we had indeed become "a happening place."

Even more importantly, I felt that people had opened up theologically, that through my preaching and teaching they felt empowered to question their faith, to be open about the places where they had doubts, and to push back a bit on church traditions that seemed outmoded. Certainly I could have done more. I regretted then, and still do, that I didn't spend more time developing additional adult Christian education opportunities. I didn't wade into the issue of how much the conventional Prayer Book liturgies are out of sync with what so many people believe about God and about sin, heaven and faith. Even the 1979 Prayer Book, bemoaned by many when it came out because the language was fairly contemporary, was beginning to seem stuffily outmoded to me. I had one parishioner who had been active in all areas of lay leadership and who was a dedicated student of theology and worship come to me to tell me that he could no more come to church because the words of the liturgy just didn't reflect his actual beliefs. He could not pray to a God presented as a seemingly supernatural being before whom we must grovel to win favor, and all the language about a heavenly kingdom on high somewhere just stuck in his craw. My remonstrances with him about just accepting this language as metaphor proved unconvincing, and I realized that there was so much more to be done. I also realized that I shared his theological objections! I too had begun to let go of any belief in God as a separate being and of heaven as a separate place and of prayer as an attempt to get God to do something. I was reading Bishop John Spong's books, notably *Why Christianity Must Change or Die*, and I agreed with him. I too was beginning to understand God as a presence within all of us and in and beyond the whole creation, God as a presence we ourselves are called to express in the way we live. But I had not really tried to change the words of the liturgy or experiment much with alternative forms. People were going through the motions, saying things they didn't understand or believe just because that was what church services entailed. Even if the theology they heard from the pulpit made sense and opened up their faith, what they said and sang was in a different theological key. I had a growing awareness that even as a rector, even in a parish that was thriving in so many ways, there was so much more that could have been done in terms of spiritual and theological leadership. Too often administrative duties absorbed my time and energy; too often the demands of a few complainers could drain my spirit. This work was an enterprise that demanded so much, gave back so much, engrossed me almost fully. I loved it while at the same time, I realized I would never achieve all I could hope, all I could dream for that faith community. I also had my private life to live.

24

"Turning, Turning . . ."

"'Tis the gift to be simple, 'tis the gift to be free, 'tis the gift to come down
where we ought to be, and when we find ourselves in the place just right,
'twill be in the valley of love and delight . . . to turn, turn, will be our
delight till by turning, turning we come round right."

Simple Gifts, Joseph Bracket, Jr. (1797–1882)

Through those first five years of getting settled in my ministry at St. John's, I had not taken much time for life away from the parish. Tom and I had been legally separated since 1999, after it became clear that we would not be able to resolve our differences about the house and taxes and that, at least for me, there was no emotional life left there. Our divorce was not final, still pending financial issues to be ironed out, but there seemed no urgency to push ahead, and it seemed to me that if we moved slowly it would be less painful for our sons. Meanwhile, I was open to dating but found extremely little opportunity. The occasional well-meaning friend would introduce me to someone but nothing ever clicked. I still loved the peaceful uncluttered solitude of the rectory and its quiet neighborhood, my walks morning and evening with my little brown and white spaniel, Tyler. Work was a six-day occupation, but I loved doing it, loved my role, loved almost every aspect of being a rector and spiritual leader. The parish provided ample social life and plenty of companionship including some real friendships. I also had a circle of friends from my days at St. Mark's, including a women's group and a theological book group. I felt as though the story of my life was still very much open-ended, and I had no clear vision of what the long term future might hold.

Meanwhile, the life of my family had been changing. My sons had proved resilient despite their pain over Tom's and my separation. They were growing up and launching themselves as adults. Chris had married Felicia Clark in 1999, and in 2002 their daughter, Emma was born. The arrival of this first grandchild was a huge thrill, and because her birth came a bit later than expected, my planned visit to San Francisco began on the very day she was born. I was actually going through security at BWI airport, taking off my boots, when my cell phone rang. Snatching it up, I heard from Chris, "Mom, we have a little girl!" No texting in those days, all this was out loud, my jubilant "Oh that's so great! What's her name? I can't wait to get there and see her" were shouted with abandon for all around me to hear. Six hours later I was in the car with Chris, speeding over the Oakland Bay Bridge as he went over every detail of the labor and delivery, the gorgeous skyline of San Francisco looming up ahead. We went to the hospital, and there I soon held this tiny little girl with a mass of dark hair, dark blue eyes gazing around at her strange new world, my tired daughter-in-law and son feeling so happy and proud. Four days later I was back home, but little Emma was always close to my heart, and even the St. John's parishioners delighted in this big event in my life, especially the first time she came there and I could carry her proudly down the aisle.

By 2003, my own life began to change even more. Chris and Felicia decided that after nine years of living in San Francisco, they wanted to move back to Washington where Chris had been born and raised. Housing prices in San Francisco were way beyond their budget, and their small one bedroom rented apartment had grown tight for them now that Emma was an active one-year-old. They hoped to be able to afford a house in the Washington market, and they wanted to be near the many family members who lived in the area. As if by some kind of shared intuition, they and I realized in the fall of 2002 that I had plenty of room in my house, enough for them to have two rooms and a bath to themselves. I loved this idea. I welcomed their company and the idea of being a household together. Furthermore, I had no financial resources to help them with housing, but by having them live rent free with me for awhile, they could set aside money for an eventual down payment on a house. Over several months we ironed out the details, and on April 11, 2003, Chris, Felicia and Emma Floyd moved into the rectory with me in Chevy Chase, Maryland.

It was a huge change for all of us, but we soon developed compatible rhythms. Chris found a job opening a new high-end restaurant with a chef friend, and Felicia got a good job doing the kind of consulting and editing she'd been doing in San Francisco. They found quality local day-care for Emma, and I loved the opportunities to drop her off or pick her up on occasion. We came up with a cost-sharing plan for utilities, food and other living expenses, and in general, for a young family living with their mother/mother-in-law, I think we sailed along beautifully.

Ironically, after four years of being single and living alone, my social life took a turn only about a month after the kids moved in. I was actually invited out for dinner! Bill Flanders, who had been a clergy colleague and friend at St. Mark's had been recently widowed. His wife, Claire, and he and I had seen each other socially over the years, and it was she who had welcomed me so warmly into her family in France back in 1992 when I was on sabbatical. We had kept in touch after I left St. Mark's, and Bill had filled in for me occasionally at St. John's. Claire Flanders had died of a rare and aggressive cancer, and for a year and a half, Bill had walked every step of the way through that dark valley with her. I had met him for coffee at some point during that time and seen his tears of grief well up even then as he talked of her impending death. So when he called, I wasn't sure whether I would be acting as pastor and grief counselor or whether this would in fact be a date. Felicia asked the same question before I left that evening. It was clear after one very simple quiet dinner at our neighborhood Greek restaurant, that Bill was not seeking me out as a pastor. We faced each other across the small table, Greek salads, moussaka, some wine. After a bit Bill probed.

"Are you seeing anyone or involved romantically?" I was surprised at his directness, and he noticed.

"I see you are blushing," causing me to blush harder, something I almost never do!

"No," but my daughter-in-law is wondering whether this is actually a date," signalling, I guess, that this was something I had wondered as well.

Two days later, I received a lovely note from Bill, telling me of his interest in reaching beyond our friendship to the possibility of a closer bond. I was walking Tyler as I read this note, and I felt the ground kind of spinning. Bill was seriously interested in a deeper connection with me! All the implications of this came flooding in. He was pretty recently widowed; it was too soon to start in with a steady relationship. He was ten years older. I had always found him terrifically handsome. In fact when he had come to serve as a substitute priest a couple of times at St. John's when I was away, people there had commented that he looked like Paul Newman. We had known each other since 1987; we were both Episcopal priests. I couldn't help letting my mind race ahead; what if we got married? It was all new and scary, and of course there was so much we didn't yet know about each other.

Fortunately, timing was favorable. Both of us had plans that took up most of the summer and would prevent us seeing each other more than a few times. I had several conferences coming up in June, and Bill was going to France for a whole month to visit with Claire's French family and all the people who hadn't been able to visit her or come to her service. Then he would come back and join his four grown children and their families at their summer place on Cape Cod, and I would be off to Maine for my three weeks rental in late July and early August. That summer we had just a few more dinners, phone talks, letters and finally three days in Maine together. Even at that early stage, we found more and more in common; we laughed at so many things; we loved learning about the long lives we'd already lived. That summer gave us time to reflect, time for Bill to continue grieving, time for each of us to consider how we might move forward. I was still legally married, although most people didn't realize this, and it was clearly something I had to address. Early on I just wasn't sure about getting involved with Bill. I'd had two failed marriages; perhaps I wasn't a very good judge about these commitments. I worried about our age difference. I couldn't help but welcome the prospect of more financial security than my paycheck-to-paycheck existence allowed. We realized we both needed breathing space, and fortunately, we got it.

As summer moved into fall, we eagerly looked forward to my first sabbatical from St. John's. It was set for mid-April through mid-Sept. of 2004. Until then, Bill and I saw each other regularly, but not very publicly, and the demands of work before leaving for five months were prodigious. Chris and

Felicia weren't at all thrilled with my dating. I think they had expected me to be more of a doting Granny, with my non-work life revolving around our little household. Both had complicated feelings about my divorces, so their response to Bill was certainly ambivalent at first. Even so, my trust in my own feelings for Bill and for his commitment to me grew steadily through that fall and winter.

Bill did have a chance to meet my parents early on. He went with me to Pittsburgh in the fall of 2003 for two nights at my mother's apartment and to visit my father in the Alzheimer's unit where he had lived for several years. I had told Mom that Bill was just a friend but was coming along for companionship on the drive, not in a "meet the parents" role. Whether or not she believed this, she liked him right away, especially when he greeted her European style with a kiss on either cheek. The next time she saw him the first words out of her mouth were, "Are you going to do that French thing again?" Our visit to my father was a small turning point for me. Dad had fairly advanced dementia by then. I was never quite sure if he knew me, and our conversations were limited and repetitive. He had no idea who Bill was, but he still loved music and could remember lots of songs, even their words. My typical visit would always be a trip to the room in the nursing home where they had a piano so that I could play for him. On this day, I asked Bill to play, beginning with Dad's Cornell alma mater. Dad sat close to the keyboard in his wheelchair while I stood looking over Bill's shoulder. As Bill played the song, a glimmer of recognition shone on my father's face, and he actually began to sing along, engaged, connected, at least in this way. "Far above Cayuga's waters . . ." Bill continued with various other songs Dad would have known, and as I watched his large capable hands moving on the keys, giving something that brought my father more alive, I just loved both of them with all my heart. And about then, a stooped over old figure in the far corner of the room who had been listening piped up, "Sir, can you play 'My Wild Irish Rose?'" And of course Bill could, and the other man moved closer, and the music held us all together. I was so glad for that time, as the only other time Bill would see my dad was about a week before he died. I've always so regretted that he never knew him when he was healthy, as they were much alike and would have hugely enjoyed each other.

25

Loss and Relief

My father finally died on January 22, 2004, of pneumonia. My mother called me and my siblings early in the morning, fatigued and weepy. She had gone with my sister who lived in Pittsburgh to see and identify Dad's body in the middle of the night just after they received the call from the care center. Even though for at least a year, all of us had felt that Dad's death would be a mercy for him and for us, the news still swept over me like a cascade of longing and sadness. The Dad who was had been long gone, and the afflicted, demented Dad he became was not someone he would have ever wanted to be. But now the suspension between the first loss and this final one was bridged; he was really gone. My father was dead. A huge presence in my life was no more, and we were at last free to both grieve fully and celebrate the life that had been.

I called Bill right away and then went downstairs where Felicia and Chris and Emma were already up and told them. Even as we all knew we'd been hoping for this ending, they knew to embrace me and share some tears, to recognize the feelings welling up in us all. And Bill knew to simply show up about an hour later, to sit with me and talk, to just be in that morning in my house that seemed especially quiet, as I suppose all houses do on the morning of a death.

We began making plans for a service in Sewickley, the suburb of Pittsburgh where my mother lived. It would be at the Presbyterian Church where she belonged and where all of us had gone to Sunday School growing up. My four siblings and spouses and children all gathered for what would be a warm, almost joyous family reunion. Bill offered to come with me, and I realized then how much a part of my life he'd become, so much so that I wanted him to be there and meet and be part of my larger family. I was happy to let Jeanne, the pastor at Mom's church guide, us through plans for the service, happy to be the daughter and not the minister for a change. I loved seeing us all assembled on several front pews, with Bill beside me. I loved watching my mother, who adored reading the scriptures in church, walk forward with brave determination to read a psalm we'd chosen and do it with the clear enunciation she so much valued. I loved hearing what my two brothers had to say in their remembrances of Dad, and I loved adding my own offering. That night we all gathered back at my mother's apartment for a family dinner, for photos, for funny, touching stories about Dad, for savoring four generations there, ranging in age from 85 to 2. It was a fitting final farewell to a man we'd loved and then lost gradually, over years he would probably never have wanted to live had he had any choice.

My feelings about Alzheimer's grew strong during those years as I searched for acceptable ways to spare my father the continuation of a life he had said clearly he never wanted. About 10 years before he died, at dinner in a restaurant with family, my father turned to me at some point in the conversation and said "If I ever lose my mind, I don't want to go on living." I agreed with him, but had no idea then of how much this desire would have to go unmet. He did lose his mind, exactly the thing he had so dreaded. For at least the last two years of his life, I am convinced that the person he was was so mentally deteriorated from what he would have considered a life worth living that he would have welcomed a way to end his life, as he had indicated to me years before. But that was not possible. We, his five children and our mother, had hung in helplessly as he became incontinent, lived in diapers, as his conversation became more and more disorganized and meaningless, as he asked the same questions over and over, and as he increasingly didn't know who we were, not even his wife. The cost of his care, mostly not covered by insurance, ran through a significant portion of the money he had earned and carefully put away to provide for his own and my mother's support, leaving her now, still alive at 95, dependent on a small social security stipend and borrowing against the value of her condominium. My father would not have wanted any of this, but he had lost his mind, and we felt we could do nothing but wait for his death.

Alzheimer's is a disease that our society will have to contend with in increasing numbers of people, and our notions about euthanasia and assisted suicide will be challenged as we watch folks in near vegetative states live on as their minds and personalities die while their bodies linger on. In my working life, I made frequent visits to demented parishioners, or just old people living out their days in nursing homes. For the patients with dementia, these homes were like warehouses for bodies whose personhood was reduced to the most basic physical needs and incoherent utterances. Many were in far worse shape than my father ever was, and for a longer time, sitting propped in chairs, heads back, mouths hanging open, staring blankly as days, weeks, months and years unfolded. Their existence was an ongoing tragic slog for those who loved them, and their deaths were always a blessing.

When a person is not of sound mind and is not physically dying, except for in his brain, how can that person, either on his own, or with some cooperation or help from loved ones, hasten death and find relief from living out the course of dementia all the way through its extreme stages until some other malady rescues him?

It seems to me that the compassion extended to those with terminal disease who wish to shorten their lives to avoid severe pain and humiliating debilitation should also be offered to those suffering extreme dementia, based on their clearly expressed desires and intentions while still of sound mind. The ability to stop treatment, including feeding, in order to shorten or end one's life would lessen the terrible fear of late-stage dementia shared by patients and their caregivers alike, give more control over how these long stories end to those who must live them, and conserve resources of money and caring that can severely diminish the lives of all concerned. I still wrestle with these questions and hope that more options will become available to families caught in this tragic downward spiral. I hope they will be available to me.

Dad's death relieved all of us of the onus of visiting him, wondering if he knew us, wanting to help, hoping he'd die and guilt about that hope. His funeral had given us a way to remember and celebrate all that we'd loved about him and bring back, in a way, the person he was before he became sick. Dad had always wanted his ashes scattered in the Caribbean, and, a year after he died, my two brothers went to Puerto Rico and did this for him.

About two months after Dad died, I had a very intense, very personal experience. It was something I certainly didn't know I needed or wanted until it happened, but when it did, I was overwhelmed, happy and shaken at the same time. One night, probably as a dream, I met Dad. I walked down a long corridor to an apartment door, knocked, and it was opened by a smiling, healthy Dad in a brown tweed jacket, white shirt, red tie. This encounter was no vague, ghostly vision; it was really Dad. He said "Hi, Sue, I'm fine." That's all; we didn't even touch, but it was everything. I had met the Dad that was, one more time, and I believe this encounter came from God. I have no literal belief in an afterlife, but in that meeting, I felt reassured that my Dad was indeed, "fine."

26

Sabbatical Again

It was now 2004 and my sixth year as rector at St. John's, and I was due for a five-month sabbatical, my first since the one from St. Mark's back in 1992, and was I ready! My plans had been taking shape for months. The church had very little expectation of any particular project I should undertake. The Biblical meaning of sabbatical goes back to agricultural roots in Leviticus. Land for farming was to be given a rest, time to lie fallow every seven years to protect and refresh the soil. So too, people were supposed to honor the seventh day of the week and do no work, to simply rest, as the creation story in Genesis tells us that even God did. I had looked forward to a time of complete change of scene and of being away from parish life long before Bill was part of my life. I had planned to go hiking in the French Alps with the same group of friends I'd hiked with as part of vacation in 2000. I'd planned to return to my brother's house in Nantucket for two months as I'd done during my first sabbatical and where I had so enjoyed the solitude. This time I did have one project in mind. That was to write a manual about functional education in order to make it more accessible to other churches and to further develop this program at St. John's. I also planned to spend my usual three weeks in Tenants Harbor, Maine with children and now my granddaughter. Other than that, the five months were open. Gradually, Bill and I decided to spend more and more of those months together. He was planning on visiting family in France anyway, so it was easy to include him in the hiking week. We debated whether it was too soon for me to meet some of the French in-laws, but after a couple of low-key email inquiries, we were assured that this would be fine. I had already met several of them way back in 1992 when I had visited Claire's family at their home in Lèves, and I think that connection made it a bit easier—less like I was a complete stranger that Bill had taken up with. We also decided to visit my friends in Lichfield, England whom I'd not seen for several years. They too were open to meeting Bill, but Nita did have to ask "And is this a serious relationship?" By then I felt comfortable saying "Yes," and so our trip planning continued. We would have these visits, and we would also visit Bill's oldest son, John, and his wife and two young children who lived in Brussels.

We next discussed spending the time in Nantucket together. Here I was hesitant. I had such strong memories about being there on my own; I wondered if I didn't need another time of solitude. But Bill was persistent, and I realized that staying there together for two whole months would be a good test of our relationship—a time to see how well we meshed in the simple dailiness of ordinary life, but without the pull of my work.

Finally, we agreed that I would go to Cape Cod for part of Bill's time there, and he would come to Maine with me. In both places, we would spend time with each other's grown children, and in his case grandchildren, a further test of family dynamics.

As the sabbatical unfolded, all of these plans worked even better than expected. Yet one huge difficulty loomed, and for Bill it was nonnegotiable. I needed to finalize my divorce. I did not want a contested divorce and did not want to do anything to cause Tom greater trouble with his tax situation. I did not want half of his house, or any financial assets from him, nor did I want him to share in my pension. I just wanted to end the marriage. We had been together for 24 years, and then separated for five; it was time to get things settled. This became the real project of the sabbatical, although I did write the education manual while we were in Nantucket. I worked with lawyers and accountants and tax experts, all at vast expense, but I did eventually manage to eliminate my liability to the IRS and come to an agreement with Tom about assets. Finally, our uncontested divorce hearing was set for February 2005.

Meanwhile, during the whole sabbatical, my confidence in my growing love for Bill increased steadily, and I became sure of his for me. One beautiful spring morning, early, as we walked along our usual path through the meadows towards Nantucket town to get the paper, we began to talk of marriage. We knew we had all that legal stuff ahead, but by then, we both knew we wanted to be married. It was a magical walk through the early green spring fields. We imagined where we might be married, who would be there, who would officiate. We talked about a date in the spring of 2005 and about whether our families could all get free then to come to Washington, and about how beautiful the azaleas and dogwood are at that time of year. As our talks continued we decided a small family wedding at Bill's home would be best. A wedding at St. John's would pretty much necessitate inviting the whole parish and would lack the intimacy of just family. And Bill still went to St. Mark's, so they might feel slighted. And certainly we couldn't get married there or the people at St. John's would have been jealous! We hoped the new bishop of Washington, John Chane would agree to marry us and thereby clear any stigma about clergy entering into a third marriage after divorce, something that had been forbidden under the previous bishop. As our anticipation grew and buoyed us through the tedious demands of my divorce process, I was tremendously grateful that the sabbatical had come just at that time. Being away from St. John's and out of my rector's role gave me invaluable freedom and privacy to focus on a life with Bill, away from the constraints of parish life. It was a heady five months and an important time. I returned full of hope and confidence in our future and eager to resume my work despite the various legal and financial hurdles to be surmounted.

27

A New Season

I was so glad to be with Bill. I remember sitting in the old Thai Room restaurant after a long drive back from Pittsburgh to see my mother and saying to Bill, "I feel completely happy right now!" I realized this gladness, this unabashed happiness was fairly new for me at least in an ongoing way. I was learning, along with my feelings of love, a sense of regard, of respect and admiration for the goodness and loyalty of Bill. His life had given him a long and happy marriage, and it was as though he could draw on those deep wells of love and commitment and give that to me. He knew how to be married; he knew how to be a good husband. He also, because of his own priesthood, understood my work and its demands and was not put off by them; he knew how churches functioned. Bill had spent only a few years in parish ministry when he was young before devoting himself to his real passion which was music. He had been a popular Christian singer in the folk tradition for a number of years in the late 60s and early 70s. He composed his own songs and lyrics, made several records and had quite a run. After that he continued to sing and compose and to teach singing, finally retiring from the teaching part when his wife became ill. He still sings and writes hymns and songs and has a head and heart full of music. Though he stopped working in churches, Bill had never lost his interest in theology, and we delighted then as now in long conversations about how to think about, how to talk about God. We read and discussed theology, argued our views and eagerly sought out a more progressive approach than the usual current church jargon. We were discovering that in living together, our interests would be compatible, but that each of us would have room to continue to be who we were and do what we did.

When we returned from sabbatical, most people in the parish were still unaware that the rector had a "boyfriend," although there had been a few sightings of us at the Kennedy Center and the movies and at one dinner party before the sabbatical, attended by about a dozen very curious but kindly folks. I had let the entire parish know by means of a letter back in 1999 when it was clear that Tom and I were formally separating. Since then, people had been remarkably restrained in terms of monitoring my private life, and I think they figured that if I had any news for them, I'd let them know.

Finally I had some news. A divorce was granted to me and Tom in Montgomery County on February 4, 2005. On Saturday, February 5, before going out to dinner, Bill asked me to be his wife. It was a formal proposal, complete with ring, even though we'd discussed marriage for months, and I treasured this traditional piece of our courtship. The next morning, I was preaching and doing my usual Sunday morning leadership. I asked the Junior and Senior wardens if I could have a few minutes with them between the services, intending to tell them my news. Immediately Richard Saltsman, the Senior warden and by then a good friend, said "Would it have anything to do with that sparkly new ring I see on your left hand?" Both these lay leaders were delighted with our news, and so the following Sunday Bill was in church and stood up with me at all four services to announce our wedding plans. People were so obviously pleased for us, applauding, congratulating, happy for the way my life was unfolding after six years alone; it was deeply touching to both of us. We had agreed on April 30th as a wedding date and on a small gathering of family at our home, and soon we had Bishop Chane's agreement to preside at the ceremony at 2 pm that afternoon in the garden.

As wedding planning went, ours was pretty simple. The Bishop did want each of us to write a letter to him stating our reasons for wanting to marry, and, in my case, to tell him a bit about my two failed marriages and what I understood about them and why I felt confident in this one. As with most weddings in the Episcopal Church, particularly those of divorced persons, we were required to receive at least three hours of counseling with a therapist. We did this with a trusted, licensed pastoral counselor, Benjamin Pratt, who had known both of us over the years and was very good at drawing us out. He asked about Bill's continuing grief over the loss of his first wife and helped us recognize that this was healthy and could co-exist with his love for me. I came to realize that Bill's grief was not a detraction, but an integral part of his capacity for love and for expressing that even after great loss. Ben helped both of us talk about our children and their varying degrees of acceptance of our union. Oddly enough, to me, it was Bill's children, who had lost their mother, who seemed completely ready to embrace me into their family. My own sons were more hesitant, perhaps because of worries about Tom's being alone and some feelings of blame towards me, as if perhaps I didn't really deserve this. Or maybe they just found it hard to feel close to Bill. I've never been sure, and these relationships with our grown children and their spouses have been complicated as they've unfolded over the years. In our counseling sessions with Ben, we began to face some of these issues, especially our own temptations to judge each other's children. He gave us some good tools for dealing with conflict and talking straight even as he let us feel his blessing and support for our marriage.

Finally the wedding weekend came and our families gathered for the celebration, beginning with a seated dinner at the rectory on Friday night for all of our families. Thirty-one of us were arranged at four tables in the living and dining rooms, a complete mix of our siblings, grown children and young grandchildren. I remember a particularly sweet moment, sitting at a table in the middle where I could see all the other tables and feeling so happy and proud to be hosting this dinner here on my last night in this house where I'd lived as rector for six years. All the beloved faces, from my mother, then 87, to my granddaughter Emma, then 3, in my family, plus all of Bill's family whom I was just coming to know, all talking and laughing and connecting with one another. And before that, I remember seeing Bill as he came in the front door, almost glowing as he looked around at his gathered children and grandchildren even as he searched to find me. He was a splendid bridegroom, adorned and expectant on the eve of his wedding, one of my very best memories.

The logistics had been easy and fun. Son Chris was our culinary advisor and arranged with a caterer friend of his to provide the dinner on Friday night and then a less formal buffet gathering on the wedding day at Bill's house. A case of Veuve Cliquot champagne was ready along with the full-bodied red

Rhone wines Bill and I both love. My wonderful friend Nellie from the St. John's flower guild had arranged all the flowers. We depended on our family to take pictures, no formal portraits.

The weather, unlike all these plans, was beyond our control. The azaleas and dogwoods in Bill's garden were in full and perfect bloom, whites and pinks and reds forming a beautiful backdrop for where the ceremony was to be; the garden had never looked lovelier. But it poured rain the whole day, not drizzles, not occasional showers, but a steady downpour, no letups. So the men of the family completely rearranged the furniture in Bill's house, clearing the dining room so all 31 of us could stand in it, except for a chair for my mother. At 2 pm, dressed in a sage green dress, pearls and carrying a bouquet of lilacs and creamy roses, I made my way downstairs into our front hall, carefully avoiding the steps I knew would creak. Bill awaited me, along with three pretty granddaughters holding baskets of roses, and together we walked into the circle of family filling the dining room and took our places with Bishop Chane.

Bill and I had come up with a marriage liturgy that was more theologically liberal than the standard prayer book form but not a wild departure. We left out the part about marriage being somehow analogous to "the union between Christ and his church," and several other passages that we found off-putting, but we used the traditional vows. Each of us had a sister read a passage, one from the Bible, one from a favorite David Whyte poem. There were still enough church trappings to puzzle some of the young grandchildren, none of whom went to church. We had explained that the bishop would come and would wear some long red and white robes and a big pointed hat as part of the service. When he arrived and appeared in this traditional Episcopal garb, little Madeleine, then about nine, looked up at him in awe and asked, "Are you the archduke?"

Bill and I held each other's hands and made our promises, which we'd managed to memorize. The bishop said nice things I don't remember. Bill's two sons were "best men," one of them dressed in a tuxedo jacket and wearing flip-flops, the other battling jet lag after his flight over from Brussels. My sister Marty was my witness, wearing the very dress she had been married in only three years earlier, with me as the minister—wonderful connections and interweaving of these family stories! This wedding was everything Bill and I had wanted, intimate, just family, not highly scripted. It was very much a gathering and combination of two large and dynamic families, full of humor and love and the poignancy of something that has come about after and because of death and divorce, loss and failure.

The next morning, I showed up at church as planned. Harrison was preaching, of course, so that I could take the following Sunday off as part of our honeymoon, a week's trip to Paris. It was fun being in church that morning, happily tired, still on a high from all of the family and festivity, still surrounded by the love of my church community. I truly felt that things in my life had "come round right," and my world seemed full of promise and opportunity.

The last stage of this huge transition was my move from the rectory to Bill's house. I'd been a bit apprehensive that the folks at St. John's would be disappointed. They were proud of their rectory and loved having me there and using it for parish open houses and other gatherings. Happily for Bill and me, they understood our desire to live in the house Bill had lived in since 1969 and in which so much of the life of his family had unfolded. It never made sense to us to find a new house together; I didn't want to take that rootedness from Bill, and I loved the house. We agreed to rearrange, redecorate, repaint and accommodate furniture and artwork from my house so that it would reflect both of us, and eventually the house had a new and different feel, comfortable to us both. After a chaotic couple of weeks of sorting and packing and throwing out and giving away, Chris and Felicia and Emma moved to their newly purchased home on Capitol Hill, and I moved to Harrison Street in Washington, just a ten-minute drive from St. John's. The Rector was home!

28

Music

Through all of my courtship with Bill, from before sabbatical and through the months afterwards, the music program at St. John's had occupied much of my energy at work. After several years of struggling to develop a good working relationship with the music director, by early 2004 I was ready to give up, and many others in the parish were more than ready. My decision to keep him in place when I came there, and my failure to replace him were in part a reflection of my belief that churches are, and should be, different from life in the ordinary business world. Churches can be training grounds for getting along with people with whom we differ; they can teach us patience and forgiveness. I was also extremely fearful of actually firing someone, or hurting this person and alienating his supporters, and I think I drifted along avoiding the problem for too long. He and I could not see eye-to-eye on so many things. I can't stand hymns played at a slow dragging pace, but no matter how often I mentioned this, he refused to go along. I would find large textbooks on church music in my mailbox with whole chapters on hymn tempo marked for my perusal. I think he felt that if only I knew as much as he did, I would agree with his approach. I wanted us to have large, enthusiastic choirs and a music program that actually brought people into the church. His choirs were pathetically small, and folks were driven away by our music! People found him difficult to work with, and he was inept at recruiting new singers. We also disagreed on how much new or less formal music we would use in order to make our singing accessible to more children and newcomers. None of this is unusual in churches, and I feel there is a good reason. Except for the music directors, the members of a church staff are expected to have great people skills, to be ministers, and the clergy are called to be this and trained to do it. Meanwhile, the musicians spend years of training in playing the organ and piano and perhaps choral conducting, but often have limited skill in connecting easily and graciously with people. Certainly our director was a lonely, unhappy man, and although I had tried to accommodate his temperament, I realized that he was keeping St. John's from growing a vibrant music ministry, a commitment I shared with the congregation. Of course, there were supporters of the director, a loyal dozen or so who protested loudly and then left once we had severed our ties with the musician. He himself threatened a lawsuit, and I ruefully learned that I had not kept enough of a "paper trail" to lay out the ongoing course of his failures to meet expectations and respect my authority.

But finally, the separation was made, an interim musician came onboard, and a talented search committee went to work on finding a replacement. Even with an interim, interest in music perked up and a few new singers joined the choirs. Staff meetings became lively and fun again, and I was relieved to have this behind me and a bit regretful that I hadn't acted sooner.

From 2004 through 2006, we experienced a roller coaster as we established a new music program. First of all, a highly qualified and seemingly perfect match of a candidate was chosen to take over, a young man whom the children loved, whose talent was prodigious and whose taste in music and approach to his ministry suited us well. Things took off! The 9 am choir of children and parents grew hugely; the 11 o'clock adult choir with 4 paid section leaders grew and improved, and things looked rosy.

However, we had learned during our search that our organ had significant problems. It was over 40 years old and had not had proper maintenance. Small repairs were frequent, and the candidates had warned us that this instrument was no asset for recruiting good musicians. So with our new director, we began to explore whether to repair the current organ or replace it. We began talking to organ experts and organ builders and to pore over exhaustive analyses telling us our existing organ was hardly worth fixing. Within months, I was forced to get my head around a figure of perhaps $250,000 to repair our organ to up over a million to replace it. This was major capital campaign material, and I wondered if we were ready.

On Easter Eve, 2006, either the Holy Spirit or perhaps Satan himself entered in. First of all, the new organist put a letter of resignation under my door only about 3 hours before the long Easter Vigil service, probably the loveliest liturgy on the whole church year. He indicated that he had some better options, but was not specific, and I was taken completely by surprise. I knew he was eager for a new organ and perhaps felt we were moving too slowly, but I had no idea he was considering leaving after being with us barely a year. Then that evening, right in the middle of the Vigil, the organ made a horrible loud noise and stopped, completely; it was impossible to play it. With a hasty move to the piano, we made it through the service, but I was reeling with the implications of what was happening.

From that night on, St. John's embarked in earnest on a thorough examination of all our options for music. We managed to get the old organ functioning, literally using wire and duct tape and some minimal professional repairs, but we knew we had to do something major. We considered doing away with any pipe organ, repairing the old organ, purchasing an electronic organ, or having a new organ built to fit our space. The new organist left, as he had threatened to do, and we began another search. This time, we were incredibly blessed. A young woman with three small children who had not been ready to return to full-time work until just then (and hence wasn't available in the former search) decided to respond to our job posting. Anne Timpane was everything St. John's hoped for and more. She was an immediate hit with the whole parish, especially the young families with children who could easily identify with her. She in turn was terrific with children and a winning presence with folks of all ages. A talented organist and pianist, she impressed all of us with her superb keyboard skills. More than that, her choices of music and leadership of the choirs, even her willingness to provide music for the 5 pm service were just exactly what we needed to propel us through the long process of replacing the organ and building a first rate music program. The whole staff liked Anne immediately, and I found her easy to work with and grew to like her very much personally.

29

"Lift High the Cross"

Meanwhile, our deliberations about what to do about an organ proceeded at what felt like a glacial pace. We eventually figured out the best way forward would be to replace our organ with a new one, and we embarked on a campaign that was entitled "Lift High the Cross," quoting from a favorite hymn. We chose the name because a central feature of the eventual renovation of the chancel was literally lifting and suspending our gilded cross high over a new altar and chancel platform, moving it from the dark shadows of the old chancel wall. The process would require a world of committees. An Organ Search Committee, an Architectural Review Committee, the two consecutive Music Director Search Committees, and eventually a Capital Campaign Committee to raise the needed funds. My part was to recruit leadership for all of these groups, to determine who would be good at what, who wanted to do what, and in some cases, wheedle and cajole people to step into these roles. A really important part of the process was bringing the wider parish along, having a transparent process so people knew what was happening and what was involved in the various decision-making processes. There were those who swore they would leave if we put a new organ at the east end of the chancel where the big gold cross had hung against a simple white wall. That was their focus for worship, and taking the long walk up to the altar rail not far from that wall was integral to their very faith! It was their encounter with the holy, not to be changed.

All the various organ builders, and we consulted with four extensively, urged us to have a new organ built and placed on the long axis of the nave for the best sound quality. The "neutral" organ experts we talked to, those not trying to sell us an organ, agreed. The existing organ stood in chambers on either side of the chancel, mostly encased in concrete walls so that it sounded at right angles to the congregation and with the two different organ chambers sort of arguing with each other across the space. I and most of our leadership were in agreement about placing a new organ at the east wall for these reasons of sound quality. Even more important for me was the opportunity such placement would afford. The new organ at the back wall of the chancel would take up all of the space where the current altar and platform and rail lived. We would need to build out our chancel with a large platform extending out into the nave, even sacrificing a couple of pews. The altar would be moved to the front of the existing chancel, at the top of the steps of the new platform. It would be a free-standing wooden table with lots of space around it. The altar rail would form a large curving arc at the front of the chancel platform, and the whole flavor of our worship would be changed. Instead of moving far away from the congregation for communion to a remote altar at one end of a deep chancel, the clergy would move front and center to this new altar, close to the congregation. People would come forward to receive communion, standing or kneeling as they preferred, but gathered in a sweeping half circle, able to see one another and feel themselves much more a part of the community. The old way represented private devotion, "me and my Jesus" at communion. The new configuration would be that of a community of disciples, gathered around a table, sharing an experience. This new chancel design was something I'd wanted for years, but only when the organ broke and we had to consider a new arrangement in order to provide the best quality of sound, was I able to realize that dream.

Finally, by October of 2006, St. John's signed an agreement to purchase a new organ, built for our space by the Berghaus Organ Company outside of Chicago. The committees had done their work well, and we had a design for the placement of the organ that was very handsomely in keeping with the rest of the worship space. The broad open-chancel platform was just as I had hoped, pale grey limestone from Indiana. The altar rail was a warm satiny brown wood, curving around from the sides with a wide welcoming opening at the center. The beloved cross would now be suspended dramatically from a central arch over the altar. Two new skylights would bring natural light into what had once been a dark altar and choir space. Extensive cost analyses had been done, and the vestry had finally given the go-ahead to move forward to the tune of $1.7 million. We hoped to raise $1.5 million in a capital campaign, and a preliminary feasibility study indicated this was a reasonable expectation. So we were off! It would be over a year before the money was raised, the construction finished, the organ built and installed, and each of its 3529 pipes hand-tuned on site. I was thrilled that we were able to do this project. I felt it would contribute so much to the quality and feeling of our worship and so much to our music program. Even though really smart talented lay leaders had counseled and supported me in launching the campaign, as the rector I also allowed myself to take real credit for bringing it about. I was grateful to have been a part of such campaigns at both St. Patrick's and at St. Mark's and to have that prior experience with construction projects and capital fund raising. It allowed me to be mostly confident as we moved forward, even when others were occasionally fearful and reluctant to move. It let me realize that despite initial opposition and griping from those who were resisting such a change, once the project was finished, they would probably come around and actually find the new space appealing. Even so, I'd had my own anxious moments and sleepless nights worrying that we'd never get on an organ builder's schedule any time soon at a price we could afford, that we'd end up paying several hundred thousand dollars more than original proposals. I had worried that things would be delayed by several years, stalling our music program and lessening our impetus and enthusiasm. But I managed to be patient and trust the process. I had to let the committees do their work, had to let them gather enough information and take enough time to gradually sell the project to the whole parish, to pursue the project with enough transparency that people could buy in and understand what we were doing and why. I had to remember that I needed to be the pastor to my community while this was going on. I needed to attend to people's concerns, fears, doubts and hopes in a respectful way. I couldn't just forge ahead and pursue my vision on what I thought was the most expeditious timetable, although there were times when I was so tempted to do exactly that! All this while presiding over the everyday workings of parish life, writing sermons, planning worship, visiting the sick, going to meetings, the usual rhythms. It was an intense, bracing time.

For me this was not just about dealing with a broken organ. It was an opportunity to express my theology of worship and to make a significant and lasting change in the way St. John's Norwood would look, sound and feel. Our success would affirm the vitality and strength of the parish and its leadership and ready us for another phase of growth in membership. I hoped that our worship would feel much more interactive with the altar out closer to the people. I hoped that our ideal of radical hospitality as one way of communicating the Gospel would be well served by this newly inviting space. I hoped that our image of God would move from one of a distant, mighty power on high to one of a loving presence in our midst, a part of each of us. During the months leading up to and during the campaign, I would preach on these themes, sometimes wondering if it was too much, other times wondering if any of it was sinking in.

There were some wonderful high points along the way. One was a quick trip to Chicago to see and hear the completed organ at the factory. What a beauty it was, in every way, from its polished wooden cabinetry to the thousands of pipes, the intricacy of the wiring, the sheer complexity of the finished product. No wonder the pipe organ is called "the royal instrument!" After our visit, the entire organ was dismantled and trucked to Chevy Chase where it arrived one bright November Sunday morning. After a combined worship service at ten, the whole congregation trooped out front to see the tractor trailer and actually get to carry some of the smaller pipes into the nave. Hours later, every single pipe, plus the organ console and myriads of internal parts were laid out in the church, on the floor, over the pews, filling the entire space, while the tired but exhilarated organ builders and those who stayed on all afternoon to help shared pizza in the parish hall.

By Christmas of 2007, the organ was all in place, but not playable, as the lengthy process of tuning each pipe would not begin until January. Even so, our Christmas Eve services using the piano were especially lovely as the new surroundings for the organ had all been nearly finished, including the large, dramatic altar platform and the handsome, custom-built mahogany altar. Even without the final limestone covering of the platform, even without the cross in place, we could still experience the beauty and openness of the new space, the closeness of clergy and congregation. An added joy for me that night was the presence of Bill's two daughters and their husbands and three children apiece who were with us for Christmas and decided to come to church. They were not regular church goers, but I think they were curious to see me in action. I looked out into the candle-lit church as we finished the opening hymn, "O Come All Ye Faithful," and there the adults all were, lined up in the very first row, right in front of me! I thought perhaps the preteen and teen-aged children had decided not to come, but then I spotted them too, also in the first row, but way up in the balcony. I was still a relatively new member of their family, and this loving support meant a lot. I remember daughter Lili, a writer herself, responding to my sermon by taking my face in her hands just after the service and saying "You were wonderful!" A Christmas gift indeed.

By April of 2008, the painstaking tuning process was finally finished, and the organ was ready to sing. I could feel the buzz in church the minute I entered on the Sunday of the dedication. The church was full; the parish hall was all set for the reception; the choirs were rehearsing, and I was exuberant to be presiding over all of this. The Bishop came to bless the whole project. All the participants, a very long list, architects, contractors, organ builders, fund-raisers, committee members, were duly thanked, and the magnificent Berghaus organ sounded forth with Anne Timpane at the console, reveling in the depth and variety of sound she could now produce. There was also a special concert in which a number of leading church organists in the Washington area were asked to come and play our new instrument—again a stunning display of its quality by a wonderful array of talented musicians. These dedications were the glorious culmination after our long and painstaking process, a time to savor what had come into being and to feel grateful for the way it had all fallen into place.

30

Conflict and Forgiveness

The organ project was definitely a fruitful, meaningful and highly satisfying period of my time at St. John's. But during the fall of 2006, other darker currents swirled. Those several months turned out to be the hardest of my whole ten years at St. John's. I believe this was a combination of some missteps of my own and the anxiety and control needs of a few parishioners that led to some very painful turmoil. As things were moving along on the organ project, I was having a terrible time working with a newly formed personnel committee as well as with the finance committee, never a good situation. We came to a bitter impasse over my hiring a secretary without their approval, especially since I changed my mind during the process, leading some of these people to feel I had lied to them. Things escalated; both committees quit and did this on email. All of my attempts to meet in person, apologize, get together and sort things out were rejected. When vestries call a rector, part of that person's authority is to hire what staff she needs as long as this is within the budget. However, in recent years, more and more parishes, especially larger ones, have personnel committees to provide guidance to the rector in personnel decisions. Not surprisingly, this can lead to power struggles over who has the final say in decisions, and that's what happened, all very quickly. Some of the disaffected were even folks I'd been fairly close to, but I felt some of the others had had it in for me for awhile. One evening, during a vestry meeting, this simmering animosity came to a head.

As the meeting began, I asked for a vote to approve the agenda, which did include a brief report on the personnel situation with the secretary, at the end. One man, part of the finance committee who had resigned, insisted that we discuss this matter right up front, but this was overruled and we continued with the agenda as presented. My anxiety grew as the meeting went on and this dissident member and a couple of others murmured among themselves down at a far corner of our large meeting table. Finally, when the personnel issue came up, they attacked. Their spokesperson, a big man, was red-faced with anger by this point and accused me of lying to the committees and recklessly spending money that was not in the budget. I tried to defend myself, but suddenly he shouted across the table at me, "You are obnoxious!" There was a sort of gasp around the room; I turned to the senior warden at my side, saying, "I can't lead this; you take over." But then I realized I had to lead; I couldn't give in to this shocking verbal attack. And prayer came to my rescue, "Let us pray," I implored. My plea was one of desperation; I was so in over my head, but it helped me to steady my voice and speak words of humility. I said something about how we all needed help to overcome these differences and find a way forward. I spoke slowly, feeling my way and feeling too that I was being spiritually upheld and given voice. Although I've never thought of prayer as a bail-out in a bad situation, that's how prayer worked for me that night, as a lifeline at the end of that terrible meeting. Immediately following it, the senior warden moved to adjourn, and you never saw a quicker exit. A few supporters comforted me, but I too raced home to unload to Bill and to flounder in a messy pool of self-righteous anger and sorrow and indignation.

After that upsetting night, we resorted to an outside counselor from the diocese to help us resolve our issues. Others in the parish heard about these difficulties, and it all just added to my own stress and anxiety and that of the parish as we were trying to move ahead with a very big project. Forgiveness became a very real challenge for me.

I've always grappled with the idea of forgiveness, and I know it is a huge issue for many faithful people, one of the hardest of Jesus' teachings to follow. From what Jesus is reported to have said in the Gospels, forgiveness should be unconditional. We should forgive someone who wrongs us, whether or not he apologizes, whether or not the harm was intended, whether or not the person actually repents and changes his ways. This is different from what I understand from the Jewish tradition in which forgiveness is inextricably tied to repentance and cannot be given in isolation; there must be a transaction. But this divide is really more of a spectrum, with many nuances, many variations of gray rather than a black-and-white separation. I have found forgiveness to be one of the biggest stumbling blocks in the whole faith enterprise. People who are in so many other ways good and generous find themselves unable to forgive, unable to set aside judgment. One man in a class I taught was typical:

"If I just forgive someone without any accountability, what's to keep him from doing the same thing again, over and over. What's the incentive to be good if forgiveness is freely available?"

I was hard pressed to answer him satisfactorily, but I said something like this:

"Chuck, if you really feel you are loved by God, and if forgiveness signifies that, then perhaps you'll want to be good in response to that gift. Perhaps the neighbor who hurts you will respond that way too. Being forgiven doesn't give you or him license to go out and sin all over again, just the opposite. It is a gift that calls for his response, and yours. It calls for gratitude and the desire to be worthy of the gift."

I then added that forgiveness is good for the giver, even if there is no response from the offender. It allows one to put the hurt behind and move on; it's good for the soul. My student was unconvinced. Throughout my ministry people have come to me saying they have tried to forgive and simply can't, while others have felt themselves forgiven when they didn't feel they deserved it, and others have really been able to forgive without conditions, such a mystery!

My own feelings about forgiveness have changed from a formulaic understanding based on apologies and changed behavior to a deep appreciation of forgiveness as a matter of spirit, and thus never entirely in our control. I don't think forgiveness is something we can make ourselves feel, even if we say the words. Nor do I think we can make ourselves accept forgiveness from another or from God. For me, forgiveness remains a mystery of grace, something to which we need be open but find hard to achieve on our own. I want to hold out for radical forgiveness and for a connection between our willingness to forgive and our capacity to experience forgiveness. I believe the connection Jesus makes in the Lord's Prayer: "Forgive us our sins as we forgive those who sin against us." But I struggle along with so many to actually be able to forgive freely, without strings. In small matters, where I haven't much at stake or where an important relationship is not involved, I manage to be pretty forgiving. That is fairly easy. A careless teenager backs into our car and smashes the fender. Her parents are friends, insurance will take care of it, the girl is groveling with apologies; forgiveness awarded!

Forgiveness has been much harder for me when more is at stake, when relationships are wounded. Forgiving those few committee members back at St. John's for their hurtful words and failure to apologize fully was really a struggle. It did come, but only much later, when the chief perpetrator offered an olive branch in the form of some very kind words at the time of my retirement. I realized that he indeed cared for me, and finally, I forgave him and meant it.

Forgiveness when there is divorce is another really difficult struggle. In my case, in both prior marriages, there was hurt on both sides, plenty of room for forgiveness to be given and received. I can't speak for my former husbands, only for myself. I can say this. My first husband and I are friends. We are not close; we seldom see each other, but we have a fondness for much of the history of our very young lives that we shared, a tenderness for the mistakes, and a mutual love for our son and granddaughters. With Tom, things are more gingerly, and I have less of a sense that he's forgiven me for leaving and for the other ways I hurt him. I used to think I'd forgiven him, but then at times our past issues and difficulties would crop up, and I would realize I'd not fully cleansed my soul of anger. I guess in one sense, the failure to forgive is what ultimately leads to divorce in the first place. If a couple could mutually forgive while their marriage was crumbling, perhaps they could restore the love that had first brought and held them together.

For me, in the hard cases, I've found it in me to forgive, but only much later, long after the hurt. Fifteen years after we separated, I have finally felt at peace with Tom. This came as an unexpected gift when all three sons and their families gathered with Bill and me and Tom and his wife Sheila for Thanksgiving dinner. There were no other guests, and as we went around, each offering something he or she was thankful for, I realized how glad we all were to be able to be together like that, almost like an intact family. Tom is facing a pretty serious cancer, and when he quietly offered that he was thankful to "still be here," my heart went to him as I realized I cared for him and valued him despite it all. Ever since that family dinner, I just don't harbor the old negative feelings. We have had a long history together, and two sons, and I am grateful for the end of resentment and the ease and warmth I now feel with him. I have indeed forgiven Tom.

Finally, forgiveness is often misunderstood as saying that whatever happened is over, that it didn't matter, that the hurt that was caused is erased. I think this belittles the very real ways we cause hurt to others and elevates forgiveness to a magical process that denies emotional reality. When I forgive, I am not denying that you have wronged me or that I was hurt by that. I'm simply willing to put it in the past and not let it define our relationship. Forgiving is of course much easier if you acknowledge the wrong, apologize and at least try to behave differently, but I still want to be able to forgive even when there is no response. I want to follow Jesus' radical teaching on this, but I certainly do need the help of time and grace to do it.

Accepting forgiveness is the other side of this coin, and for some this is even harder than being the forgiver. Our own sins can torture us; we can't stand facing these. And so we often deny any responsibility, no sin to be forgiven. Or, if we do admit our fault, we sometimes have a really hard time accepting that another, or God, could actually forgive us and still love us. Like offering forgiveness, this takes faith that it can happen and an openness to the grace which helps us get there. Forgiveness is ultimately a spiritual matter and one of the knottiest of them all. Sometimes for me the only path forward has been pretense at first, acting forgiving or forgiven as best I can until the real experience comes. And maybe it is that very process of living as if forgiveness has happened that opens us up to the reality.

Perhaps because forgiveness is so difficult, the church has always had ritual ways to address it. These have taken the form of confession and then absolution, another word for forgiveness. In most Episcopal churches on most Sundays, people say a general confession, and then the priest declares that they are forgiven. This ritual can feel pretty mechanical and meaningless, and some folks resist even this rather bland acknowledgment that we are in any way sinful and in need of forgiveness. Too often we think of sins as various destructive acts or vices or even crimes and so let ourselves off the hook most of the time. Another way of thinking about sin is more inclusive, and that is to describe sin as missing the mark by falling short of what we should be at our best. Seen this way, we all participate, and we can't claim that we have no need of forgiveness. When we live in denial of our own sins, we can so easily fall into self-righteousness, a big missing of the mark, a sin in itself!

I remember George, whom I met early in my seminary career at a dinner party. He was curious about my vocation as he was an Episcopalian and had not yet run across any women priests. He assured me that although he went to church occasionally, he felt confession to be unnecessary. He really didn't feel in need of any kind of salvation or forgiveness. He told me he led a good life as a successful businessman, had a happy marriage, three talented and lovely daughters, good health, and really nothing to confess on Sunday mornings. I was shocked by George's complacency but too timid and inarticulate in my theology back then to challenge him. If I were to meet George now, I would politely convey my understanding of sin as a missing of the mark by failing to do and be all that we could, not just big black evil deeds that others do. I would also suggest that all of us are caught up in sinful behaviors and social structures just by being human, just by being American, and especially just by being rich. We don't deliberately hurt others, but there are many things done on our behalf that do cause hurt and injury; wars, lax gun control, an economy and tax laws tilted towards the affluent are a few that come to mind. Just by paying taxes, we provide financial support for all kinds of things we probably wouldn't do, things that would never pass the "Love your neighbor as yourself" test. We are so often unaware, insensitive and careless, and just saying we mean well is not an excuse. Public, corporate confession is a way of reminding ourselves of our complicity in the ways of our world, and forgiveness is a way of reminding us that God's love and grace are still there for us; we are not condemned. Confession is not about groveling to win approval from an angry God. It is about facing the reality of our situation, which is that we are implicated in sin; we are flawed and can never be perfectly good. Confession is for all of us, good for our spiritual health. Absolution is not wiping the slate clean, giving us license to continue in sin. Absolution is the assurance that we are accepted by God. We could put it another way for those who shy away from anthropomorphic statements about God and say that we are part of the essential goodness of creation despite our failings. Hence we are free to live as the beloved members of this creation that we all are. I find saying a general confession in church, surrounded by my community, to be bracing and humbling, an affirmation of our common humanity and a release from some of the ills that beset us.

Many others have told me they object to confession because "it's depressing to dwell on sin and judgment." They want church to be about praise and celebration, about God's and our own goodness, about joy and peace. Even in Lent and Advent, traditionally penitential seasons in the church year, some folks resist confession, and they just don't like the word sin. Some have come from church backgrounds where sin seemed to be the predominant theme, and where guilt hung heavily in the air, where punishment and even hell were used as clumsy goads towards good behavior. I can understand their desire to be out from under that kind of religion, but if our religion is to be authentic, it needs to encompass who we really are and what life is really like. To do that, we all need to grapple with sin. We will be the better for it; we will probably live more constructive lives, and our times of celebration will be all the more joyous when forgiveness, given and received, is part of the mix.

The Episcopal Church also offers private confession between a priest and an individual. Confession is an ongoing requirement in the Roman Catholic Church, while in the Episcopal Church it is an option, usually exercised by someone who feels he has committed a grave sin. There is a rite in the Prayer Book called The Reconciliation of a Penitent which provides for someone to meet with a priest, either at the altar rail in church or in the priest's office. There is opportunity for the person to tell the priest what is on his conscience, for the priest to provide "counsel, direction and comfort," and then to offer absolution. The secrecy of this confession is a moral absolute for the priest. I have been asked only a few times to hear a private confession, although I know people who make this kind of confession on a regular basis, say yearly. I myself have sought this one time. I was in despair about something I had done, without meaning to, and felt helpless to somehow fix the hurt I'd caused. Making a confession to a trusted colleague was at least one act I could do, one way of opening myself in a ritual way to God's forgiveness when I felt my own apologies and remorse didn't go far enough.

I have also suggested private confession in a very unexpected way. A woman called me to ask whether the Episcopal Church had some kind of liturgy for divorce, some way of acknowledging this major turning point.

"They ought to have something for divorce, just the way they do for marriage," she said.

"Well, first of all," said I, "if you're looking for some kind of celebration, it seems odd to ask the church to bless the failure of a marriage which it had celebrated in the first place. But actually," I continued, "there is a ritual, already in the Prayer Book that can be used for divorce."

"There is?" she said, incredulously.

"Yes, it's called the Reconciliation of a Penitent, a form of confession." Shocked silence.

"So, you think divorce is a sin?"

"Well, it's at least a sin of promise breaking." I continued with my thoughts about how divorce is always the failure of one or two people to keep lifelong promises they made, either because they cannot or will not, so perhaps that deserves a confession and forgiveness. Even if divorce is the best decision people can make, an agonizing, lesser of two evils kind of decision.

" I think the promise breaking needs to be acknowledged before the celebration begins, if that's what you're looking for." Chagrined, she wouldn't accept my suggestion, but I persist in my thinking that divorce is a situation calling for humility and sorrow before there can eventually be relief and new life. And in my experience, very few divorces are actually completely mutual; usually there is a leaver and a leavee, and I have been both. There is one who wants to keep the promises and one who won't or can't. But confession as an acknowledgement of this failure (whether or not one actually does this with a priest) seems an important spiritual step in the difficult passage out of a marriage.

I continue to feel that forgiveness is one of the biggest spiritual challenges we face, whether or not we are church-goers or people of faith. To be able to forgive, and to accept forgiveness are great blessings, and not always possible for us. But to open ourselves, to reach for these capacities is something we must do if we are ever to live at peace with ourselves and others.

31

Darkness into Light

The spring of 2007 was buoyant with anticipation as our organ and chancel project proceeded towards completion. April was in full bloom in Washington; Easter was approaching, and Bill and I had a short getaway trip to Paris planned for a week after that. Palm Sunday began with an unusual but not alarming phone call. Harrison was the preacher that morning, and he was running late for the 8 am service, caught in traffic and not feeling too well. Would I be able to go over and lead the service until he got there? I quickly finished dressing, gulped my coffee and raced to St. John's, actually making it there by 8 but beginning to worry about what I could come up with as a sermon if Harrison didn't get there soon. But he did, walking in just as we finished reading the gospel and the sermon was to begin. He preached without notes that morning, and I remember being impressed at his brief, powerful Palm Sunday message, which, like most sermons, even my own, I have forgotten. And so the morning services continued with the usual processions into the church waving palms, and then the triumph to tragedy account of Jesus' arrest, trial and crucifixion. Since Harrison was on for the 5 pm service, I enjoyed the free afternoon and evening and was already thinking my way into the upcoming Holy Week with all its special services, sermons and complicated liturgies, certainly the most intense and demanding in terms of worship of the whole church year. We

had a 7 am communion service every morning as part of our observance, and
Harrison and I took turns with that one.

Around 9 pm Sunday evening Harrison called again. Sounding weary and
tentative, he said he wasn't feeling quite normal and was driving himself to
Suburban Hospital to get checked out. He wanted to let me know and ask if
I could take 7 am service the next morning. Going to the hospital sounded
pretty serious, and I asked if he'd like me to meet him there and keep him
company, but he had already arranged for his good friend, a local Lutheran
pastor, to come and be with him. The next morning I led the early service,
came home and called Harrison at home to see how he was. No answer. I
called the hospital, expecting to talk to him. Instead, I was told that he was in
the ICU on life support and in very serious condition with a heart problem!
They were probably going to Med-Evac him to Johns Hopkins Hospital in
Baltimore to receive treatment they couldn't provide at Suburban. I went
tearing up to the hospital and talked my way into the ICU thanks to my clerical collar, explaining that I was his colleague and he had no local family. And
there was Harrison, pale and unshaven, breathing with a respirator, heavily
sedated, eyes closed, IV's all over the place. I was just stunned; it was so
shocking to see my usually rather jovial looking, animated, bright-eyed colleague looking like, well, looking like he could die. I took his hand, spoke to
him, wondering if he could hear me, saying a prayer in case he could because
I knew he would want that, having no idea really what to do or what was
going to happen. Fortunately, a doctor came by and explained some of the
situation. Harrison's heart was pumping at only a small fraction of capacity,
and his situation was very grave. At Hopkins they could use some kind of artificial pump to restore blood flow, and perhaps he would need heart surgery.
I could barely take in whatever details were offered. And, they were already
preparing him for his first helicopter ride.

I came home, talked to Bill, headed for the office. I didn't even know
how to begin to let people know and to make plans for how to get through
this Holy Week which had suddenly turned so decidedly unholy. What if
Harrison should die? How would the parish and I deal with whatever was
going to happen? How could I be a pastor to him and a pastor to my whole
flock and somehow help us all move through Good Friday and Easter in these
next days? I soon was able to get in touch with Harrison's brother, Kevin, in

Portland Oregon. He, as next of kin, was to be the one to receive medical information, and all my news would have to come through him. Kevin was unsure whether to come East immediately, as their aging and frail mother was in Portland with heart problems of her own, and Kevin also had a wife and teen-aged son.

Day-by-day, a pattern emerged. I let the parish know by email to all who had access what had happened and assured them I would keep them posted daily as I got information from Kevin. I would go to the hospital to see Harrison, not every day, but most, sometimes with Bill, sometimes with my dear friend and part-time pastoral associate at St. John's, Emily Stribling. Often one of Harrison's closest friends would be there, the busy Lutheran for a short visit, the faithful Ray often for much longer vigils. Harrison remained on life support for ten days, and his condition remained uncertain. Slowly, the heart pump was working, but the various doctors were still unsure about when and if he could undergo bypass surgery. Each night, after it got late enough for Kevin to get home from work in Oregon and talk to the hospital, he and I would talk. He would pass along any news, which was scant at first, and he and I would discuss whether he should come or wait, his own feelings of fear and anxiety and what was the best thing to do for Harrison. I had never met Kevin, but his voice sounded so much like his brother's that it was eerie, sitting in my home office, often fairly late at night, talking with this man 3000 miles away about this other man, dear to both of us, lying in an ICU in Baltimore, unaware of any of it.

At church, people were incredibly kind and helpful and stepped in eagerly to help manage all the holy week activities. Bill functioned as assisting priest at all the big services, and having him vested and at my side on Maundy Thursday evening and through the long Easter vigil on Saturday night and then on Easter morning was strong comfort. I somehow faced the challenge of preparing a sermon that would be adequate to the circumstances and still be a true Easter message despite the sad waiting gloom of that strange week.

As if all of this wasn't enough, a personal crisis of my own was handed to me by phone on the afternoon of Good Friday, right after the long three-hour service from noon until 3 pm. The secretary said I'd had a call from a doctor, requesting I call back. For a couple of weeks I'd been harboring some anxiety after an abnormal mammogram which led to a biopsy on the Tuesday before

Easter. I'd had a benign breast biopsy in 2003 and wasn't particularly worried, just wanting to get it over with and hating its timing right while all this was going on with Harrison. In fact once he was stricken, I confess to some magical thinking along the lines of "well, God would never let me have cancer just now when Harrison is so seriously ill, something bad couldn't happen to both of us at the same time." Also, Bill's first wife had died of cancer, so this couldn't happen again to him, could it? I in no way believed in such a puppeteer kind of God, but during that time, it was tempting.

I called the doctor back.

"I'm so sorry to have to tell you this, and I didn't expect it, but I wanted to get to you before the weekend. It's cancer."

As my tears began, I asked desperately, "What do I do now?"

"Well, you'll need a breast surgeon. This is a very small, early stage cancer, but it must be treated. I can give you some names." And she did, and I wrote them down, and I left for home, knowing I had to tell Bill in person and dreading it. At home, arms around each other, both crying a little, we faced this first really hard blow in our young marriage. And, as people do, we started to try to plan, as if by having a plan we could determine a good outcome. Close friends were right there for us. One was a psychiatrist who came over armed with a helpful book on all sorts of alternative treatments and supplements for battling cancer or its return. Although I chose traditional treatment, Joe gave me confidence in keeping my body healthy and trusting in its power to heal and move beyond cancer. The other friend was Ellen across the street who had faced the same diagnosis a year earlier. She directed me to the surgeon, oncologist and radiologist she had used and to the whole Sibley Hospital team, and again, gave me confidence in these doctors and in a good outcome. Soon I had made appointments and chosen the recommended course of treatment: a surgical "lumpectomy" and radiation. It seemed this was indeed a very small, early stage tumor, probably had not spread to lymph glands, so no chemotherapy, and a very good likelihood of not recurring. However, we wouldn't really know about the prognosis until the surgery, which we scheduled for May 18.

One huge question for Bill and me was whom to tell, and how much, and when. Had Harrison not been sick, I probably would have let the parish in on my situation, but it seemed out of the question to burden them with it at least until we knew more, at least until after the surgery. Even with my children and siblings and mother, I just wanted to wait until after the surgery rather than have them go through several weeks of not having a clear prognosis. In hindsight, I wish I'd told my family right away, even though I felt I had a good reason for not doing so. This kind of decision comes as a dilemma. You want to be open with those closest to you so that in either suffering or cele-bration, they can share it with you, be there for you. I had always counseled people in the parish to allow at least close family and friends in on what was really going on in their lives and put aside that whole "best foot forward" thing that had been prevalent in the church of my childhood. Now here I was, masking my own fear and uncertainty, wanting to protect others, at least until I knew more.

As it turned out, my surgery proved highly reassuring. The tumor was indeed small, completely removed, with what are called "clear margins," and a lymph node biopsy was negative—so no sign of spread. Radiation was to be daily for about four weeks, followed by a course of adjunct therapy in the form of pills for five years that had proven highly effective in preventing re-currences. Even though this was exactly as the doctors had predicted, it was still a huge relief to have it confirmed and the surgery over. Bill and I went ahead and told our children and other relatives, all of whom expressed dismay that we'd kept it to ourselves but were relieved at the good prospects for full recovery. I let the parish know through a small, low-key article in the weekly Parish newsletter, "Crossroads." Here again, people were shocked and con-cerned at first, also amazed that I'd been facing this while Harrison was so sick, but finally relieved and lovingly supportive. Several much older women confessed to me along these lines, "Dear, I had just what you had years ago, and I'm fine. I expect to die of something else."

Meanwhile, Harrison had come out of the woods, but only after those long days of life support and deep sedation and then quadruple bypass sur-gery followed by a lengthy recovery from that. My daily talks with Kevin and then parish emails had kept us all in the loop, and I continued to visit Harrison in Baltimore every few days. It was such a joy to arrive one day and see his eyes open, hear his voice. Harrison was back, having emerged from his cloud of drugs and anesthesia and some really amazing dreams. He'd lost a great deal of weight, and it would take him weeks of recovery at his friend's house to regain the stamina to return to work, but he'd made it, and his doctor had been pretty candid that it hadn't been a sure thing.

It isn't often that the season of Lent followed by Easter coincides with the actual events of our lives, but for Harrison, for me, and for the people of St. John's, we lived through both Lent and Easter in more than a symbolic way that year. There is a lot of what can feel like jargon in the church about new life coming out of death and darkness, a lot of talk about the small resurrections of our life connecting us with the Resurrection of Jesus. And certainly all Christians struggle with how to understand both resurrection and The Resurrection, along with many who have dropped out or never gone near church because they can't embrace any such belief. I have struggled as well, and my sense of this central mystery has both changed and strengthened.

Resurrection faith. I do not believe in a physical resuscitation of Jesus' body after he died on the cross. I have no idea what happened in the tomb or what a video camera would have shown. I'm not sure about the empty tomb, although it is certainly a necessary part of the story for a literal interpretation. I do believe that Jesus' disciples experienced his risen presence in absolutely convincing ways, though I'm not sure about the sight and hearing and even touch that are recounted in the gospels. But I do believe they encountered Jesus, and they were changed. They were changed from fearful, cowering frail men and women who felt abandoned and perhaps betrayed. Instead, they became joyful, newly energized followers who started a movement that changed the world. They were newly alive, and that was because they had experienced Jesus as risen; they'd experienced the power of God to bring new life out of death.

I believe in that power with my whole heart. I believe that as things in us or our world die, God does bring forth new life, not usually in the way we hope or pray, but new life, surprising and refueling our hope and our capacity to face hardship, tragedy and despair. I felt that way after my late miscarriage in 1977 when an unsought vocation grew out of my sad, empty time, and a new kind of generativity was born in me. I felt that way after my second marriage had slowly withered and died, and my life opened to new love and a new chance at being truly married. I believe that Harrison really did walk through the valley of the shadow of death, and we who loved him went along, me with my own dark tumor. And then came our Easter, for me, for Harrison and for St. John's. After a complicated two years of focus on a capital project, on fund raising, on settling conflicts about my leadership, we came through, into a new day. That time of illness brought us all together and reminded us of why we were there, why we even have church. So much mutual support and love poured out in those weeks just after Easter that it really did seem like we'd come newly alive into the church we'd envisioned. We really had and really were "Building Community at the Crossroads of Faith and Life."

At our Annual Meeting, some three weeks after Easter, I had these words to offer as part of my sermon:

"This spring has been a life-changing experience for Harrison and has had a profound impact on our community, on me, on our vestry, on all of you. The vulnerability of our Associate Rector, so well loved here, reminds us of the human frailty we all share, the ways that life can surprise us and dissolve our illusions of control. Suddenly, what is most important about our community becomes clear. We are here to be in loving relationship with each other and with God. We are here to share and explore faith and to connect it with the real lives we live. We are here to celebrate our experiences of God and to wonder together about the times when God seems absent or too mysterious to fathom. How do we live out our sense of God as shown to us in Jesus Christ?

To me, what the Resurrection of Jesus shows us about God, regardless of what you believe actually happened, is that God's presence, God's love, God's being, are stronger than death. Jesus' new life that began on Easter Sunday stands for me as a powerful story about new life open to all of us and about the meaning and influence every life can have, even beyond the grave. The spring of 2007 was a real, lived Easter following a dark and fearful Lent, an intense, shared experience for our whole community. We might have sunk into a nice complacent sense of satisfaction at the success of our organ project and perhaps the let-down that sometimes occurs in parishes after such a campaign. Instead we were given, through the shadowy passage of Harrison's illness and my own scare, a kind of new birth as a community, new confidence in how we could care for each other and a clearer sense of what was really important in our lives together. From darkness into light, from a cross to resurrection."

32

Retirement

Before I married Bill in 2005, I had imagined that I would stay at St. John's until about 2011 and then retire at 68. In the Episcopal Church, priests in full-time positions can retire with their full pensions at 65 and are required to do so at 72. But once we married, I began to consider retiring earlier so that we would have more time together during the years when we could expect to both remain healthy. Bill had been wonderful about supporting me in my 50–60 hour work weeks with 2–3 nights out and few real weekends, but we were definitely limited in the time we could spend traveling, seeing our adult children and grandchildren and just being retired together. The events of 2007 helped us to decide that 2008, when I would be 65, would be best for me and Bill and for St. John's. My cancer scare reminded us of how good health is not a given. We were ten years apart in age; both of us healthy, and then I wasn't. Who knew what other difficulties would arise and how soon? So there was my strong feeling that I wanted Bill and me to have as much good time together as we could, that in a sense I owed him that after three years of long days and evenings alone while I was at St. John's.

In addition, the end of the capital campaign and renovation at St. John's made 2008 a good time for me to leave and open the doors for them to seek new leadership. I would have been there ten years, and we'd accomplished a great deal. The parish was healthy and in a very good place to seek a new rector. Bill and I debated all the pros and cons of various retirement dates and finally decided at Christmas of 2007 that October of 2008, just exactly ten years after I'd begun, would be the best time for me to step down. I would not announce my retirement until May, after the organ had been dedicated and celebrated and when just a few months would remain for me to say good-bye, and planning for the 2008–9 program year would be well underway.

Once we had made this decision, my remaining months at St. John's were poignantly full. Moving through Christmas, and then into Easter and Spring, knowing they would be my last at St. John's filled me with emotion, kept under wraps because I hadn't yet announced my retirement. The familiar rhythms, pressures, tensions and preparations for these holiest holidays had been part of my life not only for the ten years at St. John's but ever since I began training for the priesthood. I would miss them, even as I would welcome having those holidays free to enjoy with my family.

Finally, on the first weekend in May, I made my plans known. This was at the annual Vestry retreat in Rehoboth and it was indeed a momentous weekend for me both personally and professionally. Bill's 75th birthday was on the Saturday, and of course I wanted to organize some kind of special celebration, but I also had to be at the retreat. That weekend was just one of the many times over the course of my life as a priest that I'd wanted or felt I needed to be in two places at once. This time, I decided to surprise Bill on Friday night with a small dinner for friends and at least two of his children who would fly in and surprise him. The vestry agreed that I could show up in Rehoboth by 9 the next morning. I could hardly contain my excitement as the details for both the birthday dinner and the vestry retreat took shape. The look on Bill's face late Thursday night when I, having said I was going to a women's group, instead arrived home from Dulles airport with son John and Anne from Brussels, was worth every moment of planning. Daughter Sonia's arrival the next day completed the surprise, and our dinner that night was festive and warm and a true celebration of family and friends celebrating Bill's life. I would not have missed it for anything.

Next morning, however, as I drove towards the beach, my apprehension about how my news would be received came to the fore. Would some feel I was leaving too soon after the big organ project? Would some feel I was bailing out before they had a clear vision of where St. John's was headed next? Both of my predecessors had stayed much longer. I so hoped people would see this as a good time, not only for me, but for St. John's. I hoped they would embrace the challenge and adventure of seeking an interim rector and then rector who would continue and build upon the fruitful ten years we'd had together.

At approximately 9:10 am, we were all gathered in our meeting room, finishing our coffee and ready to get started. Despite my full evening Friday and very early rising, I was all keyed up, anxious and eager to get to my announcement. After a brief prayer, the wardens turned the meeting over to me. There was a tense silence, but the minute I began speaking, I think folks realized what was coming. I told them that I would retire at the end of October, almost six months hence, and about how Bill and I had arrived at this decision as being best for us and hopefully for them as well. I also told them of my mixed feelings about leaving St. John's, how I'd loved my time with them but was also ready to lay aside the mantle of rector. Some were indeed surprised, but others were not, and in general, the group was supportive, loving and eager to begin planning for a smooth transition. We had arranged for someone from the diocese to join us later in the day to go over the transition process—the timeline, rules and guidance we would receive from the Bishop's office.

I had already told the staff in close confidence a few days before and had arranged for an all parish letter to be mailed out on Saturday so that everyone would have the news right after the weekend. From then on, I was in public retirement mode. It was at times unnerving because I would realize during some planning meeting that I wouldn't even be there for whatever we were discussing. I kept realizing various things I was doing were for the last time. The last Pentecost Sunday, the last annual parish meeting, the last newcomers' welcome and brunch, the last baptisms, and on the day before the last day, the last wedding. These were heady, emotional days, full of anticipation looking forward, and nostalgia for all that I would miss, especially so many people to whom I'd grown close over these years. In the Episcopal Church it was expected, and sensibly so, that I would no longer attend services or be part of the life of the parish once I'd left, and that I would not come back to do funerals, weddings or other special services. For some this was big and unwelcome news, and for some it felt like a betrayal. I really took care to explain that we needed to say our good-byes thoroughly, but that then I needed to get out of the way and give them room and time to open their hearts to new clergy leadership. A new season would begin for St. John's with my retirement, and we all needed to honor that. Meanwhile, I invited anyone who wanted some time with me to to please schedule a lunch or a coffee or just a short good-bye. I found those occasions to be precious, full of kind words on both sides and mutual savoring of times we'd shared.

Finally, October 26, my last Sunday and last day arrived. There had been a gala dinner party the night before for the whole parish, both joyous and bittersweet, both celebration and letting go. I was given a gigantic scrapbook full of photos and mementos of my time at St. John's, a handmade pine needle cushion pointing to my beloved times in Maine as well as a beautiful print of a Maine meadow. The dark wooden gavel with which I'd chaired vestry and annual meetings was handed over with much flourish—it had become a symbol of my growing sense of how to handle the administrative part of the rector's role.

I was to preach and celebrate at all four services. At the end of each service was a Liturgy of Departure in which I would hand over symbols of my office, a priest's stole to Harrison, the keys of the church to the senior warden. Most of the words were the same as those used when regular parishioners said good-bye and moved on.

Harrison: *"Susan, during your time with us, where there has been growth and joy, let us be thankful; where there has been hurt or sorrow, let it be forgiven. Now go in peace."*

Congregation: *Go in peace, Susan. Our prayers will be with you wherever you go.*

Rector: *And mine with you.*

The music director had invited me to choose all the hymns for that day, so of course I included my favorites, ending with one I can scarcely ever get through with dry eyes: "Come, labor on." Here are the last three verses:

Come, labor on. Away with gloomy doubts and faithless fear!
No arm so weak but may do service here:
By feeblest agents, may our God fulfill his righteous will.

Come, labor on. Claim the high calling angels cannot share –
to young and old the Gospel gladness bear: redeem the time;
its hours too swiftly fly. The night draws nigh.

Come, labor on. No time for rest, till glows the western sky,
till the long shadows o'er our pathway lie,
and a glad sound comes with the setting sun, "Servants, well done."

At the end of each service, as I made my way down the aisle to the back of the church, with each last time, my eyes did fill up and my heart with them, seeing all the dear faces I wouldn't see again in this way, moving through the space itself which had housed so much of my and our life together. It all felt glorious, full of glory, God's, I suppose, that spirit of love which moves in us all, so keenly alive in St. John's, Norwood Parish on that last day.

My family had surprised me by all showing up in church in the morning, and then that evening we gathered at son Chris' for champagne and dinner and the beginning of a new chapter. It was one of the fullest and happiest days of my life, and the tinge of sadness at what had ended made it only more precious.

33

A New Chapter Indeed!

Any accounts of retirement risk sounding like a series of clichés. People always ask "So what are you going to DO?" "How do you like retirement?" this latter even if it's only been three days. They look at you expectantly as if a well-constructed plan is about to pour forth. Some are wildly envious; others ecstatic that they get to keep their current life work. My own clichés were the usual: "I love retirement; it's great." "No, I don't have a plan yet; I've always heard you're not supposed to make lasting commitments for six months to a year." "Well, I'll really miss some parts of my job, but not all, and yes, of course I'll miss the people" (essential when talking to parishioners). I participated in all these sorts of exchanges, and, I expect, like many others, I really had very little idea of what I would be doing and how much I would miss, or not miss, working.

Bill and I did celebrate with a trip out to California to visit my old haunts in San Francisco and drive down the coast to Los Angeles to visit one of Bill's daughters. After that we savored both the Thanksgiving and Christmas holidays free from the constraints of church ministry and made plans for a longer, six-week trip to Italy and France in March and April. I remember how odd it felt on Christmas Eve at the late service, sitting at another neighborhood Episcopal Church in the candlelight. It felt a bit like exile, being in this other church, not far from St. John's, but it was not painful. There was no longer the sermon anxiety, the responsibility to provide a great worship experience, just the pleasant coziness of sitting between my sons and daughter-in-law, singing the familiar carols, being an observer.

From the beginning, being an observer was a tricky role for me as a retired priest. I think perhaps chefs who visit other restaurants may experience something similar. I really didn't worship; I would just observe, and not uncritically! I watched everything, and, being me, judged. "I could have done this better; they should have sung this; that sermon was boring; there aren't many people here," and on and on. Of course I came across wonderful preaching, and lovely music and churches full of life, but they were a rarity, and it was easy to see why my own children and so many other people had just given up on going to church. It's such a different experience when you're not being paid to be there and be heavily involved. For at least a full year, I never really settled in to going to any church on a regular basis, and although I enjoyed that freedom, I also missed the discipline and spiritual nourishment of Sunday worship.

Very gradually, over the early months of retirement, I began to envision the contours of this new life. I imagined four very general areas of focus: family, intellectual pursuits (reading and writing), volunteer service and church involvement. It took at least the first two years to settle in to a kind of balance and regular rhythm, and even now, several years later, my patterns are shifting and evolving.

The family part has been pretty easy. Two of my sons live here in Washington, DC, and I have the good fortune of seeing them and my four grandchildren regularly, for family dinners or short impromptu visits and occasional baby-sitting. A third son and his wife live close to New York in Connecticut and come to visit often as well as housing us on our way through to Cape Cod and Maine in the summer. Bill's children live in Brussels, Chicago, Los Angeles and San Francisco with ten grandchildren between them. We see them mainly in the summer when they all manage to come to Truro on the Cape for what feels like an experiment in communal housing, short or longer, harmonious or less so, but always important for renewing the bonds of this far-flung family. Holidays in Washington are usually a mixture of Bill's family and mine, a mingling of traditions and personalities that can be prickly but is for me, most of the time, a delight. I particularly love sitting at our oval table surrounded by all these people of all ages, our physical and emotional offspring. Here are the next two generations of our families, a huge variety of personalities and traits and life trajectories. I watch and interact with awe as these new stories unfold, stretching into a future beyond me, carrying my genes, my hopes and my love.

The reading and writing focus has emerged very gradually, and this memoir has been one of its fruits. I have always loved reading, literature, biography, theology, books on church leadership. With a full-time job, I had far too little time to read, not only books of professional interest, but all the vast riches of the world of fiction and personal narrative. Once I retired, it was easy to begin reading much more widely and deeply, and I have. The only challenge has been choosing books and finding a good balance between fiction and nonfiction and avoiding spending way too much time on the depressing daily fare in the newspapers. I've also become a crossword puzzle addict. Before retirement, this habit was limited to the Washington Post, but once I retired, I confess to converting to the New York Times puzzle and to working it daily, especially once I discovered the app for doing this on my iPad! This can be a real time-waster, although I justify it by hoping it hones my mental acuity. It does occasionally help me in Scrabble. But puzzles and games aside, much more time to read has been one of the true delights of retirement.

Writing has been more of a challenge, but more of a pull, something tugging at me, an endeavor to be risked, a muscle to be exercised. I'd never thought of myself as a writer. Other than sermons, I wrote regular articles for the parish newsletter, and I'd kept a journal from around 1984 until 2005 when Bill and I married. The latter was highly personal, mostly my wandering, confused, sometimes angry, sometimes resigned, sometimes grateful and hopeful musings on my marriage and how that whole side of my life was unfolding.

Once I retired, I realized that I had been a writer in all these ways, and I missed it. I also felt I had things to say, and I began to explore the possibility of memoir, articles, even a blog, although I've not yet pursued that. For now, this memoir has been an important part of whatever balance of energies I'm developing in retirement. I've participated in a couple of writers' workshops, read numerous other memoirs, reviewed all my own journals. I've learned a lot along the way, about writing, about giving and receiving criticism, about careful reading, and however successful these early efforts at authorship prove, they have enormously enriched these past few years.

Long before I retired, I wanted to do something in a direct way to make lives better for disadvantaged people. I almost never got involved in various outreach projects during my time in the parish. I felt it was my role to inspire and encourage lay people in these endeavors but that my time needed to be spent in the overall care and maintenance of the church where I served. Christianity is so much a religion of work in the world, and I do think churches need to be very pro-active in encouraging folks to get out there and help tackle problems, both with their money and their time. I had always tried to give away 10% of my income to charities, including church, but I hadn't done the time part.

So once I retired, I was ready for volunteer service. However, finding just the right place was a stumbling block. Once faced with actually doing something, like many other retirees I've talked to, I had a hard time deciding. Should it be through a church, or not? How many hours per week? In what, exactly, kind of service did I want to get involved? Bill has volunteered two mornings a week for years at Samaritan Ministry of Greater Washington which helps people take the steps they need to move out of poverty. He is a caseworker there and counsels clients. It's a wonderful program, and Bill finds his work there enormously satisfying. But I wanted to find something different.

One day, almost a whole year after I retired, I remembered a neighbor telling me about the Water Ministry at St. Columba's Episcopal Church, right in our neighborhood. This is a program providing showers and laundry and snacks and lunch four mornings a week. I liked it because it was very basic and direct—offering something that all people need. It sounded simple and unbureaucratic. That very day, I got on my bike and rode over to check it out. Once there, the director and volunteers welcomed me openly. It didn't matter that I wasn't a member of St. Columba's, and they could use help on Thursday mornings. The hours were from 10:30–1:30. I agreed to come the next week, and from the start it just seemed a fine fit. I began by helping with the showers and laundry. Two of us fold and lay out towels, washcloths, soap and other toilet articles. Most of the clients are men, mostly young to middle age, about half African American, about half Latino and with a very few women and white people. Some are homeless, many are marginally housed; most are unemployed. We greet each client and list those who want showers—we can handle about 14 a day and two loads of laundry, for which people sign up in advance. All the rest of the clients, usually 30–40 a day, come for the ample home-cooked lunch at noon and the coffee, tea and snacks beforehand, at 11 am. When I got there, the program had been going for over 15 years and was already well thought through and well run. There is now a solid core of regular volunteers, a woman who makes up the schedules each month, and a paid director. They have an intake form for new visitors including various guidelines about no smoking, drinking or drugs, no violence or cursing, but otherwise, all were welcome. This is a no-strings, no questions asked radical hospitality ministry—food and a shower and laundry for anyone who needs it. One of us offers a prayer before lunch, but otherwise, there is no specific religious input.

The Water Ministry is a unique program in my part of the city. It has turned out to be just right for me, and I continue to love my Thursday morning and occasional other fill-in slots. I've gotten to know a number of the volunteers well and now help out both with the shower/laundry part and in the kitchen setting out the snacks and helping to prepare and serve lunch. Talking as we cut carrots or refill the coffee pots builds surprisingly close ties over time, and I'm grateful to be part of a community that is not part of my parish, family or social network. We are a varied, quirky lot. Most of us have been through some tough times, and maybe that's why we're drawn to the work. Clarence, who died in early 2013, helped check people in for showers and laundry. He walked with a cane and spoke with a slur, and one eye was cocked off at an angle all due to a stroke suffered when he was at the peak of his career as a lawyer. He loved to tell jokes to anyone available, and as I was new, he could recycle a lot of his material that the others had all heard. His mind remained keen; he missed nothing, and the clients loved this thin limping black man with his warmth and empathy for them. Geoffrey towers over all of us, and his British accent and quirky smile are endearing to guests and volunteers alike. He manages to remember the names of almost all the regular guests. Jim shows up even when it's not his day, filling in and relating easily to one and all. He is always quick with practical suggestions to help things run better. He visited Clarence when he was dying and read a psalm at his funeral. Adele chats easily in Spanish with our Latino guests as she supplies them with towels and toiletries. JoAnne and Cathy, our chief cook and meal planner, and I delight in catching up each week, whether on new recipes we've tried or the various life issues our children and grandchildren confront. We volunteers are divorced, widowed, single, married, well-off, struggling, young, retired and in between. We are a community drawn together by a common desire to reach out and engage with folks who would otherwise be strangers to us. On good days, it feels like Christianity at its substantive, concrete best—loving our neighbors as ourselves. On bad days, it can feel boring or tiring, or worse, the intractable problems of homelessness and unemployment that parade before our eyes week in and week out make me wonder if we make much of a dent and if more than a few of those we serve will ever break out of poverty.

The final intentional aspect of my retirement is continuing church involvement. Episcopal priests retain their ordained status even when they are no longer working for the institution. This reflects, accurately, I believe, my felt reality that priesthood is something I am, not just something I do or have done. And so I welcome various ways of continuing to function as a priest. One of these is providing "supply clergy" services for colleagues who need a substitute for a Sunday or two, usually in the summer when they are away. This is fun, but infrequent, as I am away most of the summer as well. I do preside on one Sunday in August at the tiny summer-only chapel in Tenants Harbor, Maine, something I began well before retirement when I was vacationing there. A small congregation of 20–30 gathers in a tiny wooden church nestled in a pine forest for a simple 10 am service. Bill usually leads the music with his guitar, and we both love the quiet intimacy of this simple rustic space with the sound of the wind rustling in the pines just outside the screened windows. The whole scene is a combination of a highly traditional, old quaint setting with theologically sophisticated city folks on vacation who seem very open to my progressive theology and even liberties with the Prayer Book liturgy.

One of the real freedoms for me in retirement is being able to tailor services quite carefully to reflect what is spiritually real for those where I visit, and sometimes to invite them to stretch or at least experience something quite different. They can't fire me, and their rector isn't held accountable if I depart from traditional norms. As I continue to explore the challenge of how our services express the actual beliefs and concerns of the worshipers, these opportunities at other churches are invaluable.

Once free from the weekly Sunday obligation, I became available to do more out-of-town weddings, specifically, my sons' friends' "destination weddings" in fancy places! These friends, unlike my sons, were mostly unchurched and so didn't have any connections with parishes or clergy. But they all knew the Chris, Tom and Rob's mom was a priest, and to some extent, I think they perceived me as "cool" compared with the more stuffy clergy they had encountered elsewhere. So they would call and ask if I would preside at their weddings, one at a lovely resort on the Eastern Shore of Maryland, one at another beautiful resort on the coast of South Carolina. I would do the pre-marriage counseling here in my home, and then off I would go, as a guest of the couple, to a delightful weekend in which my contribution would be to lead the rehearsal and then celebrate and bless the marriage the next day. Bill would come too, and my sons would be there as well, usually as members of the wedding party; these were treasured occasions for both this priest and this mom.

The main way in which I continue my involvement with church is back at St. Mark's, Capitol Hill, where I began my ministry, this time as a member. Bill and I serve there in the capacity of "adjunct clergy," meaning we help out on Sundays as needed, including the occasional sermon, maybe three times a year. It took a while to return to St.Mark's. Right after retirement, I really wanted to explore other parishes and also take a lot of Sundays off. I wanted to see what was out there in churches I didn't know and how much I missed regular church. Along with the difficulties of getting out of the critic mode I described earlier, I found much that was off-putting in some of the parishes I visited, mostly the tedium of very traditional worship offered with not much energy to shrinking congregations of mostly older people. I happened across a couple of fine preachers, and I did find a few churches that were full of life, had beautiful music and seemed to be healthy communities of faith. I had avoided St. Mark's at first, because I didn't want to simply return, after St. John's, to the place I'd come from. St. Mark's had changed, and so had I since I had left in 1997. Unfortunately, when we did visit a few times, well-meaning folks would come up and say "Oh, we're so glad you're back!" as if now everything would be just the way it was before. And some of this was from the very people who had been instrumental in not keeping me there or calling me as rector. I needed to find a parish home based on present reality, not memories, on their side or mine.

Over time, I have found this home at St. Mark's. I have a deep respect for and friendship with the rector Paul Abernathy, who will retire in early 2015. He has welcomed both Bill and me as kindred sprits at St. Mark's. He shares our progressive theology and impatience with liturgies that do not reflect this. And so, we have settled in there and attend most Sundays when we are in town. From the beginning, however, I had criticisms. At first I would just grumble to Bill and a few others, complaining about how things were better in this area or that back at St. John's. One of these areas was ministry to young children, another was liturgy planning. Finally, after about a year of whining, I decided to try to help make changes. I volunteered to start a Children's Chapel along the lines of the one we started at St. John's. I had noticed how few families with young children were in church at St. Mark's, even though I knew they were members. I would see them with these children on Easter, suffering through an interminable service with nothing age appropriate for the little ones, and it would make me both sad and mad. So in early 2011 with the eager support of Paul and the help of a small group of parents, we launched a St. Mark's Children's Chapel, and I'm so pleased to see that it has continued and flourishes now without my involvement. I also worked with the Liturgy Planning Task Force for a couple of years trying to make sense for myself of how they function and what their role is or should be. Here I was definitely in the role of critic and probably not entirely welcome, but I enjoyed providing input, even if as a provocateur to push for change.

I've also gotten back into the Christian Education program at St. Mark's by teaching their current version of the long confirmation class I taught so many years back. It is now called "Life, Community and Faith" and is similar to the "Faith and Values" class I led at St. John's. It is now far less rigidly structured but continues to offer folks a chance to really look at the issues and questions that matter to them in their busy daily lives and to find some spiritual grounding. I've led this course twice recently, each time with three other teachers and have loved serving as a mentor as well as a colleague in this enterprise. Through it, I've gotten to know many members beyond my circle of old friends and thus feel I've found a new place in the St. Mark's community—no longer as the old Associate Rector come back, but as the seasoned retired clergywoman I've become. I feel sort of like a consultant, sort of a mentor to the current Associate Rector, a colleague to Paul and a pastor and priest still to the people in that place. This feels good; it feeds me in my continuing vocation and gives me a place from which to continue my prickly love affair with the Episcopal Church.

Recently, I sat in the pew of a large and beautiful Presbyterian Church in Atlanta at the wedding of a cousin of Bill's. I didn't know the couple or the minister; I'd never been there before, and it had been a long time since I'd even been in a Presbyterian church. The organ preludes and processional were some of my favorites, and as the bride and her father moved down the aisle towards the graciously smiling female minister, I felt the same shivery thrill I would feel when I was doing a wedding. So much hope and idealism and love and expectation all focused on that moment as the young bride moved forward to join the groom, his own face shining with adoration. The minister had a lovely, warm manner that made the formal language of the service less remote, and she preached a brief, powerful, well-structured homily using fire as a metaphor for five important aspects of marriage. "I used to do that," I thought with a bit of longing, noticing how easily she preached without notes, connecting not only with the bride and groom but with the rest of the hushed church. Finally, we sang a hymn together, a familiar, beloved hymn. The minister was singing out, loving her role as leader. My husband sang next to me, with his deep sonorous voice, and I was singing my own heart out. And then my voice quavered and stopped, and what washed over me was a flood of nostalgia for my old role, for what I used to do so often, for being in the center of joyous worship. How I missed it! Letting myself feel that, even as I knew I didn't regret retiring, was a blessing, a recognition of the meaning and value of all those years of active ministry and of how much they had meant to me and always will.

34

Dreams and Theology

As my life in the church has unfolded in new ways, so have my dreams and concerns for its future, and so has my theology. Mainline Protestant churches are in trouble, and the Episcopal church is in as much trouble as any. We are a declining denomination, and attendance gets lower every year, while the average age of worshipers gets higher. As I've noted, Bill's and my children and grandchildren do not go to church except very occasionally on Christmas and Easter. I baptized two of my grandchildren at their parents' home in the spring of 2013, using a liturgy I wrote myself, but I have no illusions that this will lead to regular Sunday School and church attendance. Most of our closest friends and neighbors do not go to church. Both anecdotal evidence such as this and myriads of articles and studies confirm that Christianity is in decline at least in its liberal, middle-of-the-road form. Even Evangelical Christianity, including the fundamentalist segment, seems to be leveling off in its growth except for in the Southern Hemisphere which is full of new Christians and growing churches. But these are not the churches I've known, not the Episcopal Church of my time as a parish priest. As progressive retired Bishop John Spong notes, ". . . contemporary people, who think with modern minds, began to be repelled and to drop out of their faith commitments into the Church Alumni Association. Between these two poles of mindless fundamentalism and empty secularism are found the mainline churches of Christendom, both Catholic and Protestant . . . The renewal of Christianity will not come from fundamentalism, secularism or the irrelevant mainline tradition. If there is nothing more than this on the horizon then I see no future for the enterprise we call the Christian faith." I agree with Bishop Spong's bleak outlook, but I have hope as well.

From what they tell me, the church that no longer appeals to my family and friends, fails to do so mainly because the belief system, at least as it is expressed in worship services, is off-putting to contemporary thinking people. I remember a recent funeral service for a friend, the father of one of my sons' best friends. My oldest son, Chris, sat next to me. The service, led by an elderly priest, came straight from the *Book of Common Prayer*, using the traditional language so beloved by many old timers in the church. It includes a lot of flowery words about an actual heavenly resting place after death, a place where we'll see Jesus face to face and where we'll experience a bodily resurrection ourselves if we believe in Jesus. The Biblical readings expressed this same kind of hope, and the priest simply affirmed all this in his homily. Only when the grown children of the deceased man spoke of their father, was anyone at all moved. Only then, were there tears and laughter and fond love, not only for the one who died but for each other, gathered there with our memories of a life now lost to us. When the service was over, my son leaned towards me:

> "Mom, I'm sure you understood all that symbolically and maybe it meant something to you, but I don't believe any of that and it made no sense to me and was just boring—all except when the family members spoke."

I nodded, understanding completely. His reaction, unfortunately, is all too common when people come to church for a wedding or a funeral, on Easter or Christmas or just every once in a while, seeking some kind of connection with God through worship. Our services focus almost entirely on the needs of those who already come, or worse, on maintaining a certain traditional form. Most do not focus on the growing Church Alumni Association out there or those who have never darkened the door of a church. In fact, I don't think our services really speak much to those who come regularly except through good sermons and perhaps excellence in music. I know a few people who absolutely love the cadences of the Episcopal Church liturgy, but I feel this is an aesthetic rather than a faith response. There is a beauty in the Elizabethan language and in the old beloved hymns, but what is actually being said is more than most people can either understand or accept in any way that is helpful for day to day living. We need to ask ourselves, "What is church for?" "Why do we go?" "What are the spiritual needs of people today, and how can they be met in communities of faith?"

Even at St. Mark's, which has always prided itself on progressive theology and innovative liturgy, there has been an ongoing struggle until recently to offer liturgies that do not present God as a supernatural being who has a plan for us and who rewards or punishes us according to the quality and frequency of our prayers and good works. Most people there don't believe these things. Fortunately, there are finally some exciting new liturgies being written by the present clergy and an ongoing project to include many of the hymns Bill has written over the years using language that is consistent with our beliefs. Changing the liturgy is slow work, and sometimes we still sing hymns and say and listen to prayers that point to a God most people no longer believe in. It seems that more and more, what draws people who do go to church to show up on Sundays is the desire to get together with their community and to support various outreach or other parish projects. It is the community, not the theology or even the spirituality that is important. And although church communities can be some of the best, many other groups can satisfy our need for community, and many church communities can be insular, cliquish, bigoted and mean-spirited. What goes on in the name of God can be a very mixed bag! And for increasing numbers of people, they just don't believe any more—they don't see religion as life-giving, and too often, they see it as death dealing.

This growing antipathy towards going to church saddens and frustrates me. I long to see the Christian church not only survive but flourish again in ways that truly feed people and make our world better. So many of us believe in God, search for God, yearn to have our spirits nourished with hope and meaning and fullness of life. I have never not believed in God, even in my younger years when I stayed away from church, but I have such a hard time now with the services in many churches—services that grate on my intellect, bore me with their sameness and almost never help me feel close to God.

What kind of churches and worship services might do this? I would so love to see a Christianity that is both more serious and more relaxed than what most churches offer today. I'd love to see rigorous theological and Biblical education. Once the downward spiral of church attendance began in the '60s, fewer and fewer people got even a Sunday School background and are quite shockingly ignorant of what's in the Bible and of what Christianity has to offer. I'd love to let folks in on all the good work of contemporary, nonthe-istic theologians going back to Paul Tillich but moving on into post-modern, process, and liberation theologies and an embrace of evolution and the whole cosmos as the realm of God. We also need good thinking about how as Chris-tians, we can be connected with Jesus in more convincing ways. And then, given these alternatives to traditional orthodox theology, the language of worship could take wings and lift both our hearts and our minds. It could offer spiritual substance that people long for; worship could be both under-standable and believable! I'd love to hear readings in church from sources other than the Bible. So often a lot of Biblical material is incomprehensible and off-putting—even those passages selected for the yearly cycles of read-ings on Sundays. The Bible is not the only channel for God's word! How much great literature and poetry convey profound spiritual truths and do so in exciting, interesting or evocative ways. We should hear many more authors in church than the Biblical scribes. Powerful prophetic voices have spoken throughout history and speak today. We should hear these in church.

I know liturgical innovation is going on all the time; it's just not hap-pening in any officially organized or structured way, at least not yet. As far as I know, no new Prayer Book is on the horizon, but there are signs of change. A robust "Emerging Church" movement exists, with authors, clergy and lay people all expressing hopes similar to mine. The grass roots are alive with individuals and groups working to bring Christianity into a new century and a new world view. Bill and I have spent many hours envisioning a house church or small worship community that would develop its own customs and rituals, and in the spring of 2014, we began one. At St. Mark's, we've had the encouragement and the blessing of the rector in developing some liturgies ourselves including several non-theistic Eucharistic services that we have used recently both at St. Mark's and at St. George's summer chapel in Maine. I'm encouraged by people's receptiveness to such experiments, and I do think we're moving glacially towards new forms and new expressions of Christianity that will steady its future, but not until long after I'm here to see it.

I do know that young children can love church and Sunday School, at least for awhile. A couple of years ago, concerned that my granddaughters, Emma and Chloe, then aged 4 and 7, had had absolutely no exposure to church, I asked their parents if Bill and I might take the girls to church on Sunday. They live very near St. Mark's, so this was an easy offer for us, and quite agreeable to them. Even they felt that at least some kind of church experience would be a good idea, and the prospect of someone coming on Sunday morning and taking the children off for a couple of hours seemed pretty appealing!

We started in the fall season, going first to the 45-minute church service with communion, then having Emma and Chloe go to Sunday School while Bill and I attended Sermon Seminar. Both girls enjoyed dressing up for this occasion, and at first they seemed awed by the large soaring space, the stained glass, the organ music. Emma immediately noticed a few other kids her age, wearing white robes, carrying candles and a cross in the procession and helping out during the service. She wanted to know: "What are they doing?" I explained that they were acolytes. "I want to be one of those! How old do you have to be?" Within weeks, Emma had been trained and fitted with a white robe and silver cross on a red ribbon. With delight and a bit of nervousness, she took her place, carrying a candle (or torch) in the opening procession. Even her nonchurch-going parents showed up. It seemed that Emma, and little sister Chloe as well, had fertile religious imaginations and did respond at first to the look and feel and sound of church worship and the teachings of Sunday School. I also realize that they looked forward to this regular weekly time with me, a time we often concluded by getting a treat at the ice cream or doughnut shop. However, after two years, Emma joined a soccer team that played on Sundays, and her interest in being an acolyte waned. Her parents felt their daughters' lives were busy enough without this Sunday obligation, and so our weekly experiment with church came to an end. I was sorry but not surprised; I'd heard this from plenty of other parents in a variety of churches. Sundays are no longer days set aside pretty much for church as they were in my youth; church must compete with sports and ballet and gymnastics and scout trips and simply the chance to have one quiet morning at home. For so many families, including my own, church is losing.

My dreams and criticisms of church remain a loving mixture, and I expect they will continue so. Meanwhile, my theology, my way of thinking and speaking about God and about Jesus Christ continues to evolve. I've always valued the space for ambiguity and questions afforded by the Episcopal Church. This freedom was one of the reasons I came to be part of it back in my thirties, and I still love the way skepticism and doubts are embraced as a necessary part of a developing faith. But out of all these years of exploration, of living the questions, what has been new for me in my retirement is, finally, a core theological understanding I can call my own, a theology that works for me. Part of it is about God, and part of it is about Jesus.

35

God and Jesus

Belief in God can never be certain knowledge. In that sense, I'm an agnostic, because I don't believe we can ever know for sure that God exists or what God is like. Belief in God is always a choice, and for me that choice has been made on the basis of both intellect and experience. My belief in God has moved beyond a belief in a spiritual being with whom I can be in relationship, a being who hears my prayers and who has plans for me and for the world. I now understand God as the essence of being itself, as presence and power permeating all that is. I see this presence and power as dynamic, unfolding, a continuing process of divine life undergirding all that is. I see the entire creation as the expression of God's being, and I see that expression as one of love and grace, a free gift. This creation, into which God pours Godself, includes evil and suffering as necessitated by the freedom inherent in creation, the freedom within the structures of the natural world and the moral freedom of human agents. One of the unique contributions of Christianity is the Cross. It symbolizes the place where incarnate God suffers and dies as we all do, where God faces evil and betrayal and yet lives through tragedy and beyond. God participates in all of it, not as the unmoved mover, but as the animating Spirit of all life. A technical theological term for this way of believing in God is "panentheism," a term currently popularized in the writings of theologian Marcus Borg and others. Panentheism goes beyond pantheism which is the belief that God is in all things but does not transcend

221

them, does not go beyond the created world. Panentheism sees God as fully immanent in all that is, but also transcendent, before and beyond all things. I think of God as an inhabiting, embracing mystery. I have experienced this God in ways profound and simple, in the grandeur of nature, the beauty of music, the amazing wonders of love given and returned, in all the various ways recounted in this book. I don't think I will ever be able to settle on any one word or definition for God. Loving Presence, Source of All Creativity, the Essence of Being are possibilities, but then how does one pray to any of these? How does one feel in relation to them except as each courses through my own life and being? And yet, and yet, I want to be able to pray and worship and talk about God as something real and of immense importance. I want to be able to tell my story as I have here, as a story in which God is a real, and not an imaginary character.

With this understanding of God has come a more radical way of believing in Jesus and in what Christian discipleship means. I have long struggled with the idea of Jesus as the divine Son of God, uniquely begotten, and, though fully human, like us, fully divine as well. I've struggled even more with the idea of God sending this Son on purpose to be tortured and killed on our behalf, to "save" us from our sins. This atonement theology suggests to me a transaction between a harsh, cruel God and an innocent victim on a cross, and I've never understood its so-called saving power.

What I have increasingly come to believe about the Jesus story is that in it God is fully present, or incarnate in the person of Jesus, and that Jesus was trying to live as God's presence in the world and to invite the rest of us to do the same. I would go so far as to say that we are different from Jesus only in the degree to which we manage to incarnate God's love and presence, but not in the way we are called to *be* this presence. I would say we are not ontologically different from Jesus, and when we worship him as divine and as "only Son of God" we rob ourselves and distance ourselves from the power of Jesus' story for our lives today. We are all children of God; Jesus was a model for this. We are not completely different from Jesus—keeping him at a divine distance lets us off the hook! We are all called to embody God's presence in the world to the extent we can. Believing this, the "Body and Blood of Christ" that we share in communion reminds me symbolically of this call and strengthens me to follow it. If the Church wants to call itself "The Body of

Christ" in the world, then we need to take this seriously as an invitation to live the incarnation, not relegate it to the Christmas Story. Discipleship becomes far more than trying to figure out how Jesus' teachings would apply today; it becomes the lifelong quest to be a loving presence in the world, always and to everyone. This is serious and tough, but I think Christianity demands no less. Our faith has much in common with the world's other great religions, but the Jesus story, with these implications is, I believe, its most powerful revelation.

Conclusion—A Religious Story

Am I religious? Sometimes, with all my reservations about churches and my impatience with traditional forms, you might think not. Sometimes, I simply agree with my unchurched family and friends and with all their reasons for not going to church. They mostly all say they're spiritual, just not religious, and that is the common claim today, so much so that SBNR has become its shorthand. But the whole idea of being spiritual, of spirituality, gets misrepresented here. It's as if spirituality were some separate trait of humans, or a distinct topic we might pursue. All of us are spiritual; it's part of being human! Being spiritual isn't an excuse for not being religious. That would be like saying that being intelligent is an excuse for not getting an education. Education equips us, give us the tools we need to use our intelligence. I want to claim here that religion equips us, give us the tools we need to express our spirituality. The question is really how we develop and express this part of our humanity and what we do to sustain it. And if one answer is through religious practice, then religion should be up to the task. Too many churches are not. And here is where I think so many folks find churches wanting and stay away.

What do our churches need in order to feed the spirits of so many who go hungry for lack of spiritual nourishment? What would going to church be like if it had the urgency, the drama, and the gravitas to beckon to those who have left it or never went? I imagine something like this. You enter a light-filled space, clear windows, a high ceiling and seats arranged on all four sides of an altar. People gather informally, dressed in whatever they feel like wearing. They greet others, take seats and look around the room, happily acknowledging each other, recognizing shared anticipation. Music, different instruments, different styles, some sung, some not, is threaded throughout the gathering. There are readings, but only some are from the Bible, while others are provocative, poems and prose writings, beautiful, challenging passages clustered around a theme for that day. There is ritual, but it is alive and meaningful, connected with the life of the community. The central Christian symbols of bread and wine are there, but they are shared without piety, without kneeling, perhaps passed from one person to another after a simple clergy blessing. People leave feeling uplifted, feeling that their time has been well spent and that they have been nourished and strengthened for the days to come.

I can't stay away from church. Ever since my earliest years in the Presbyterian church, there has been an allure that has called to me, even during the years when I didn't respond. I am indeed spiritual, and church doesn't answer all of my spiritual needs, nor should it. I don't look to church to give me a spiritual life; I believe I have this as a gift of God's grace. But over the years it is the regular practice of religion that has helped me grow and expand my spirituality, helped me grope my way into the mysteries of a mature faith. I have looked to church to tend and nurture this gift. The word religion comes from the Latin verb *"religere"* meaning to re-tie or bind together. My religious life is a way to give structure to my spiritual life, a way of tying together and trying to make sense of what otherwise might seem a fragmented, even meaningless existence. In many ways I feel my life has been made up of many strands, many weavings that have gradually been coming together into a consistent story that seems true to who I am. I have wrestled with both faith and life, and it has not been in vain. I look back now on a lot of years of struggling to find my own place and voice in the church and peace in my family life. But these wrestlings were not miserable, not failures, not a waste of time. Despite marital difficulties, career and financial concerns, a lot of years of wondering how my life would ever come around, I've known a happiness and sense of faith that have sustained me all along. I don't believe this would have been possible without religion, without church.

So yes, I am religious. I go to church and hold fast to the Christian story as I understand it. I feel myself a part of a growing community of people who call themselves progressive Christians and who seek to revive, refresh and reinvent our ancient faith. I would love it if my children and grandchildren sometime along the pathways of their lives find a sense of God and a religious framework that sustains them. But that time and that sense will come or not; it is beyond me, beyond my love for them. Ineffable gifts of love and grace will pour out on them, and tragedies will darken their hearts as with all of us. Their stories will join the great cascade that is life in its infinite richness and sadness and hope, and whether religious or not, they will try to make sense of them and find meaning.

Making sense, finding meaning. They are the spiritual life work of each of us, seeing our story as one worth living, one worth telling. For now, my story lives and breathes and sings of a God who is real for me. It is a story that seems true to who I am, a story I can claim with compassion for the journey and gratitude for all its blessings.

APPENDIX A

Sermon on the Will of God

After these things God tested Abraham. He said to him, "Abraham!" And he said, "Here I am." He said, "Take your son, your only son Isaac, whom you love, and go to the land of Moriah, and offer him there as a burnt-offering on one of the mountains that I shall show you." So Abraham rose early in the morning, saddled his donkey, and took two of his young men with him, and his son Isaac; he cut the wood for the burnt-offering, and set out and went to the place in the distance that God had shown him. On the third day Abraham looked up and saw the place far away. Then Abraham said to his young men, "Stay here with the donkey; the boy and I will go over there; we will worship, and then we will come back to you." Abraham took the wood of the burnt-offering and laid it on his son Isaac, and he himself carried the fire and the knife. So the two of them walked on together. Isaac said to his father Abraham, "Father!" And he said, "Here I am, my son." He said, "The fire and the wood are here, but where is the lamb for a burnt-offering?" Abraham said, "God himself will provide the lamb for a burnt-offering, my son." So the two of them walked on together.

When they came to the place that God had shown him, Abraham built an altar there and laid the wood in order. He bound his son Isaac, and

laid him on the altar, on top of the wood. Then Abraham reached out his
hand and took the knife to kill his son. But the angel of the Lord called to
him from heaven, and said, "Abraham, Abraham!" And he said, "Here I
am." He said, "Do not lay your hand on the boy or do anything to him; for
now I know that you fear God, since you have not withheld your son, your
only son, from me." And Abraham looked up and saw a ram, caught in
a thicket by its horns. Abraham went and took the ram and offered it up
as a burnt-offering instead of his son. So Abraham called that place "The
Lord will provide;" as it is said to this day, "On the mount of the Lord it
shall be provided."

Genesis 22:1-14

THE WILL OF GOD

The theme I chose some weeks ago for this sermon is The Will of God. It was
a difficult choice, given the deeply troubling story from Genesis, about the
binding of Isaac. As someone in the Wednesday Bible Study class said: "It's
an appalling story—a grown up story. Not for the faint of heart. It's not "G"
rated. It's not "X"; it is definitely R"—but, she goes on, aren't we supposed
to put away childish things and to think and reason and puzzle through and
tease out and get all shook up by God?"

She is right. I've found myself grasped by this story, compelled to wrestle
with it and finally to try to make some sense, especially in connection with
how we might think of God's will as having any part in it. We know the
story. It's told in Sunday School, scary as that might seem. But I don't remember being scared back then, probably because the ending, like that of
a fairy tale, erased the scary parts. The ram was provided and they all lived
happily ever after.

But now, as an adult, as a mother, I find it horrifying. Horrifying in its
presentation of God, horrifying in its presentation of Abraham. The narrator
tells us up front that this is a test by God, but *Abraham* doesn't know that!
A God who makes cruel demands, causes horrible punishments (like all the
trials of Job) just to test people's faith? Isn't there enough pain and suffering

built into the fabric of existence without such testing? What about God's grace and the loving acceptance I've been talking about and how our faith is a response to *that*? Can it be God's will to put us to the test and make us prove ourselves in this way—to demand sacrifice of what is most dear to us just to see if we'll do it—even though God knows we won't have to actually go through with it? This seems utterly cruel and manipulative. This portrayal of God seems good fodder for atheists. If faith involves resigning oneself to what is asked of Abraham as God's will, I find myself unwilling and unable.

Which brings us to Abraham. What in the world was going on with him? The same God who asked him to leave his home and ancestry, his whole past, and journey to a new place, and who promised him and Sarah a child in their old age who would begin a whole new nation and future—now this God is telling Abraham he must *sacrifice* Isaac—murder the child given by God, destroy the fulfillment of the promise.

I find the stark telling of the walk to the mountain chilling. How could Abraham bear it? What were the wonderings and fears of the little boy—and finally terror as he was bound and placed on the altar? Wouldn't he have been screaming? Shouldn't Abraham have been sweating, shaking, throwing up even, as he made the murderous preparations? Shouldn't *he* have pulled back, never reached for the knife, *refused* to obey the command of his God?

Instead, he's ready to go through with it, and only at that point the angel intervenes, revealing the test, and the ram in the thicket is provided. Knowing this ending, we preachers can seek to explain the story in reassuring terms, something along the lines of how when we face the worst, God will come to the rescue. And maybe it *is* a story of radical trust—that because God had kept God's earlier promise of a son, God would spare Isaac.

I don't buy it. I don't buy a transactional God who demands a blind faith and sets us up for murder to prove it. I don't buy a God who wills his followers through Jim Jones to drink the lethal Kool-Aid. I don't buy telling a parent who has lost a child to leukemia or had a son blown up in Iraq that it was God's will. I soured on that theology a long time ago—most poignantly on a hot summer night in 1983 at Children's Hospital where I was doing chaplain training.

A very young couple came in with their ten day old daughter, Nicoletta, who was near death from an untreated fever and infection. They hadn't realized how ill she was, and now it was too late. She died in a couple of hours. A grandmother was with them and tried to console them by saying it was God's will, and that God would send another child, a boy next time. They were from another Christian tradition, and I held my tongue, trying to simply comfort and be with them. Part of this was to be with them as they held the small body one last time. The grandmother handed her to me to put back on the bed—it was actually the first time I'd ever seen or touched a dead body. She was so limp and light, such a tragic little bundle. I'll never forget how she felt. Later, alone and awash in tears, I also grew angry—seeing the death as the *opposite* of God's will. I saw it instead as the result of young and inexperienced and ignorant parents and a lack of social support. The death shouldn't have happened, needn't have happened, but when it is too difficult to lay blame, or find a reason, claiming God's will is inadequate. It makes a monster of God and is no help as an explanation.

Back to our story about Abraham and Isaac and God. I want to examine it in a different way. As in many Bible stories, God is personified, speaks, appears in the form of an angel. There is dialogue between Abraham and God, just as there is dialogue between Abraham and Isaac. Abraham gives the same answer, "Here I am" to God, to Isaac and to the angel calling from heaven, as if all three exchanges were of the same kind. What if we have lost that way of believing in God as some celestial personage? What if the story is about Abraham's devastating *internal* confrontation with something he is doing based on some primitive tribal custom? What if, suddenly, from the deepest well of his being, the heart of his love for his son, he just can't continue? There *must* be another way to serve God! The agony of trying to fulfill the sacrifice is too great, and something *within* him stays his hand, and he says "No, No!" to his God—and, in the next moment, the ram, a new option, appears. Is God there in the midst of Abraham's tortured struggle? Is the test a challenge to evolve in his understanding of what God requires? Maybe God's will is for us to grow and change in our understandings of what love demands.

I'm trying to understand this story as one about our own collective and individual development towards new insights and behavior in our time, and in our history. We go about living one way—keeping slaves, until, fueled by violence and sacrifice and bloody war, we no longer can. We were willing to go along, and then we weren't.

We oppressed women and used the Bible to justify it, until we no longer could sacrifice the intelligence and energy and intuition of half of humanity on the altar of male dominance. We were willing to go along, and then we weren't. We've kept gay and lesbian people in the closet and discriminated against them—stifling their unique identity, disqualifying their loves—until we can't anymore, and, in its wisdom, the majority of the Episcopal Church is no longer willing to sacrifice the dignity of gay and lesbian people on the altar of a rigid and unchanging orthodoxy.

All of these conditions—slavery, oppression of women and of gay people—were once thought to be God's will. Now, they're not. We evolve in our humanity, and, as we do, our understanding of God and God's will changes as well. (And because God is indeed hidden, invisible and never fully knowable to us, this is not to say that God or God's will is shaped or changed by us—rather that our own intuitions of this God can and do change—and that perhaps it is indeed God who reshapes them—the angel who stops the knife—offers a new way.)

And so we come to our contemporary Abraham and Isaac situation. Our continuing willingness to sacrifice our sons and daughters, although mostly not ours, but the sons and daughters of others, in war. And yes, there are, or have been, just wars, and sometimes the sacrifice is deemed worth it, even by the soldiers, even by their parents. We send them off, uniformed and armed and trained, to sacrifice them on the altar of national interest, in service to the god of patriotism and American hegemony. Or, more charitably—we make this sacrifice to spread democracy and freedom. Maybe it's worth it. There are things worth fighting and dying for, and sometimes even the most painful sacrifice is worth it to bring about a greater good.

But maybe, just as with other forms of human brutality, God's will is for us to come to a different understanding about this contemporary form of child sacrifice and to find a new way to settle the struggles among nations and peoples over power and wealth and resources. Where is the ram in the thicket for our time—what will stay our hands?

Perhaps God's way of testing us is not as cruel as it seems in the story of Abraham and Isaac. Perhaps God's challenge and God's will is for us to look honestly, to be awake and aware, truly present to how we live and behave. Perhaps God's challenge and God's will is for us is to question ourselves about how love is served in the ways we treat each other. And perhaps these challenges, these tests, are not to set us up, but to transform and free us. Maybe it's not about Abraham trusting God to spare Isaac, but God trusting Abraham to hold the knife. Maybe it's not about us trusting God to make wars to cease, but about God trusting *us* to find new ways to live together. That is a test worth taking, a trust we dare not betray. Amen.

Index